C000279327

# IN SEARCH OF AMRIT KAUR

BY THE SAME AUTHOR

*Non Scrivere Di Me*

# In Search of Amrit Kaur

## An Indian Princess in Wartime Paris

LIVIA MANERA SAMBUY

Translated by Todd Portnowitz

Chatto & Windus
LONDON

1 3 5 7 9 10 8 6 4 2

Chatto & Windus, an imprint of Vintage, is part of the Penguin Random House group of companies whose addresses can be found at global.penguinrandomhouse.com

Penguin
Random House
UK

First published by Chatto & Windus in 2023

Copyright © Livia Manera Sambuy 2023
Translation copyright © Todd Portnowitz 2023

Livia Manera Sambuy has asserted their right to be identified as the author of this Work in accordance with the Copyright, Designs and Patents Act 1988

Epigraph taken from *The Sense of an Ending* by Julian Barnes, published by Vintage. Copyright © Julian Barnes 2011

Epigraph taken from *Autumn* by Ali Smith, published by Hamish Hamilton. Copyright © Ali Smith 2016

Epilogue epigraph: 'maggie and milly and molly and may'. Copyright © 1956, 1984, 1991 by the Trustees for the E. E. Cummings Trust, from *Complete Poems: 1904–1962* by E. E. Cummings, edited by George J. Firmage. Used by permission of Liveright Publishing Corporation

penguin.co.uk/vintage

A CIP catalogue record for this book is available from the British Library

HB ISBN 9781784741198
TPB ISBN 9781784741204

Typeset in 12/14.75pt Dante MT Std by Jouve (UK), Milton Keynes
Printed and bound in Great Britain by Clays Ltd, Elcograf S.p.A.

The authorised representative in the EEA is Penguin Random House Ireland, Morrison Chambers, 32 Nassau Street, Dublin D02 YH68

Penguin Random House is committed to a sustainable future
for our business, our readers and our planet. This book is made
from Forest Stewardship Council® certified paper.

MIX
Paper from
responsible sources
FSC® C018179

*for Maria Edmée*

'I certainly believe we all suffer damage, one way or another. How could we not, except in a world of perfect parents, siblings, neighbours, companions? And then there is the question on which so much depends, of how we react to the damage: whether we admit it or repress it, and how this affects our dealings with others. Some admit the damage, and try to mitigate it; some spend their lives trying to help others who are damaged; and there are those whose main concern is to avoid further damage to themselves, at whatever cost. And those are the ones who are ruthless, and the ones to be careful of.'

Julian Barnes, *The Sense of an Ending*

'Whoever makes up the story, makes up the world . . . So always try to welcome people into the home of your story.'

Ali Smith, *Autumn*

# Contents

# A Note from the Author

In 1995, the Indian government changed the name of Bombay, the capital of the state of Maharashtra, to Mumbai: a word that refers back to the Hindu goddess Mumbadevi and is in alignment with the nation's shift towards Hindu nationalism. Bombay, a name that carries no religious connotations, was instead considered by some to be an undesirable legacy of the colonial era. Today, in spoken language, the local population uses both Bombay and Mumbai indifferently. For clarity, I chose to use 'Bombay' for past events and 'Mumbai' for the modern-day city. Just as I do for Poona, which became Pune in 1978.

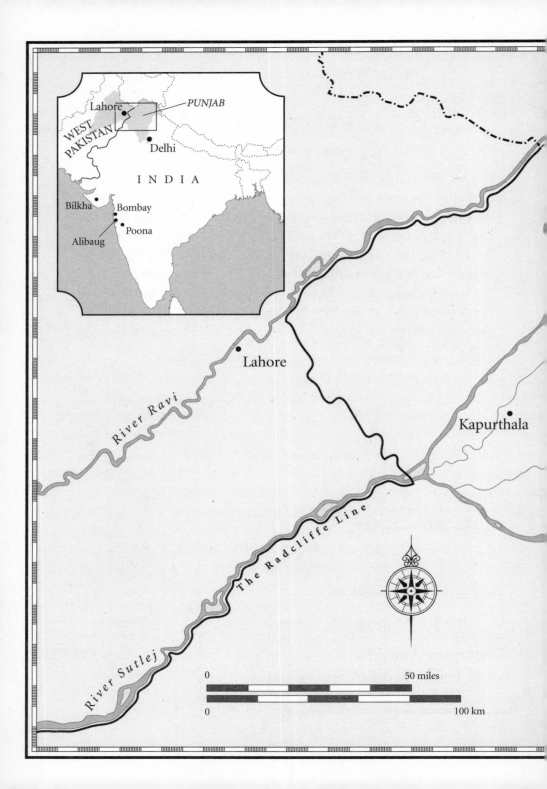

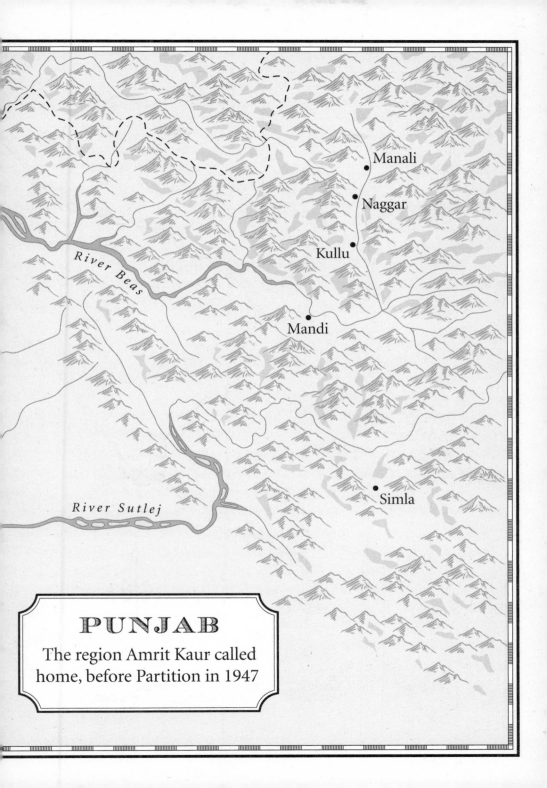

Manali

Naggar

Kullu

*River Beas*

Mandi

*River Sutlej*

Simla

# PUNJAB

The region Amrit Kaur called
home, before Partition in 1947

# IN SEARCH OF AMRIT KAUR

# Prologue: An Unusual Day

Mumbai, early March 2007

What I remember about that day is the dust-filled air, the blue sky, my white dress, and the curiosity that kept me walking, despite my exhaustion on arriving in Mumbai. I wandered between stark skyscrapers and Portuguese villas in disrepair. I chased the shade under Moorish colonnades and skirted cricket fields turning yellow in the heat. And as the sun baked my skin, I fought to overcome the lethargy that had been weighing me down since I'd left Italy.

I had boarded the plane for India just a few days after my brother's funeral – a ferocious disease had torn through him, far too young, in a matter of months. And for eleven hours I drifted over the snow-capped peaks of Central Asia in a drugged state of drowsiness – the same drowsiness that had possessed me a few years earlier, when my body reacted to another separation, from the love of my life, refusing to stay awake. It was in that somnambulant state that I'd arrived in Mumbai, for a work assignment I couldn't postpone: to write a profile of the Indian novelist Vikram Chandra.

Cheerful and welcoming, Vikram spent a few days showing me around the city that had inspired his most ambitious novel, *Sacred Games*, together with two other colleagues. We wove our way through the ragged denizens and small-time craftsmen of a slum that was to be demolished to make way for a middle-class residential neighbourhood; he gained us entry into the den of a gangster who was preparing to run for mayor; and into the lurid office of a pockmarked policeman, said to have knocked off 200 'suspects'. Evenings

I

we dined in fashionable restaurants – I remember one, in particular, 'Mediterranean', filled with foppish men dressed all in black, their hair tied up in ponytails, and Bollywood starlets who moved with the levity of nymphs, in full possession of their seductive powers. Such assignments didn't come around very often in my experience as a literary journalist. It was the winter of 2007 and Mumbai was evolving at a whirlwind pace: just breathing the air made you dizzy.

But from the minute I arrived at the hyper-modern hotel in the neighbourhood of Bandra, it took every ounce of my energy just to keep up with Vikram, as he showed me the spirit and contradictions of a metropolis whose colonial architecture was making a valiant stand against the miles of new cement besieging it on all sides; where beauty queens whizzed past in Mercedes-Benzes piloted by chauffeurs; and young men who fancied themselves warriors wore skin-tight T-shirts, their muscles stretching the seams. 'If you want to get an idea of the identity crisis that Indian men are facing today, just look at how the image of Rama has changed,' he said to me, pointing to a technicolour poster of the Hindu god, armed with a bow and arrow. 'He used to be skinny; now he looks like Arnold Schwarzenegger,' he laughed. Even the wetlands that surrounded the city were transforming – into construction yards, the mangroves fighting for life in a mechanical forest of cranes. The only thing that hadn't changed, in that most ancient, most modern of worlds, were the hundreds of families that poured in every day from the country to lay a mat down on the pavement.

After finishing my assignment, I had twenty-four hours to spend on my own. And I began that sweltering day by doing something that, for me, was highly unusual. I'd been packing my suitcase, back in Italy, when the man I had separated from, said to me: 'When you're in Mumbai you should go see Ramesh Balsekar. He is a very interesting philosopher, I picked up his essays by chance at the bookshop and they're truly radical. He's very old now, but he still receives guests, once a week. I'd like to go see him myself.' And, noticing that

I was hardly paying attention, he'd added, 'Please, do it for me'; even though, thinking back, I sensed what he was really saying was 'do it for yourself'. So, partly out of curiosity, partly out of inertia, that Saturday morning I stepped out of the hotel and asked a taxi driver to take me to Malabar Hill, land of Mumbai's upper crust, with its elegant homes surrounded by gardens overlooking the Arabian Sea. Though just a few miles, the trip was a kind of homecoming: I'd treasured the memory of Salman Rushdie's Malabar Hill ever since my lover and I, before getting married, travelled around the Mediterranean on a tiny sailing boat, a Picador edition of *Midnight's Children* curling in the humid sea air, transforming our cruise into a voyage towards an exhilarating new world and way of storytelling.

It took an hour and a half to reach Balsekar's address, thanks to the knot of traffic that's a feature of India's new economic boom. And when the taxi finally stopped in front of a two-storey house with fading white paint there were already thirty or so people waiting in the street, beneath the shade of a few leafy branches. It was a beautiful late-winter day, and up on the hill the scent of frangipani blended with the odour of dust. I'd read that Balsekar, almost ninety, held a two-hour open house on Saturday mornings for anyone interested in his 'conversations'. And at precisely ten o'clock, two assistants appeared at the top of a stairway and ushered us disciples into a sober living room, where I shuffled to a corner to make myself invisible. I'd only just settled in when one of Balsekar's assistants signalled for me to stand and take a seat on an empty stool, directly in front of the guru's chair. This, as I'd later learn, was the fate of newcomers. In the time it took me to reluctantly change seats, the room had grown still. And it was then that a man entered from the door behind us – slight, with a beautiful aquiline profile and smooth silver hair, his stark white kurta and pants freshly ironed. After greeting us, Ramesh Balsekar sat down in a rocking chair, glanced around the room, turned his gaze to me, and asked: 'Why are you here?'

All it took was that simple question to expose me as an intruder. What could I say to him? I felt so vacant and paralysed by shock that I couldn't bring myself to utter a single word. But my silence had no impact on the guru. He moved along and turned to a young man with sandy blond hair, sitting to my right, who readily responded: 'I'm here in search of myself.'

How bold, I thought, with the haughty impatience of one who hasn't yet forgotten the spiritual supermarket of the 1970s, when the doors of India's ashrams opened to welcome a generation of the lost and confused, on the run from ideologies. Meanwhile, in that crowded room on Malabar Hill, the teacher began to speak of love, greed, passion and other afflictions of the human soul, offering his interpretation of the Advaita Vedanta, a school of Hindu philosophy based on the idea that the world is guided only by divine and natural laws, and that, despite our conviction that we're the agents of our own decisions, free will is an illusion. Balsekar enunciated each word slowly, building his argument around a series of interesting counterpoints. But the result struck me as a cold and intellectualised view of the world. I was also struck by the fact that, before inheriting his mission to spread the word of the Advaita Vedanta from his dying teacher, Ramesh Balsekar was a banker. And not just any banker, but president of the Bank of India.

Nearly forty-five minutes later, having exhausted his response to my neighbour, he turned his gaze back to me and asked for a second time: 'Why are you here?' And though my heart again skipped a beat, I now understood that I wasn't there, in the house of this aloof and learned gentleman, only because someone else had begged me to go in his place. 'My brother died a few days ago,' I responded, surrendering to the tears. 'And I've learned that death is unacceptable. That I can't find the tools to accept it, not in myself and not in my culture.'

Ramesh Balsekar spoke again, following the same line of reasoning: first the viewpoints of other religions, then that of the Advaita

Vedanta. But his words were too radical to provide me with any relief. While on the one hand he was saying that it was natural to feel pain at the death of a loved one, on the other he considered the prolonging of suffering to be an act of ignorance. The problem, he explained, lies in our refusal to recognise that the entity we refer to as mind-body is an illusion, as is identifying ourselves with our own body and our own actions. In other words, individual human beings, though certain of their ability to exercise their own will, in truth possess no such autonomy and are an infinitesimal part of a consciousness that encompasses all.

I listened, hoping to find some hidden truth I could cling to. But there was no way for me to adopt a dogma that at its root denied the individuality of my mind, my will, my attachment to my own body. And yet something in this man's voice, something in this bourgeois-living-room-turned-temple, began to elicit a change. And as I listened to the music of his words, I could feel the ravenous beast of sleep within begin to loosen its jaws.

When it was all over I joined the stream of disciples flowing back out into the street and asked a taxi driver to take me to Colaba, in the heart of Old Bombay overlooking the iron-coloured ocean. And in a tea room at the Taj Mahal Palace Hotel I took a seat at a table by the window, letting the time slip as I observed the water crashing against the walls behind the basalt arch of the Gateway of India; the red-faced tourists staggering, drunk from the heat, and the boats lined up along the dock, waiting to ferry them out to Elephanta Island.

I paid the bill and set off on foot towards the old Prince of Wales Museum – now known as the Chhatrapati Shivaji Maharaj Vastu Sangrahalaya – its majestic imperial architecture looming over a toxic traffic circle that wrings it like a noose around a neck. And there, in that Indo-Saracenic-style building surrounded by the thinnest of palm trees, I saw a poster for a photography exhibition featuring portraits of maharajas and maharanis, on loan from the Victoria and Albert Museum.

Not for me, I told myself. There was so much to see in Mumbai. I had better things to do than linger around an exhibition on loan from London, which was just a short trip for me. But when I stepped back outside and felt the smack of the early-afternoon sun, I had no choice but to retreat and take cover for a little longer beneath the museum's enormous fans. The exhibition's fifty or so photographs were attributed to Lafayette, a studio opened in London in the late 1800s by an Irish photographer who'd adopted a French moniker. A first glance seemed to confirm my suspicions that the show wasn't worth the little time I had left in Mumbai. Those plump maharajas, with their stiff moustaches and sombre gazes, did little to excite my curiosity; in fact, all that ostentation – their chests covered in pearls, diamonds and precious stones – seemed almost vulgar to my European tastes. But when I'd just about convinced myself that I was better off braving the heat and moving on to the next destination, one photograph changed my mind.

It was a full-length portrait of a slender young woman, whose grace, in that setting, shone like a ray of light. Tall, dark-skinned, her hair tied up, she wore an impalpable, translucent sari, its edges embroidered with gold or silver thread – hard to say, in a black and white photo. The label identified her as 'Her Royal Highness Rani Shri Amrit Kaur Sahib', the sole female child of Maharaja Jagatjit Singh Bahadur of Kapurthala and his fourth wife, Rani Kanari. The photograph was dated 24 June 1924, one year after the princess's marriage to the Raja Joginder Sen Bahadur of Mandi, when the young newlyweds visited London and were received by King George and Queen Mary.

There was one detail in particular, according to the exhibition's curator, Russell Harris, that set this portrait apart. In contrast to the splendour of her sari and the theatricality of the setting, the Rani wore relatively little jewellery: the sign of a certain originality, 'since

HH Rani Shri Amrit Kaur Sahib, only daughter of the Maharaja of Kapurthala, on her visit to England with her husband, Raja Joginder Sen Bahadur of Mandi.

her father annually spent up to a quarter of his revenue buying swags of pearls and heavy emeralds to adorn himself'.

There was no question that, amid the dazzling display of princes surrounding her, the Rani of Mandi's choice to wear 'only' a necklace of diamond cabochons and two long strings of pearls did seem almost like an act of modesty – or else, as the curator suggested, the sign of a singular character. But what really caught my attention was the last part of the photograph's description: 'A letter received by her father's fifth wife, the former flamenco dancer Anita Delgado, contained a report that the Rani of Mandi had been arrested by the Gestapo in occupied Paris on the accusation of having sold her jewellery to help Jews leave the country. The letter stated that the Rani survived less than a year of Nazi imprisonment.'

An incredible story, I remember thinking, as I stepped back to get a better look at this alluring woman. How could such an act have gone unnoticed? A gorgeous Punjabi princess, a Sikh by faith, who risks her life, in occupied Paris, to help Jews and ends up murdered by Nazis.

What struck me wasn't just the heroic nature of the act. I longed to know more. I longed to understand what led a princess of the Raj to leave India for Paris in the 1930s; and more than all else, I longed to discover what it was that kept her there until it was too late.

In that moment, I could never have imagined just how firmly the desire to answer these questions had taken hold of me; nor that the search I'd soon embark upon would lead me towards the discovery of a lost world, down a meandering trail full of winding paths, dead-end offshoots, hairpin turns, and revelations. I was entering a realm where stories led to stories that led to more stories: a labyrinth in which I'd encounter a host of unusual characters. Bankers with utopian ambitions and venturesome jewellers; young lions of the Resistance and shrewd secret agents; ill-fated explorers and pearl fishers reduced to slavery; joyful widows and heiresses; magicians and charlatans; and a throng of unhappy princesses and powerless princes.

And so this adventure began: as a jolt of curiosity amid a haze of lingering grief, when a pervading sense of loss had obscured my past and future. Little did I imagine that the desire to solve the mystery tied to that inscrutable face would take me into the new life I was poised to begin.

# Rue du Bac

By then I had little connection to my home town. Milan, the sober industrial metropolis of Italy's north – home, beginning in the 1950s, to a series of enlightened entrepreneurs and a sophisticated intellectual life – had long since folded in on itself and become drab and provincial.

A few years before that trip to Mumbai, I had separated from the artist I'd fallen in love with at nineteen, when his freewheeling lifestyle, his old-world manners and his lack of interest in all things material had presented me with an irresistible alternative to my own bourgeois upbringing. Marriage was never part of my plan, because I had no desire to replicate the family I'd come from. My father, a brilliant executive at a major corporation, was loving but mostly absent due to work. My brother and I, six years apart, had grown up as single children. And the intense bond I shared with my beautiful and idle mother suffered a huge blow just as I was entering adolescence.

In any case, the independent streak I shared with my lover seemed to bar us from repeating those mistakes. For years we lived in separate houses, me writing my articles and he painting his expansive watercolours of archeological ruins – and later, the large canvases of remote cargo ships on the high seas that would become his spiritual refuge. But then something changed and we tied the knot. Later, when our children were born, I found myself enchanted by my son's impatient curiosity and my daughter's inquisitive grace. And I became so attached to my family that for years I navigated the treacherous waters of marriage with both hands firmly on the helm.

When the separation came, it was both civilised and devastating.

Perhaps I should have pursued my interests and left immediately. Instead I lingered for another five years in the home we'd all shared, my instinct pressing me to keep our family united, in whatever way possible. I was determined to be the kind of parents who can live up to the commitment they've made, even under different roofs. And it worked. Until my son left to study in England. Until my brother fell sick and died. And suddenly our beautiful home – with its grand ships sailing on motionless seas, my colourful suzani embroideries, our library in such disarray that I often had to rebuy books we already owned – had become a monument to absence. That's when I surrendered.

It was therefore in a moment of rebellion, when it seemed like the future had nothing in store for me but more loss – my father had already passed away, my mother was in her late seventies and my teenage daughter would leave home after secondary school, just like her brother – that I decided to move to Paris. Perhaps it was recklessness: I was going to live in a place where I knew no one and could not even speak the language. And yet it was precisely this lack that motivated me. I wanted a new language, a new city, a new culture, a new beginning.

Then, in a stroke of luck, I found a lovely apartment in the building that was once home to a *grande dame* of Parisian literary society, Madame de Staël. 'It's a bit bizarre,' said the friend who'd gone to take a look at it for me. 'The walls are crooked, and I can't promise you the floors are straight either, but there's charm and fireplaces to spare.'

The day we left Milan, my daughter Maria Edmée and our terrier Ombra were wearing the same expression, somewhere between excitement for the new and fear of the unknown. As for me, I recognised that we were saying goodbye not only to our family life but to all the comforts that came with it: longtime friendships, a support network, our beautiful apartment with its gold-inlaid Art Nouveau doors and windows facing out on to a sprawling garden, and a spacious farmhouse kitchen, where so many of our friends had gathered. And yet I knew that I would miss none of it.

Paris was still caught in the languor of late August. So it was that I found myself sitting on the parquet floor of our new home on the rue du Bac, intent on dealing with the ungodly number of boxes we'd dragged along with us, when, slicing one open, I found a green folder with the words 'Rani of Mandi' written on it. It had been some months since I'd thought of that ill-fated princess whose portrait had captured my imagination in Mumbai. As soon as I'd returned from that trip, I'd asked an Indian friend to help dig up more details about her story. The Rani of Mandi had had two children, one boy and one girl, she wrote. The son had died several years ago, but the daughter was still alive – she was now a seventy-eight-year-old woman, and she'd said that the information accompanying the portrait of her mother in the exhibition I'd seen was incorrect. So the story wasn't true after all? My friend had enclosed an address and phone number, along with a photo of a petite woman with shoulder-length silver hair wearing a turquoise sari and posing timidly before an enlarged portrait of her mother. Rani Nirvana Devi of Bilkha, it read. The address listed was in Pune, in Maharashtra, the large central state of India.

Of course, I'd thought, with a pang of disappointment. If the story about the Rani of Mandi and her jewellery were true, it would be well known. Then I'd tucked the letter back in the folder and stashed it who knows where.

Only when the note resurfaced in the chaos of my move to Paris did I realise how many questions remained unanswered; but trying to juggle all the pressing needs of my new life left me with no time to pursue them. Still, every day when I took Ombra for a run along the banks of the Seine, I couldn't shake the feeling that I'd left something unresolved. However, the thought of dialling the mobile phone number of an old lady who lived on the other side of the world to tell her I was an Italian calling from Paris to find out if her mother really died in a Nazi prison camp was shameful even to consider. So I let it drop.

Then, one afternoon, seated at my desk, staring out the window at a patch of shifting sky, I reached for my phone. Outside the gulls were circling nervously, presaging bad weather. To my surprise, a friendly voice responded. 'Yes . . . who did you say you are?'

In a flash, the rani's sing-song English brought back memories of my sleepwalking days in Mumbai: when, during breakfast one morning, I'd watched a team of workers demolish a building between the ocean and my hotel using just one hammer each; when I'd discovered that the vultures, who for centuries had been picking Zoroastrian corpses clean atop Malabar Hill's Tower of Silence, had flown elsewhere to escape the pollution. I remembered the chaste couples who sat along the crescent-shaped Marine Drive, staring out at the sea, growing less chaste as the night wore on until the police came to shoo them away; and the day that Vikram took us to a movie set, where, after an acrobatic duel, Aishwarya Rai, Bollywood's most heavenly diva, came over to say hello, bewitching us with her impossibly green eyes while shyly extending her hand.

All of this rushed through my mind as an elderly woman's childish voice explained to me that, unfortunately, certain information included in the exhibition deviated from the truth. The story of her mother's arrest in Paris, yes, that was true. And it was true that she'd been sent to a prison camp. Except that the camp was in France – her daughter couldn't remember where. And either way, Amrit Kaur didn't die in 1941 but was freed after a few months. 'I believe my grandfather, the Maharaja of Kapurthala, was able to organise a prisoner exchange,' she said. 'But captivity had taken a terrible toll on my mother's health, and I think in the end it killed her. In any case, she died in London in 1948.'

When I asked about the jewels, whether her mother had really traded them to save others' lives, she told me that she didn't have the slightest clue.

'Come to see me,' she said, just when I thought the conversation was at an end.

I must have sat there silent, because she repeated herself: 'It would be nice if you came to see me.'

There was something about her tone of voice that made the invitation feel like more than just a courteous gesture.

I turned my gaze back to the window; the sky was now shrouded in dark clouds.

'I would love to,' I replied, as the first raindrops began to strike the panes.

# PART ONE
## *Glimpses*

# The World in a Garden

Setting off anytime soon, however, would have been impossible. I had a city to discover, a daughter to put through school, a job to keep up and a life to rebuild. Nevertheless, that brief conversation with the Rani of Bilkha had piqued my curiosity. On the web, you could find only a handful of facts about Amrit Kaur: she was born in 1904 in the small kingdom of Kapurthala, in north-west India; she was the fifth – and only daughter – of the maharaja's six children, whom he'd had with as many wives; she'd gone to a boarding school for girls in Sussex; and, rather intriguingly, she'd posed for the camera of Lee Miller, in the days when Man Ray's American muse was taking her first steps as a photographer at an atelier in Montparnasse.

A few days later, I went to do some reconnaissance at the Bibliothèque Nationale de France. But there was nothing in the general catalogue under Amrit Kaur, Rani of Mandi.

On the other hand, the French newspapers abounded with articles on Amrit's relatives, who paid regular visits to Paris between the 1920s and 1930s. I learned that her father, Maharaja Jagatjit Singh of Kapurthala, had purchased a home on a corner of the Bois de Boulogne, bordering the gardens of the Château de Bagatelle – a gem of Neoclassical architecture commissioned by Louis XVI's brother, the Comte d'Artois, as an outpost for hunting trips in the Bois. The charming 'Pavillon de Kapurthala', now owned by the city, was under restoration, but where I found a construction site there once stood a garden with rows of grape vines – yet another of Paris's bizarre traditions, these urban vineyards, a few of which are still flourishing, like the vineyard on the hill of Montmartre. In the age of Louis XVI, it appears, the most celebrated wine was produced by the multi-ethnic neighbourhood of La Goutte d'Or. Determined to make Paris his adopted home, in the interwar years Amrit Kaur's father had even experimented a little with his own winemaking.

The newspaper clippings told of a gregarious and widely travelled maharaja: a tall man with a commanding moustache and an expression that, on account of the dark patches around his eyes, seemed grave even when he was laughing. In most of the photos he wore an *achkan*, a long brocade jacket buttoned up to his neck, with a belt studded with precious gems, trousers that tapered at his ankles, and a turban. But his face was clean-shaven. The fact that from middle age on he didn't wear a beard, which Sikhs were forbidden to shave off, was a brazen sign of Westernisation, and it brought him no shortage of criticism in India.

Other photographs showed him in a top hat and tails, flanked by members of France's elite such as Baron Robert de Rothschild, Princess Marie de Broglie and Countess Élisabeth Greffulhe. To his dear friend Marie de Broglie he presented a pet elephant named Miss Pundji – greatly appreciated until they found out she had the appetite of a dozen horses. So it was, after a while, that the princess entrusted Miss Pundji to the Jardin d'Acclimatation – a park with peacocks and other free-roaming animals in the Bois de Boulogne. However, the elephant must have maintained a special place in her heart, since the princess later had her buried in the castle gardens in Chaumont-sur-Loire, beside the graves of their family dogs. On the headstone, to this day, is a medallion with a photograph of Miss Pundji surrounded by the princess's children, along with an epitaph that reads like a Proustian flourish: '*Ô tristes que nous sommes / notre fantaisie ici enfouie*' (How sorrowful we are / our fantasy here buried).

The articles on Amrit Kaur's polygamous father spoke of shooting parties, horse races at the track in Longchamp, evening concerts; of his Indian fourth wife, Rani Kanari, dressed like a Frenchwoman, in

Amrit's father and mother: Maharaja Jagatjit Singh of Kapurthala and Rani Kanari, *c.*1890.

accordance with the Belle Époque's latest whim; and of his Spanish fifth wife, Anita Delgado, dressed like an Indian woman, with a crescent-shaped emerald on her forehead. Much ink was also spilled on the social escapades of Brinda of Kapurthala, spouse of Paramjit Singh, the maharaja's firstborn and Amrit Kaur's half-brother – a gadabout who seems never to have missed a soirée, from the faubourg Saint-Honoré to the faubourg Saint-Germain. But the family member most admired by the French press was Sita Devi, known also as 'Princess Karam'. Married to the maharaja's fourth son, Karamjit Singh, she was a petite woman with a keen sense of style, whose delicate features lent an air of exoticism to the fashion magazines of the day. One sumptuous photograph taken by Cecil Beaton in 1934 shows her with eyes closed, as if dreaming, beneath a cascade of peony petals.

Amrit's sister-in-law, Sita Devi of Kapurthala, also known as Princess Karam.

All of which attested to the wide renown of the Kapurthala family in France, though none of it revealed a thing about the maharaja's daughter. What was she doing in Paris in the 1930s? I'd read somewhere that her husband was appointed ambassador. Did it mean that she was following him on some sort of diplomatic assignment? Most disappointing was to find no record of the portrait featured in Lee Miller's first solo show in Manhattan, in 1933, mentioned in a review. Whatever connection Miller had had with Amrit Kaur was to remain a mystery, and not the last when it came to this story. The only interesting hit that cropped up was the Wikipedia page for the Clovelly-Kepplestone boarding school for girls in Sussex, where the princess's name figured among the institute's most famous alumnae – a rather vivacious student, it struck me, given that she'd directed an all-girl five-piece jazz band. Clo-Kepp, as it was nicknamed, wasn't just any school, I came to learn. Its founder, Frances Anna Browne, was the sister of the theatre impresario Maurice Browne. Thanks to the Brownes' connections, several noteworthy guests had paid a visit to the students at Clo-Kepp, including the great African American baritone and actor Paul Robeson, who starred in *Othello* at London's Savoy Theatre; or Sir Ernest Shackleton, who lived nearby and gave frequent talks there on his expeditions in Antarctica. Tuesday evenings at Clo-Kepp were dedicated to needlework, but Mondays were spent rehearsing comedies for the stage, and on Saturday evenings they danced. Under the banner of religious tolerance, the school welcomed pupils from all over the world, with Jewish girls making up a third of the student body. I read this as a sign of a connection between the Indian princess and the Jewish world.

Just a week after my rather frustrating trip to the library chasing a ghost, Amrit Kaur took it upon herself to appear before me, in a group photograph.

I was out discovering Paris and had decided to visit the extravagant gardens of Albert Kahn, a Jewish banker born in 1860 in a Hebrew enclave of French Alsace. The son of a humble livestock merchant, Kahn had built himself an immense fortune from a sequence of formidable investments, allowing him to set up his own investment bank at the age of thirty-eight. He would eventually suffer huge losses in the 1929 stock market crash and die in poverty at the age of eighty, in his house in Boulogne, on Paris's western outskirts – with the Germans at the door and just a few hours before bailiffs came to repossess even the bed he died on.

This visionary banker, who valued discretion over money, lived in a *hôtel particulier* overlooking a ten-acre park. Today, visitors enter the park through a building that houses a permanent exhibition on Kahn's life. The evidence paints the portrait of a secular, frugal vegetarian, a nature lover and tireless spirit who spoke French with a strong Alsatian accent, avoided the salons, and never married. His

Albert Kahn standing on the balcony of his Parisian office, 1914; the only photograph he ever posed for.

ideal evening, according to those who knew him, was to have his driver take him outside Paris, roll the top down, and sleep beneath the stars – preferably somewhere near the sea.

The building also houses a rotating exhibition of his unparalleled collection of 'autochromes'. The predecessors of colour photographs, 'autochromes' were glass plates coated with dyed grains of potato starch and lampblack, producing a granular, watercolour-like effect, which had been invented by the Lumière brothers in 1903. Kahn invested a large chunk of his capital in a visionary project that took advantage of this new technology.

It had all begun in 1908, on a trip around the world, accompanied by his driver-engineer Alfred Dutertre and more than 4,000 stereotype plates. Together they photographed Japan, China and the United States. Then, a few months after his return to Paris, Kahn set off again, this time for Uruguay, Argentina and Brazil, along with a professional photographer, Auguste Léon. Together they'd experiment with the first autochromes.

Out of those experiences came the idea for an immense archive of colour images depicting the entire planet. By showing the human geography of every country and continent – customs, practices, beliefs, habits, expressions that now seem astonishing, with Ireland and the Balkans looking like realms from a fantasy novel – this archive, Kahn hoped, would become a means of bringing men closer together and pushing war further away. The historical context was one of colonial conquest – getting to know the 'other' was a means of managing and governing them more effectively – but Kahn remained a sincere utopian, convinced that the knowledge of humanity in all its various expressions stood at the foundation of building a culture of tolerance. All of his efforts from that 1908 trip on would be directed towards this goal.

Thus was born one of the most extraordinary endeavours in the history of photography. For over twenty years, from 1909 to 1931, when the economic crisis brought the project to a halt, Kahn deployed his resources to send five photographers and cameramen to map the entire planet. The result was a truly singular collection: 72,000 autochromes and 100 hours of film that together form the Archives de la Planète.

It was this project that served as the source of the rotating autochrome exhibition at Kahn's gardens in Boulogne, and as fate would have it my visit coincided with a show centred on Kapurthala – the home of Amrit Kaur herself, in the region of Punjab.

The autochromes on display had been captured in 1927 by Roger Dumas, a photographer commissioned by Albert Kahn. The occasion was a golden jubilee party for Maharaja Jagatjit Singh, a Bois de Boulogne neighbour with whom Kahn had formed a lasting friendship. Fifty or so guests – European, Indian, and several family members – posed for Dumas against the palace backdrop. Seated to the right of the maharaja was a pale, lanky man with a pith helmet balanced on the handle of his cane whom I recognised to be the viceroy, Lord Irwin. To the maharaja's left, her face obscured by the broad brim of a beige hat, in a silk duster coat worthy of a Fitzgerald heroine, sat Vicereine Lady Irwin. Next to her, in white, the Maharaja of Cooch Behar. And beside him, on the right edge of the photograph, I spotted the oval of Amrit Kaur's face, one end of her orange sari draped over her head. I did the maths: she was twenty-three at the time and had been married for four years. Her husband, Joginder Sen of Mandi, was surely there in the photo as well, but I couldn't place him.

It must have been my lucky day, because the autochrome exhibition was accompanied by a film of Jagatjit Singh's 1927 jubilee, which offered a good look at Kapurthala in those years. Dumas had filmed the maharaja's soldiers in their turbans and knickerbockers as they filed past a French-style palace: 'Un petit morceau de France au pied de l'Himalaya,' as the voice-over narrator put it, affecting a tone of admiration. Five elephants stood waiting for the guests, ready to carry them on gold and silver palanquins through the dusty provincial town, past the celebratory crowds in the streets. Another sequence showed the maharaja seated on one plate of an enormous balance scale, while on the other plate servants piled sacks of rupees and silver coins that would later be distributed to the residents. In contrast to that archaic rite, the voice-over spoke of an enlightened ruler who'd sparked industrial and agricultural development in his state, introduced administrative reforms, outlawed marriage between children and promoted free education for women. But above all else, Jagatjit Singh of Kapurthala deserved to be remembered as an enthusiastic francophile: so enthusiastic that he made French the official language of his court. He added Victor Hugo's poetry to the school curriculum; he wore Cartier jewellery at his jubilee; and he had his palace modelled on Versailles – except that, with an added touch of Indian sublimity, he had it painted pink.

Other footage showed the maharaja strolling through Albert Kahn's garden with Baroness Béatrice Ephrussi de Rothschild at his side – both the Ephrussis and the Rothschilds had homes in Boulogne. So there it was, I told myself, right before my eyes: evidence that the Kapurthalas were in with the Jewish society of the day. Though what intrigued me most was the maharaja's relationship with Kahn himself, that Alsatian banker who'd been such a major figure of his era and whom anti-Semitic France had been so eager to forget. I couldn't help wondering if Amrit Kaur might have compromised herself, at the risk of arrest, to help rescue an old family friend who'd fallen into disgrace during a time of rampant anti-Semitism in France.

I was trying to put all of this information in order, and to fully absorb just how much this extraordinary man had managed to accomplish, when I left the museum and walked out into his garden, crossing a small bridge surrounded by azaleas. And I realised that, in sending France out into the world, Albert Kahn had brought the world back to Boulogne. In the years that his photographers were exploring Persia, Italy, Turkey and Palestine, all around the *hôtel particulier* at number 6 quai du Quatre-Septembre Kahn set about unloading sand, dirt, gravel, rocks and thousands of plants, aiming to create an encyclopedic landscape. As I walked amid the crowd of families who'd come to enjoy the beautiful afternoon, I discovered that his landscape included a Japanese garden with a red lacquered bridge, a pagoda and a pavilion for tea ceremonies; a French-style garden with symmetrical boxwood hedges; a forest straight out of the Vosges, with dark greens and granite blocks from his beloved Alsace; a 'blue' forest of Atlas cedars and Colorado spruces; a wild garden; a park modelled on nineteenth-century British landscape paintings; an orchard, a rose garden and a greenhouse for tropical plants.

The young boy who'd grown up in the woods of the Lower Rhine and who'd come of age in the throes of Paris's urban transformation had maintained his old, farm-boy habits all throughout his life – up at five, a cold bath – all while keeping an eye on the many discoveries of that revolutionary age: electricity, railroads, cars, air travel, the wireless telegraph, Pasteur's vaccines, the cinema, photography, the radio. All these interests he shared with Amrit Kaur's father, a maharaja who cared deeply about the modernisation of his state.

Then, after the massacre of the First World War, Albert Kahn began to practise a militant brand of pacifism based on the belief that conflicts could be resolved through arbitration. 'Think like a man of action and act like a man of thought,' his mentor Henri Bergson had taught him. All around him lurked the fear that Europe might destroy itself in another global catastrophe.

Over the years, he created a galaxy of associations and foundations, around which revolved many of the most important figures of his time: Le Corbusier in architecture, Marcel Mauss in anthropology, titan of industry André Michelin and military mastermind Maréchal Ferdinand Foch. The more I considered the banker's life, the more clearly I understood what it meant for Amrit Kaur's father to consort with a neighbour like Albert Kahn: it meant coming into contact with a world that was far more intellectually stimulating than the horse races and masked balls that served as the main attractions of his forays into Paris society.

When he died in November 1940, Kahn had just registered himself as a Jew, obeying an ordinance issued by the Germans shortly after they occupied Paris. Not two years later, the Prefecture recast him as a dubious figure, suspected of having been at the helm of Germany's political espionage efforts during the First World War, and even of having played a key role in inciting the Bolshevik Revolution.

As I closed a book on his life, I wondered yet again if Amrit Kaur's tragic destiny was somehow tied up with this utopian who loved to sleep in his car under the stars.

It was only a beginning. A first inkling. Just enough to leave me wanting more.

# An Irishman Named Lafayette

Albert Kahn and his passion for autochromes reminded me that, in my case too, a photograph had been the starting point, the spark of what was destined to become an engrossing pursuit – and not just any sepia-toned print, but the portrait of an unconventionally beautiful woman against a hazy backdrop. Amrit Kaur commanded attention with her gleaming sari threaded with precious metals, in stark contrast to the inky blot of her hair; her gaze still imbued with the languor of early youth; her elegant hands, dotted with two rings like beads of light. If the glass plate of that young woman hadn't been buried beneath the post-war rubble, I have no doubt that someone else would have dug into her story long before her features caught my eye. But instead, that portrait, along with the entire collection it belonged to, had fallen into oblivion, only to resurface in 2002, when the British Council of New Delhi launched an exhibition dedicated to Lafayette's newly discovered archives – containing the portraits of more than 150 maharajas and maharanis who'd sat for the photographer in the 1920s and 1930s. How this archive came to be recovered and acquired by the Victoria and Albert Museum was due, in equal measure, to chance and luck, both good and bad. And it accounted, at least in part, for the obscurity in which the Rani of Mandi's tale had been shrouded for more than half a century.

James Lafayette did not in fact share a name with Gilbert du Motier de La Fayette, the aristocratic French officer whose involvement in the American Revolutionary War won him universal fame. His real name was James Jack Lauder, and he was an Irish entrepreneur who'd learned his trade at his father's daguerreotype studio in Dublin. When he struck out on his own in 1880, he adopted the name Lafayette to give the impression that he'd come from Paris, the city at the vanguard in the art of photography.

'Lafayette' opened studios in Manchester and Glasgow – though his true break came in 1897, when he established a cutting-edge studio in London, and Queen Victoria, grateful for the fine touch-up work he'd done on her chin, arms and waistline, issued him the privilege of a royal warrant.

It was then that the Duchess of Devonshire hired him to photograph the 700 guests at the costume ball she was holding in honour of the queen's Diamond Jubilee. On the evening of 2 July 1897, Lafayette set up a tent in the garden of Devonshire House in Piccadilly and turned his lens on the likes of Semiramis (Lady de Trafford); Zenobia, Queen of Palmyra (the Duchess of Devonshire); the Queen of Sheba (Daisy of Pless); and the Empress Theodora of Byzantium (Lady Randolph Churchill).

It was the ball of the century, as the press reported. The costumes alone required months of work by dressmakers, milliners and embroiderers. The intensity of the preparations bordered on hysteria. And when the evening of the party finally arrived, Lafayette went on maniacally photographing until his assistants collapsed from exhaustion. It was five in the morning.

Looking carefully through his catalogue of works, I decided that if Lafayette had won the world's favour, it was due in no small part to the uncommon depth of detail in his photographs. He had a gift for poses, for backdrops with Rembrandt-like draping; he knew how to make one's complexion look pleasantly smooth, and to create the illusion that the birds pinned in a lady's hair – like the dove with its wings spread above Countess Warwick's forehead – may be on the verge of taking flight.

But London in the early 1900s was a far cry from Poussin's Arcadia, and if a dove had flown into the studio at 179 New Bond Street it would have turned greyer than a pigeon. And this was where Lafayette demonstrated his true genius. To increase the clarity of his images, he invented an air filtration system that blocked out the London smog and all of its sooty particles. This involved a process of dehumidification and ventilation which cleared away the filthy specks and produced the little miracle that the photographer loved to describe as 'the transparent air of Southern skies'.

It was such coastal air, then, that Amrit Kaur took in many years after the triumph of the Devonshire ball, when aristocrats from all around the world – not just England – lined up behind the lens of the aspiring Frenchman. Flipping through the photographer's catalogue felt like watching a parade of crowned heads go by: first came the English royal family in lace and tails, followed by Indian princes with their cascade of rubies and pearls, then the royals from Greece, Romania, Turkey, Sumatra, Russia and Spain. The Kaiser posed in a cloak and feathered hat; the Duke of Orléans with his pipe; the Sultan of Zanzibar in a sumptuous, gold-embroidered ensemble; and the Emperor of Ethiopia's cousin, Ras Makonnen, in a sublime silver crown topped with a lion's mane.

Even for this enterprising photographer, though, the journey came to a bitter end, just as it had for Albert Kahn. Lafayette's glory days, as I came to learn, lasted only up until the end of the 1920s, when the Wall Street crash dealt a major blow to his clients. Throughout the 1930s his studio was forced to operate at a loss. Then came the war, followed by the dire financial straits of the post-war years.

Considering the rise and fall of his career, I figured that if no one had gone to the trouble of recovering the Lafayette studio archives, it must have been because they'd assumed the work had all been buried beneath the rubble of the Blitz.

But what happened instead – twenty years later – was that

someone chanced upon them. The master builder of a bricklaying crew had gone up into the glass-shard- and cobweb-filled attic of a building on Fleet Street to clear it out before renovations, when, out of curiosity, he wiped the filth off a few photographic plates. Staring up at him were the faces of Queen Victoria and David Lloyd George. Thrilled by the discovery, the builder called up the major film studios outside London who were his frequent employers, and he managed to transport 80,000 plates and negatives to the Pinewood Studio warehouses – salvaging nearly six tons of material in all. At that point, you'd think such a conspicuous collection would have attracted someone's attention. But no, the work of the now deceased Lafayette would have to wait in the shadows for another twenty years.

It wasn't until 1988 that an art director, the latest to stumble on that dust-covered treasure, set the recovery process in motion. Following negotiations with the institutions, 30,000 negatives left Pinewood and made their way into the collection of the Victoria and Albert Museum, while the remaining 50,000 went to London's National Portrait Gallery. Russell Harris, director of the V&A's photography department, had curated the exhibition I saw in Mumbai, *The Lafayette Studio and Princely India*, restoring the photographer to fame. The most internationally renowned of maharanis – Gayatri Devi of Jaipur – launched the show's premier at the British Council of New Delhi. And a shy Nirvana Devi of Bilkha struck a reluctant pose in front of her mother Amrit Kaur's portrait. 'The beauty and the beast,' she'd later say to me, breaking into one of her giggling fits.

But back then I wasn't yet familiar with her vibrant laughter. The thought of accepting Nirvana Devi's invitation to visit her in Pune had not yet crossed my mind. What I needed to do first, if I wanted to lay a solid foundation for my research, was get myself to London. The Kapurthalas may have chosen Paris as their second home, but they were a princely family of the British Empire. So I boarded a train for St Pancras International and, on a windy but clear morning, made my way to the red-brick building of the British Library.

Awaiting me there, in the peaceful enclave of the Asian and African Studies reading room, was a file from the India Office Records labelled 'Rani of Mandi'. Of course, I thought, leafing through the letters, cablegrams and typewritten minutes with notes scrawled atop them in pen, the handwriting a testament to the war's urgency: the arrest of a woman who was the daughter and the wife of two of the Empire's rulers must have been a problem not only for the Crown's representative in India but for the Foreign Office itself. The folder was thick with correspondence, the involvement of British intelligence agencies evident. And the pleas for help on behalf of Amrit from the Maharaja of Kapurthala and the Raja of Mandi conveyed what appeared to be genuine anguish.

It was now up to me to interpret those grief-laden voices by putting them in their context.

# When the Taj Mahal Was for Sale

Almost no book I read on the Raj – the period of British rule in India – could resist quoting Kipling's famous words: 'Providence created the Maharajahs to offer mankind a spectacle.' And the truth was, the more research I did, the more convinced I became that this author who'd fuelled my adolescent dreams of India and the exotic – before tumbling into an abyss of accusations of imperialism, racism and misogyny – had hit the nail on the head.

In that realm of unbridled extravagance, the Nizam of Hyderabad had used a 282-carat diamond as a paperweight; the Maharaja of Gwalior had commissioned a toy train made of silver as a centrepiece for distributing cigars, port and liqueurs around the dinner table; the Maharaja of Junagadh had celebrated the marriage of his favourite golden retriever with a banquet, illustrious guests, pearls for the bride's neck, gold for the groom's paws, and a wedding processional consisting of 250 dogs, a few of which rode atop an elephant; and the Maharaja of Patiala, a passionate collector of women, at his death left behind 322 of them in his harem.

The deeper I dived into that spectacle, the more it resembled a Wes Anderson fantasy. In the world of Indian princes, newborns played with ruby-studded balls, children with golden toys, and adults with luxury cars. In his book *H. H. or the Pathology of Princes* (1930), Kanhayalal Gauba offers an extraordinary description of the cars parked outside Metcalfe House in Delhi, on the day in 1921 when the Chamber of Princes held its first meeting – an assembly whose presumed function was to bring about reforms, though it never succeeded: 'When the Chamber of Princes is in session the display of royal cars which await their owners rivals that at the New York Automobile Show. All the most expensive makes are represented – Rolls-Royces, of course, Renaults, Mercedes, Fiats, Isottas. There are cars which are gold-plated and cars which are silver-plated, cars which have hoods of polished aluminium and bodies of costly woods, cars in purple, lavender, sky-blue, orange, emerald-green, vermilion, cars upholstered in satins, velvets, brocades. One has mounted on its roof a searchlight as large as those used on destroyers; another is fitted with steel shutters, presumably to save its owner from assassination; a third has on its running-board a small pipe-organ on which an attendant plays his master's favourite airs.'

The millennia-old form of government whereby princes offered their subjects military protection in exchange for obedience, gold, agricultural products and even women had produced a society founded upon a sinkhole of inequality and ignorance. I did, nevertheless, come across a few enlightened princes. The Maharaja of Baroda banned polygamy, permitted untouchables to attend school, and funded universities out of his own pocket. In Gwalior, the maharaja had already reformed his administration by the time he turned twenty-three. The Maharaja of Bhopal elevated the status of women through education. The Maharaja of Mysore funded a university modelled after those in Chicago, Oxford and Cambridge. In Bikaner, the maharaja invested enormous resources in the building of the Ganga Canal, an irrigation system that transformed part of the Rajasthan Desert into a breadbasket and alleviated the hunger problems in his region.

And yet Gandhi was not speaking in euphemisms when he declared, in 1930, that the system allowing princes to continue their reign under the British Empire was a stain on the Empire's reputation: 'The existence of this gigantic autocracy is the greatest disproof of British democracy and is a credit neither to the Princes nor to the unhappy people who have to live under this undiluted autocracy. It is no credit to the Princes that they allow themselves powers which no human being, conscious of his dignity, should possess. It is no credit to the people who have mutely suffered the loss of elementary human freedom.'

Amrit Kaur was born twenty-six years before Gandhi would utter these words, when the Empire was at its height.

Her entry into the world in 1904, while her father was busy travelling abroad and her mother shared the women's palace with his three previous wives, came during Lord Curzon of Kedleston's tenure as the eleventh viceroy – a formidable administrator without equal in the Raj's history, and a staunch critic of Amrit's father. Curzon governed India with an iron fist, not bothering to hide his disdain for the princes, whom he considered to be a bunch of degenerates, nor his indifference towards the Indian people, whom he saw as the inheritors of a once-extraordinary civilisation now plummeting into decay. And yet the history and culture of India were dearer to him than to any viceroy before or after. When I asked my friend Peter Curzon what his great-uncle's impression of India had been upon his arrival, he quipped: 'The Taj Mahal was for sale.'

And it was true. Today Curzon is credited with rescuing and restoring that unsurpassable mausoleum, erected in the seventeenth century by the Muslim emperor Shah Jahan for his wife Mumtaz Mahal, who died giving birth to their fourteenth child. Not to mention the viceroy's efforts to revive a gem of Mughal architecture such as Fatehpur Sikri, once the Empire's capital, abandoned in the 1600s; or the pains he took to ensure that the Archaeological Survey not only recorded but also preserved what he considered to be 'the greatest galaxy of monuments in the world'.

Nevertheless, Curzon's legacy remains a prickly subject. As the historian John Keay saw it, Curzon did everything in his power to protect India's grand imperial project not only from external dangers but also from the decay threatening to corrode it from within. 'To this end he worked heroically and unselfishly, but his example terrorised rather than inspired, his caustic wit devastated rather than delighted.' In 1915, ten years after his departure from India, Maharaja Ganga Singh of Bikaner wrote that 'the subject of Curzon was so painful for some princes that merely talking about that epoch was enough to reduce them to tears'. And the English, too, found him unbearable.

Despite it all, for an imperialist of his stature, Curzon showed impressive conviction, maintaining that England's mission was to govern the subcontinent for the benefit of the Indian people and not for the industrial manufacturing interests in Manchester. In the most comprehensive and fascinating biography of Curzon, David Gilmour reports that, over his six-year term from 1899 to 1905, the viceroy committed his resources not only to the most important monuments but also to animals on the verge of extinction, restoring lion populations to their former numbers and passing a law to protect the unlucky birds whose feathers had become the latest fashion trend among the ladies of London. He prevented Bombay's government from sacrificing the magnificent Gersoppa Falls 'for the sake of some miserable cotton mill'; and he built up an irrigation system to restore life to Punjab's increasingly desert-like landscape. Upon discovering that there were no longer any craftsmen capable of working in *pietra dura*, he brought in mosaicists from Florence to help repair the damage done to the Red Fort in Delhi during the Sepoy Mutiny. Restoration expenditures for monuments in the Agra district alone cost his government £50,000.

When it came to princes, however – and Amrit's father, Jagatjit Singh, the prince of Kapurthala, above all – Curzon was not given to such generosity. Their decadent ways irked him beyond all measure.

He wished they were all as simultaneously liberal and conservative as the Princes of Cochin and Travancore, as intelligent as the young Maharaja of Gwalior, as enlightened as the old Maharaja of Jaipur: exceptions for whom he reserved his admiration. Of the others he asked only that they fulfil their role: in other words, to dazzle in their Eastern costume while at the same time abiding by the rules of Western decorum. And when it came to the question of decorum, especially regarding women, he had plenty of bones to pick with Jagatjit Singh, whom he once lambasted in a fit of anger as a 'third-class chief of fifth-rate character'.

Queen Victoria was another story. She had a weak spot for Indians and their princes. To Victoria they were impossibly glamorous and exotic; enchanted, she treated them all, indiscriminately, as important monarchs, even when their reputations were less than exemplary. To the corrupt Maharaja of Indore, whom the English would later depose for ordering the murder of a rival lover, the empress extended her most generous friendship, merely because he'd sent her a telegram on her birthday.

'Curzon grumbled that almost anyone with a turban and jewels was regarded in Europe as a prince and treated as if he were a descendant of Nebuchadnezzar,' wrote David Gilmour. The empress's attitude towards them was maternal. Even though she never travelled to India, she did spend thirteen years studying Urdu with the aid of a Muslim servant – whom she eventually promoted to the lofty position of secretary, inciting a scandal. Curzon, on the other hand, would have liked to whip them all into shape, those rajas and maharajas ('kings' and 'great kings' respectively). He was determined to prevent them from handing their domains over to a *dewan* – that is, a prime minister – or to a Crown representative, only to slip off to the casinos on the French Riviera or the dressing rooms of the Folies Bergère. To which end he later issued a mandate requiring princes to request his approval for all travel outside

India – a ruling which a cosmopolitan traveller like Jagatjit Singh of Kapurthala must have taken as an affront, but also a provocation. No wonder, then, when he was once denied permission to bring one of his wives to Europe he sneaked Amrit's mother, Rani Kanari, out of India dressed as a boy.

We also learn from Gilmour that in 1900, after only a year in India, Curzon warned the empress that her vassals were 'frivolous and sometimes vicious spendthrifts and idlers'. Victoria may indeed have had a sympathy for her 'dark-skinned children', as her biographer Elizabeth Longford referred to them, but the viceroy was determined to open her eyes. Without mincing words, he wrote to her that the Rana of Dholpur was tumbling headlong into full-blown alcoholism; the Maharaja of Patiala was 'little better than a jockey'; the Maharaja of Indore was witless and corrupt; and Jagatjit Singh of Kapurthala thought only of his trysts with Parisian women. The truth, however, is that it was the British themselves who had encouraged the maharajas to indulge in a life of unbridled pleasure. The India that Curzon inherited from his predecessors took shape after the 1857 bloodbath of the Sepoy Mutiny, in which the British East India Company squashed the rebellion of the sepoys, the Indian infantrymen serving in the company's own army. As a result, several territories that had been controlled by the company for hundreds of years were absorbed by the Empire. The India that emerged was divided into two large zones: British India, governed directly by the Crown; and the Princely States, a mosaic of just under 600 states of varying classification and size, from Kashmir, larger than Great Britain itself, to micro-states like Jalia Manaji, hardly bigger than a courtyard. The English went about conquering these realms one by one, forming separate alliances and treaties, and granting different levels of autonomy in their internal affairs. But all states were subject to the law that paramount power, the highest rule, lay exclusively and absolutely with the British Crown.

This meant that hundreds of Indian states who'd been at war for thousands of years were suddenly faced with peace. And their princes with time to kill. Enlisting them among the ranks of the British army was out of the question, because it would mean placing whites under the command of non-white officers. So what the British did, in a sense, was offer them a deal with the devil: they could maintain their titles, honours, riches and possessions in exchange for renouncing their supreme authority. This not only stripped them of their responsibilities, it also cut the umbilical cord that had tied them to their subjects for centuries, breaking the contract between a *raja* and his *praja*, or ruler and ruled, which had long been the foundation of their shared history.

It's no surprise, then, that some of the princes left their domains in the hands of administrators while they ran off and caroused in Europe, as Jagatjit Singh did in Paris throughout the 1920s and 1930s. The Prefecture's archives had an impressive stack of accident reports involving his Hispano-Suiza around Hotel George V, though at least Amrit Kaur's father limited himself to merely wrecking his luxury car; the Maharaja of Alwar, whenever he got tired of his own Hispano-Suizas, would bury them with great ceremony in the hills around his palace.

Another thorny issue revolved around the princes' education in England. For a girl like Amrit, boarding at Clovelly-Kepplestone clearly meant a culture shift – reading Shakespeare and Voltaire, and even learning to play the music of New Orleans's Black musicians in her all-girl jazz band. But it also meant that, after such a strong dose of the cosmopolitan life, being forced to honour an arranged marriage – and as a consequence being dispatched to a very remote and traditional area of Punjab – was hardly an attractive prospect, especially when the groom chosen for her had received a more limited education than hers. Even for the young male princes, like Amrit's five brothers, it was often difficult to reassimilate back home in India after attending elite schools like Harrow, or Oxford University. Curzon himself was convinced that an Oxford graduate could never make a good ruler in India, and experience seemed to prove him right. There's an irresistible passage in David Gilmour's *The Ruling Caste* when the Crown's representative of Central India in 1888 informs the Minister of Foreign Affairs that the English education of the young princes in his region had thus far produced 'sodomites 2, idiots 1, sots 1 . . . and a gentleman . . . prevented by chronic gonorrhoea from paying his respects on the Queen's birthday'.

You can imagine, then, just how irritated the viceroy must have been to learn that Queen Victoria had on one occasion received the prince of a minor state like Kapurthala at Balmoral Castle, allowing him to treat the Kaiser and the Czar as equals. As a result of this encounter, Jagatjit Singh would take the liberty of upgrading himself from raja to maharaja: a promotion that, under traditional circumstances, would have fallen upon the British authorities to eventually bestow. This process formed a part of the package of institutional perks that the English developed to flatter the princes, along with a gun salute (each prince was granted a number of blank cannon rounds, from nine to twenty-one depending on their state's importance, to be fired in their honour on official occasions); a coat of arms, designed from scratch by the queen's heraldic experts; and knighthoods with extravagant titles like the Most Exalted Order of the Star of India.

The irony of all this is that a maharaja of the likes of Amrit Kaur's father, so openly disdained by the most formidable viceroy in the Empire's history, would win himself a position of international prestige destined to outlast Curzon's term by forty years.

Thanks to the military aid Kapurthala gave to the British during the First World War, in 1919 Jagatjit Singh had the honour of being invited to the Paris Peace Conference; and of representing India in the League of Nations in Geneva in 1926, 1927 and 1929.

His social savvy took care of the rest.

Maharaja Jagatjit Singh on the Kapurthala throne.

# The Kapurthalas and the Cradle of Mankind

It would come as no shock to the reader of the English explorer Rosita Forbes's *India of the Princes* (1939) that of the fourteen states that made up the Punjab region – which is to say, the triangle of loosely defined borders in the subcontinent's north-west corner, comprising what is today the eastern half of Pakistan all the way up to the slopes of the Himalayas – Bahawalpur was the largest, Patiala the most populated, but Kapurthala the most widely known outside India.

Like Punjab's other states, Amrit Kaur's birthplace benefited from the region's extraordinary geographic position, with five rivers flowing through it: an enormous breadbasket, ancient enough to have been the cradle of mankind, and culturally rich enough to have produced the Vedas, the remarkable body of texts that stand as the spiritual foundation of Hindu culture, expressing a knowledge that encompasses all, from a grain of sand to the edge of the universe.

It was in this region, according to the *Mahabharata* – the world's longest epic poem – that the Kurukshetra War was fought, centuries before the birth of Christ: a struggle for dynastic succession between two families of lunar descent, the Pandavas and the Kauravas. And it was here, too, on the shores of the sacred Sarasvati River, that the god Krishna passed on the teachings of the *Bhagavad Gita* to a despairing archer of the Pandava clan, Arjuna, in verses that continue to wield their influence. According to the legend, the blood spilled by those heroes produced the most fertile soil in all of India.

It wasn't until I spoke to the Sanskrit scholar Silvia D'Intino that I understood the full depth of Amrit Kaur's ties to Punjab and its rich history: 'Amrit's first name means "immortal", while Kaur is a mythical name, harking back to the Kaurava family in the *Mahabharata*.' Like 'Singh' (lion) for men, 'Kaur', meaning either 'prince' or 'princess', can be used as a title, middle name or surname. And, being both masculine and feminine, it is symbolically very important, since it indicates the equality between men and women espoused by the Sikh religion. In a country like India, where a person's last name indicates their caste, the fact that all Sikh men go by Singh and all women by Kaur symbolises a freedom from the caste system's constraints.

One myth about the origin of Punjab's fertile ground tells of an Iron Age king named Kuru. Passing through Punjab one day, the king finds that his chariot has suddenly transformed into a plough, pulled by two terrifying beasts: the Bull of Shiva, lord of destruction, and the Buffalo of Lord Yama, ruler of the underworld. Driven on by a mysterious voice, Kuru sets about ploughing the vast stretch of land before him – until, having completed the last furrow, he sees the blue-skinned god Vishnu descend to earth to speak with him. Vishnu commands the king to sow the virtues of mankind. But Kuru has no seeds. For fear of disappointing the god, he decides to sacrifice one of his own arms, chop it into thousands of pieces, and plant each piece in the earth to grow. In a spirit of generosity, he then offers his other arm as well. Then one leg. Then the other. And finally his own head. At which point the gods declare themselves satisfied and give him their blessing.

On this patch of earth enriched with the blood of a king, over the course of the millennia one group after another made their home: the people of the Indus Valley and the Aryans; the Persian kings Cyrus and Darius; Alexander the Great and Genghis Khan. Entire civilisations came and went. And from that intermingling of Asians and Europeans arose a new population, with caramel skin and delicate features. Sifting through libraries and ordering out-of-print volumes from antiquarian booksellers, I turned up still more legends. One of them claimed that Kapurthala was established in the eleventh century, between the Beas and Jalandhar Rivers, by a man named Rana Kapur of Jasailmer, a prince of the Rajput clan. The noblest of warrior castes, the Rajputs traced their lineage back to the Aryan population that gave India the *Rigveda* (the oldest of the Vedas) and, further back, to the very sun and moon.

But, lacking evidence, historians seem to have come to a different consensus: that the Kapurthala family descended from the more modest caste of the Jat Kala, or the Distillers, which, according to the English historian and diplomat Lepel H. Griffin, was no downgrade at all. 'The Rajas of Kapurthalla [*sic*] have no need of fiction to make them illustrious,' he wrote in *The Rajas of the Punjab* (1873). 'Bravery, loyalty and devotion, wise and just administration, and an example of liberality and enlightenment set to all Princes of India, would have allowed the late raja of Kapurthalla to dispense with an ancestor altogether without disgrace, had not the true founder of the family, Sardar Jassa Singh, been the leader of the Khalsa and the most distinguished of all the Sikh Chiefs north of the Satlej [*sic*],' the longest of the five rivers that flow through the region of Punjab in northern India and Pakistan.

Amrit Kaur's ancestors, therefore, descended not just from any great leader but from a head of the Khalsa itself: the spiritual and military brotherhood of initiated Sikhs, established in the late seventeenth century to combat Mughal oppression and protect the innocent from all forms of religious persecution. When I searched for an image of Sardar Jassa Singh Ahluwalia (1718–83), I found several paintings depicting a vigorous old man, not unlike Zeus, with a stark white beard, jet-black eyes and eyebrows, a dagger on his belt and his right hand clasping the hilt of a *talwar* – a traditional Indian sabre.

This man of Greek-god-like stature proved himself to be one of the most courageous and magnanimous Sikh leaders, the 'Saint-Soldiers' who devoted themselves to the religion founded in the fifteenth century in none other than Punjab by Guru Nanak – one of those irrepressible idealists who crop up now and then among the merchants and craftsmen of smaller villages, like Saint Francis of Assisi in Italy. Inspired by the idea that only one truth exists and that each prophet gleans a different aspect of that truth, Guru Nanak founded a monotheistic faith that borrowed elements from Hinduism as well as Islamic Sufism. At the centre of this faith was not a god but a holy book, the *Guru Granth Sahib*, an expression of the Creator containing the teachings of the ten principal Sikh gurus. The book condemns idolatry, breaks with the Hindu tradition of asceticism and castes, and preaches equality between men and women. When I saw the scripture with my own eyes, transported on a golden palanquin festooned with flowers, at an evening ceremony at the Golden Temple in Amritsar, the crowd was praying with such fervour that I could feel the air vibrating like the string of an enormous double bass. All around the temple, reflected in the immense mirror of the surrounding water – where Sikhs are required to bathe at least once a year – men and women of all religions were greeted openly and invited to take a purifying dip.

The population in Kapurthala was composed of different religious faiths. According to a 1921 census, 22 per cent of its 284,000 inhabitants were Sikh, like Amrit Kaur's family; 20 per cent Hindu; 56 per cent Muslim; and 2 per cent of other faiths. But there was something peculiar: one branch of the royal family had converted to Christianity, and as a consequence was cut off from the line of succession to the throne. Among that branch was a cousin of Amrit's, also named Amrit, whose full title was Rajkumari Amrit Kaur of Kapurthala. *This* Amrit Kaur, who was seventeen years older than her cousin and who never married, was a towering figure, a heroine of the Gandhian nationalist movement. She would never fade from view like the younger Amrit. As Gandhi's closest assistant, she dedicated her life to his cause and spent three years in prison with him before becoming the Health Minister of India in the new era of independence under Prime Minister Jawaharlal Nehru. But I never did find evidence of any relations between the two cousins. The dynastic squabbles stemming from that conversion to Christianity must have caused a rift between the family's two branches long before either of them was born.

In the search to restore *my* Amrit Kaur to her context, however, I had plenty to work with in Punjab's rich and troubled history. From the moment the Europeans arrived, India was almost constantly being invaded from the north-west. As a result, Punjab became a perennial object of conquest, subject to centuries of raids by populations who came to be known invariably as 'Afghani invaders'. It was in this climate of conquests and pillaging that the Kapurthalas' forefather, Jassa Singh, distinguished himself for his bravery. When the Emperor of Persia, Nader Shah, invaded Punjab in 1739, slaughtered 100,000 people, sacked Delhi and made off with a vast treasure that included the Mughal emperor's priceless Peacock Throne and the Koh-i-Noor diamond, Jassa Singh, then only twenty years old, fought to liberate the slaves who were claimed as booty. And after many other battles won and lost – always taking cover in the nearby forests – he conquered Kapurthala in 1774 and established his capital there.

Little remains today of the *lakhi*, 'the forest of a hundred thousand trees' that protected him and his soldiers during the years of wars against the Afghani invaders. In *A History of the Sikhs* (1963) Khushwant Singh writes that, in the sixteenth century, northern Punjab boasted jungles with rhinoceroses and elephants, and that until the middle of the nineteenth century the forests that gave cover to Jassa Singh and his soldiers were swarming not only with tigers and leopards but with lions, panthers, bears, wolves, hyenas, wild boar and deer. After that, everything changed. 'The flora and the fauna survived the incursions of foreign armies but succumbed to indiscriminate felling of trees and slaughter of game in the nineteenth and the present century.' Punjab, the cradle of Indian civilisation, the birthplace of Vedic culture and the land of wheat, rice, barley, cotton and sugar cane, began its slow transformation into an arid, windswept territory where only goats and camels could survive.

In any case, contrary to my first impression, the riches and possessions that comprised Amrit Kaur's family fortune were not conquered by the sword of Jassa Singh during Punjab's prosperous years, but much more recently, by the princess's great-grandfather, Randhir Singh (1831–70). As always, behind that accumulation of land and money lay a successful military campaign. When the Sepoy Mutiny broke out against the East India Company in 1857, Randhir Singh of Kapurthala was among the first to band with the English, marching at the head of an army of 1,200 infantrymen, 200 cavalrymen and five cannon. A year later, he again ran to Queen Victoria's rescue, in Oudh, in the Awadh region of northen India, where he fought for ten months. As a reward for his courage and display of loyalty to the Empire he received money, lands, the privilege of an eleven-gun military salute and the title Farzand-i-Dilband Rasikh-ul-Itiqad-i-Inglishia, meaning 'Favoured son of the English nation'. The English also granted him the perpetual right of adoption, should he lack a male heir.

After his many military victories, I discovered, this lion of Punjab set his sights on another matter close to his heart having little to do with war: his dream of visiting green England and resting in the shade of its lindens and oaks. For years he'd been forced to put this dream on hold because of a hereditary dispute that kept him bound to Kapurthala. But, having emerged victorious from this family battle, Amrit's great-grandfather set sail in 1870 to pay his respects to the queen he'd so bravely served – even though he was in poor health and his doctors had discouraged him from travelling. His plan was to spend a year in England, weather permitting. On a stop along the way in Aden, however, his condition worsened and he was quickly transferred to a ship heading back to Bombay.

It struck me as a cruel, cynical fate for a warrior of such intensity and intelligence as Randhir Singh to die at the age of only thirty-nine, in the middle of the ocean, unable to partake in what may have been the one indulgence in his life.

# A Most Parisian Maharaja

There to receive Randhir Singh's body at the Port of Bombay was his firstborn son, Kharak Singh: a twenty-year-old boy tormented by psychosis, whom doctors would later place in confinement in a home in the Himalayas, banning him from seeing another living soul until his death. It is to this most ill-fated prince that we owe the birth of Amrit Kaur's father. However, conflicting stories have emerged regarding the origins of Jagatjit Singh of Kapurthala.

The omnipresent aide-de-camp, functionary, travel companion and court gossip Diwan Jarmani Dass tells us in his memoir, *Maharaja* (1969), that Kharak Singh and his wife Anand Kaur were unable to have children (Kharak's brother Harnam, having converted to Christianity, had de facto removed himself from the line of succession). According to Dass's unofficial version, with no viable heir to the throne, Kapurthala's prime minister advised the rani to declare herself pregnant, never mind that her husband was far afield: the palace doctors and nurses would confirm her pregnancy. Nine months later – on 26 November 1872, at two o'clock in the morning, to be precise – a bundle containing the newborn child of one Lala Harichand, later rewarded with the role of Finance Minister, was taken from his family and placed in the rani's arms. Five years later, her husband Kharak Singh died in exile in the Himalayas 'under mysterious circumstances' – an expression that seemed to crop up often in histories of the Raj, though I could never tell if it was due to a lack of information, mythomania, or because someone really had been killed. Whatever the case, the title of raja fell to that newborn boy, who would grow fat and full of curiosity for the world, and the Indian government officially recognised him as the child of Kapurthala's deceased raja.

By the time he was eighteen – when he could finally take the reins from the interim regency council that had governed while he was a minor – Jagatjit Singh already knew English, French, Farsi, Sanskrit, Hindi, Urdu and Gurmukhi. At twenty, determined to realise, and surpass, his grandfather Randhir Singh's dream, he set sail for the West.

'This will ever be a memorable day,' he wrote in his diary on 11 April 1893, while in Florence. 'I had the privilege of being presented to our beloved Empress-Queen. Her Majesty is staying at the Villa Palmieri, in the environs. Although her stay in Florence is entirely private . . . Her Majesty was pleased to intimate that she would be glad to receive me.'

His meeting with the empress in that fourteenth-century villa – whose heavenly gardens inspired the setting of Boccaccio's *Decameron* – must have gone well for the young raja, who scored a success. It was afternoon when he arrived at the hilltop villa in Fiesole, where Victoria awaited him in a boudoir, along with Princess Beatrice and Prince Henry of Battenberg. There he seized the occasion to bring up his grandfather Randhir Singh, expressing his own desire to bow to the woman who'd inspired such a faithful ally of the Empire to embark on his courageous, and ultimately tragic, voyage to England. His words must have worked their magic on the empress, who extended him a highly coveted invitation to the wedding of the Duke of York and Princess Mary, to be held three months later in the Chapel Royal at St James's Palace in London, with a night's stay at Windsor Castle. After exchanging a few more pleasantries, Jagatjit Singh was given a tour of the gardens by a member of the court and sent on his way.

The true key to understanding Jagatjit Singh's character is in his diaries, published in two volumes: *My Travels in Europe and America*

(1893) and *My Travels in China, Japan and Java*, published ten years later.

From these pages I learned that, after visiting London – which disappointed him – and pursuing the empress in Florence – which delighted him – the twenty-year-old prince of Kapurthala had made his way to New York, where the public transportation system, with its elevated railway and trams, left him in awe, as did the height of the buildings. In Newport he met the Vanderbilts, in Cambridge he visited the campus of Harvard University, in Chicago he studied the efficiency of a nursery school, and at the Midway Plaisance anthropological park he met 'some genuine Red Indian Chiefs'. 'I was surprised,' he wrote, 'to find several words in their language that have a strong resemblance to Turki as spoken in Central Asia. I am inclined to think they are of Mongolian origin, having crossed over into America by way of Kamchatka.'

Ten years later, on the eve of Amrit's birth, Jagatjit Singh would leave for his second grand tour, this time travelling to the Far East. Now his diary revealed a more mature and eager ruler, looking to learn from others' experience about the art of statecraft.

In China, he found Beijing to be the 'City of Chaos and Evil Odours' and the food 'revolting', but Shanghai won him over with its modernity and its international newspapers – British, American, French and German. 'They partake more of the style of journalism current in America than anything we have in India.' He visited temples, opium dens and orphanages; and he marvelled before Guglielmo Marconi's radio, on display at the Italian delegation's residence.

In Japan, however, he liked everything he saw, starting with the ships at Nagasaki port bearing flags from all over the world. In Tokyo he sat in on naval architecture courses at the Imperial College; witnessed trials at the High Court of Justice; and joined a garden party thrown by the empress, who came out dressed in green velvet, European-style, her face 'absolutely expressionless'.

Visiting a prison, he discovered that each cell had its own sanitary services, and that the prisoners could wash themselves in a tub three times a week. 'Cleanliness is held in high esteem in Japan: even the coolies bathe every day!' In Kyoto, on the other hand, his encounter with a Buddhist high priest left him underwhelmed: 'I really wanted to ascertain the difference or resemblance between the religion in Japan and that prevailing among the Hindus in India. All I succeeded in accomplishing in this direction was the usual polite bow and smile of acquiescence.' He had more luck a few days later, at a geisha school, where they received him with just the kind of refined submissiveness that aligned with his tastes. On his way to Java he visited the psychiatric hospital in Buitenzorg, a hill station founded by Dutch colonists on the island of Batavia, a place that would hardly attract your average tourist.

These trips, undertaken with a crew of seven or eight – which invariably included an Indian chef – would not be without their consequences. The same prince who in 1889 had commissioned a majestic durbar – the council room where princes and their ministers met with their subjects – in the most traditional Indo-Saracenic style in 1917 called upon Patrick Geddes, the sociologist, geographer and pioneering city planner, to draw up a report on how to improve the capital, which would soon see the construction of new schools, hospitals and places of worship. He replaced Kapurthala's old Mughal mosque with one inspired by Marrakesh's magnificent Kutubiyya. And to help him with this new project he turned to a Frenchman, Maurice Mantout – one of the architects responsible for the Grand Mosque of Paris, whose cornerstone ceremony the prince himself attended in 1922.

This gesture of supplying Kapurthala with a new mosque was a significant one, since it stood as evidence of one of Jagatjit Singh's most agreeable and magnanimous qualities. In his 1930 inauguration speech, he took care to point out that the city had a Hindu temple built by his ancestors and a *gurdwara* that he himself had commissioned for the Sikhs. Now the time had come for his Muslim subjects to have a house of worship worthy of their religion. This ecumenism was part of an open-mindedness that paid honour to the roots of the Sikh religion, whose founder, Guru Nanak, taught that the Hindu god and the Muslim god were one and the same, and that what counted was the spirit of one's faith, not what shape it took. Jagatjit Singh may have been a secular enough ruler to forgo a beard, yet his principles of ecumenism and tolerance remained steadily in line with the teachings of Sikhism's founder.

The Western capital that really conquered his heart was Paris, which he discovered on his first trip to Europe in 1893. Young, handsome and ambitious, he made his debut into Parisian society at the grand ball of the Princess of Sagan, where he had the chance to consort with the Duchess of Aosta and the Princess of Chimay, and to strike up a friendship with the king of all socialites, André de Fouquières, who'd go on to become his companion for more than five decades of salon-hopping – duly chronicled in de Fouquières' memoir *Cinquante ans de panache* (1951). An exotic newcomer, with his diamond *sarpech* ornament pinned to a pink turban and his silk brocade *achkan*, the maharaja made an enduring impression. For the next forty years Parisian aristocracy would be pleased to open the doors of its festively lit *hôtels particuliers* to the fashionable prince. These balls – a few of which were 'in Oriental costume' – even gave Jagatjit Singh the distinct honour of dressing as himself. However, for all their splendour, for me they began to bleed into one another – with one notable exception: when the Hôtel de Beaumont was transformed into a surrealist aquarium for an evening in 1928. There, among jellyfish and goldfish, the Kapurthala prince met the cubist painter Marie Laurencin, was introduced to the Russian choreographer Léonide Massine and to the Duchesse d'Ayen, and shared a few words with the composer Francis Poulenc, who was chatting with Madame de Lubersac – all dressed as fish. In the meantime, as de Fouquières tells it, the Countesses of Andlau, Mortemart and Caumont made their appearance 'draped in fishing net, as if trapped in a trawl'. Not even Proust would have dared imagine such a luxuriantly frivolous scene.

To return the favour, Jagatjit Singh threw a number of garden parties at the Pavillon de Kapurthala, where, as de Fouquières wrote, dipping his pen in arsenic, the guests were a bit confused about how to greet him. So 'Kneels followed bows and nods followed kneels . . .' That pavilion in the Bois de Boulogne was one of Amrit's father's earliest property ventures, so to speak, and by no means his most extravagant. In fact, it appears to have been that very first jaunt in Paris that sparked Jagatjit Singh to commission a French-style palace modelled after Versailles on the Punjab Plain – complete with Aubusson rugs, Gobelins tapestries, Louis XVI furniture, and staffed by wig-wearing servants. I was surprised to discover that the maharaja's architect was, ironically, an expert in the Orientalist style: the very same Alexandre Marcel who, in 1896, had designed the Japanese-influenced *salle des fêtes* on the rue de Babylone which Parisians know as La Pagode.

That folly, built by an architect with such close ties to Amrit Kaur's father, happened to stand on the street right behind my new home, lending the block a touch of exoticism. I'd been intrigued by that peculiar structure ever since I first began exploring my new neighbourhood in Paris, when I caught sight of this small building with its comma-shaped roof, surrounded by wisteria and a bamboo garden, that would have made more sense in Kyoto than on the corner of the rue de Babylone and the rue Monsieur.

As I'd later discover, La Pagode was a central fixture of Parisian society during the Belle Époque. Marcel had designed it for a co-owner of the Bon Marché department stores, François-Émile Morin,

Kapurthala's royal palace, designed by the French architect Alexandre Marcel, was completed in 1911.

who was hoping the extravagant gift would help win back his rather distracted wife. Madame Morin accepted the gift, though she left her husband all the same for one of his business associates. And for years the new couple made La Pagode home to some of the city's most spectacular parties. Then, beginning in the 1930s, that *salle* with its gold flower-print Japanese wallpaper became home to one of France's first cinemas. And possibly the most beautiful of all.

So it happened that Marcel's design for the royal palace, completed in 1911, brought the last touch of French charm to the little capital where Amrit Kaur was born. In *India of the Princes*, Rosita Forbes described Kapurthala as an anomaly: 'It has the tinsel fragility of an exhibition. A scrap of Paris laid at the foot of the Himalayas, it has the temporary quality of exile, but the effect is enchanting. The palace of a ruler, whose spiritual home might well be Versailles,

The palace's 'French' drawing room.

resembles, with some logic, a chateau with gardens in the manner of Le Nôtre. The town at the gates is a feudal village, admirably maintained. There are some delicious pink villas to which one can imagine the Parisian bourgeois retiring in middle age. The gardens of these are as neat and as unimaginative as their prototypes in the suburbs of Fontainebleau . . . Prison or palace, law court or post office, temple or mosque, hospital, school, or co-operative credit bank, have the same charming appearance of being planned for an exhibition of decorative art. Undoubtedly the Maharajah has a talent for creation. Nothing could be more interesting than the model State he has made, an oasis, delectable and original, but not in the least typical of India, between Lahore and the Kashmiri tableland.'

Jagatjit Singh's royal palace was naturally the largest attraction in town, and it was said he'd built it as a gift for a woman, just like Monsieur Morin's Pagode: a gesture in which I recognised a fusion of

Kapurthala in 1927.

power, competition and desire. But unlike Morin's enchanting folly, which failed to win back his wife, Jagatjit Singh's pink 'Versailles', completed by Alexandre Marcel when Amrit was eight years old, brought him better luck. The maharaja dedicated it to the young Anita Delgado, the Spanish dancer who in 1908 became his fifth wife, thus entering the already crowded group of women that, in addition to the four established ranis, included at least one European lover per season. A list of these female companions – though far from complete – comprised the alluring silent-film actress Jane Renouardt; a certain Mademoiselle Séret; a Henriette Serrurier and an Arlette Serry. However, the brightest star in that firmament seemed to be the chic and beautiful daughter of a Piedmontese bricklayer whom the maharaja met at the boutique on the French Riviera where she worked, eventually sending a private boat from India to sail her back. After more than a year in Kapurthala, where she made herself known for her verve and intelligence, Mademoiselle Germaine Pellegrino returned to France and, in secret, married the founder of the

French cinema chain Cineac, Reginald Ford. On receiving a lavish pearl necklace from the oblivious maharaja, she graciously accepted it as a wedding gift.

I was beginning to understand why Lord Curzon had such an issue with Amrit Kaur's father. He was as ecumenical in his love life as he was with religions, and such behaviour was bound to get him into trouble. Playing it safe, the maharaja chose his first four wives from among young aristocrats of Rajput blood. The first, Harbans Kaur, was a princess of Paprola, a small state in the Himalayan valley of Kangra, where in 1886 Jagatjit Singh made a triumphant arrival with a nuptial court of 4,494 people and thirty-seven elephants. On the heels of this wedding, in 1891, came his marriage to Parvati Kaur of Katoch, and one year later to Lachmi Kaur of Bushahr. Unlike the first three, Amrit Kaur's mother, Rani Kanari, whom Jagatjit Singh married in 1895, was not a princess, but the daughter of a minister of Jubbal.

The fact that Rani Kanari accompanied the maharaja on his trips to Europe, while the others were confined to the *zenana*, the separate quarters where Jagatjit Singh's wives lived, seems to indicate her higher level of education. Out of these marriages came a small army of boys – four – and a single girl, Amrit, who inherited her mother's good looks and her father's physical presence. But then entered the beautiful Anita Delgado, trailed by the scent of scandal, since the British strongly disapproved of mixed marriages, and the Indian population frowned upon them too. She and the prince had first met in 1906 when Anita, a sixteen-year-old girl from a modest family, was performing Andalusian dances at a club in Madrid and Jagatjit Singh was in town for the wedding of King Alfonso XIII. The thirty-three-year-old maharaja courted her in secret, though her family would soon intervene. Unable to have her any other way, he sent Anita's parents a formal marriage request. He then sent her to be educated in Paris, married her in a quiet ceremony at the *mairie* of the seventeenth arrondissement, and in 1907 brought her back with him to Kapurthala – where, under the new name Prem Kaur, she flourished for eighteen tranquil years, arousing the jealousy of his other wives, the racism of his aristocratic daughters-in-law and the not-so-disinterested admiration of other Indian princes. When she accompanied her husband to the home of the richest man in India, the Nizam of Hyderabad, every time she sat down at the table she found more jewellery hidden in her napkin – which gave rise to a diplomatic dispute.

Anita, however, would not let herself be intimidated by this cold reception from the maharaja's family and from the women in the *zenana*. She continued to dress like a European whenever she pleased; she accompanied her husband on his travels abroad, attended his banquets and maintained a remarkable spiritual independence.

Only fourteen years stood between her and Amrit, her husband's young daughter. This might have made her a kind of older sister figure, or surrogate mother, given that Amrit's birth mother died in 1910 when the girl was just six. Meanwhile, Anita and Jagatjit Singh bore their own son, the handsome Ajit Singh, after which the maharaja's interest waned, their marriage foundered, and in 1925 the couple signed a separation agreement. It was then that Anita Delgado left for Paris, and eventually home to Madrid, where she lived a life of considerable comfort, managing to stay on good terms with the maharaja. When Amrit left for Europe in 1933, some family members took it for granted that she'd chosen Paris to be close to her beloved stepmother.

The story of Anita Delgado was, all told, a tale with a happy ending. And she for her part demonstrated an uncommon level of good sense in navigating a complex situation. Such luck, I discovered, did not befall the maharaja's sixth and final wife, the young Eugenie Grosupova, daughter of a Czechoslovakian actress and a nondescript count. Despite her reluctance, Grosupova was persuaded to marry the ageing Jagatjit Singh by her mother and grandmother, who feared that such a propitious opportunity would not come around twice.

This brown-haired, blue-eyed girl, who appeared rather unassuming in photographs, agreed to leave Prague in 1937 and arrived in Kapurthala under the guise of a mistress, with her mother and grandmother in tow as her personal housemaids. Five years would pass before Jagatjit Singh agreed to ask her hand in marriage and 'Nina' Grosupova's name changed to Tara Devi. The crestfallen girl had no luck finding a place for herself in the court, and with no official role for her (British authorities denied her the title of maharani) their marriage became a political problem for the maharaja.

Neither the British nor the Indians would forgive her her humble origins, just as they'd done with Anita. But in every other sense, the destinies of these two Cinderellas could not have been more different. Marrying the prince, for the former, meant gaining a social standing, a life of comfort, and eventually her well-financed freedom; for the latter it meant being humiliated by her new relatives, regarded with suspicion by the servants, and banned from any function where the English were present.

One summer, while the maharaja was on holiday with the court in Mussoorie – a hill station in Uttarakhand where the Kapurthalas had, and still have, a 'château' inspired by the castles in the Loire – Nina Grosupova's grandmother and mother died in quick succession, in one of those mysterious circumstances that I was coming to recognise. Nina, who by then felt she was surrounded by enemies, suspected that they'd been poisoned by the servants. Fearing for her life – Jagatjit Singh had again tired of the marriage, and this time he'd made it clear that he would not be bowing to another exorbitant separation – she attempted to flee India. The attempt failed when the British authorities refused to grant her a passport.

Depressed and seized by paranoia, she sought refuge at a hotel in Delhi – at first, it appears, accompanied by a handsome military officer. Then one day she took a taxi to the Qutb Minar, the magnificent twelfth-century minaret named after a Sufi saint, whose 240 feet of red sandstone pierces the Delhi sky like a giant smokestack.

And there, after climbing up 379 steps, she leaped to her death, clutching her two favourite Pomeranians in her arms.

Jagatjit Singh was far away when it happened. But that didn't stop the press coverage from casting a shadow over the prince.

# Wedding Extravaganza

On 13 January 1911, in Marseille, four hundred guests boarded a steamer headed for Bombay. Three hundred hailed from England, the United States and South America, the rest were French. Among these I found the names of the notorious spendthrift and blue blood Prince Antoine d'Orléans-Braganza, the Prince and Princess Amédée and Marie de Broglie, the Countess de Pracomtal, the counts Jean and Charles de Polignac, the architect Alexandre Marcel, and the ever-present André de Fouquières, who'd memorialize the trip in his 1912 book *Au Paradis des Rajahs*.

The grand occasion at hand was the wedding of Amrit Kaur's

Amrit in white aged seven, sitting with her three eldest brothers, 1911.

oldest brother: Tikka Raja Paramjit Singh, the firstborn son of the Maharaja of Kapurthala, and Princess Brinda of Jubbal. The bride was sixteen and the groom eighteen, and they'd been engaged since they were young children. In a group photo with one hundred or so of the Western guests, we find Amrit at age seven, seated at the feet of her brothers and dressed in white.

I found two very different accounts of this celebration, which Jagatjit Singh saw as an opportunity to dazzle his distinguished guests and boost his international reputation. The first was a portrait so besotted with admiration it elevated flattery to an art form; the second checked such sugary excess with the bitterness of melancholy and sadness.

André de Fouquières told of their trip across sun-scorched Punjab, with its sparse trees set against a cloudless blue, until the guests came upon a mirage: an encampment with 240 tents set up in the palace garden, arranged as a fully functioning village. 'Mine was a miniature palace, with all of the finest comforts: furniture in pure Louis XVI style, antique paintings, layers of oriental rugs . . . a marble fireplace, electric light, a bathroom . . .'

Guests' tents for Brinda and Tikka Paramjit Singh of Kapurthala's wedding celebrations, 1911.

The drawing-room tent.

This tent city on the Punjab Plain had its own post office, a barber, a large reception hall with potted plants and bridge tables, and a lunch room that could seat 300. Beneath the canopied entrance to the smoking room, guests encountered gentlemen dressed as explorers with pith helmets, *boulevardiers* in morning coats, and 'fascinating women in light dresses, holding umbrellas too delicate for such a ruthless sun'.

Lunch for 800 preceded the grand ball in Durbar Hall. And here the maharaja's self-appointed French ambassador lost all linguistic restraint: 'Imagine a mélange of glimmering fabric, stitched with gold and silver, imagine stupendous jewellery, diamond-crusted plumes, necklaces sagging with pearls, earrings of emerald, sapphire, ruby, topaz, turquoise, every gem, every stone that casts reflections, dancing light, a perpetual swirl of lights.' In the face of such exultant prose, I found myself missing Francis de Croisset, the French playwright and librettist for Massenet, who, describing the festivities for Jagatjit Singh's 1927 jubilee in the *Revue des Deux Mondes*, had the stroke of brilliance to write, 'Beneath thousands of coloured lamps, the palace, this evening, blazes like Broadway.'

As for the other account of this multi-day marriage extravaganza – during which the ladies, guarded by broad-brimmed hats, participated

The maharaja with the heir to the throne, Prince Paramjit Singh, getting
ready for the elephants' parade, 1911.

in the running of the elephants, and the Count of Polignac won the
camel-riding derby, to the utter disapproval of our Parisian chronicler
('it remains one of my most unpleasant memories') – I found it, of
all places, in the bride's memoirs.

In *Maharani: The Story of an Indian Princess* (1954), the then elderly
Brinda of Kapurthala looked back on her own wedding as a moment
of profound anxiety and conflicting emotions: pride, disorientation,
arrogance and humiliation all crashing over one another like waves
on a shore. The aristocratic Brinda, born Princess of Jubbal in the
Rajput clan, considered her marriage with a Sikh, arranged by her
father in a moment of grave difficulty, to be far beneath her status.

It would not have been easy for a devoted young Hindu woman to
return to India after five years in Paris in order to honour a promise
made by her parents when she was only seven years old. Her future

father-in-law had been the one to invite her to France, so that she could complete her education there and learn to be a worldly maharani. By a series of fortunate circumstances Brinda was entrusted to the care of a brilliant and affectionate woman, at whose table she became acquainted with the names of Marcel Proust, Émile Zola, Captain Alfred Dreyfus and Diaghilev, even before the Ballets Russes took hold of Paris. In Countess Louise de Pracomtal's home the young Brinda of Jubbal became familiar with a relatively free lifestyle, attended an excellent school, shared her aspirations and secrets with her host's daughters and lived under the same roof as her two sons. And, as teenagers do, she even fell in love with a boy – in the book she gives him a made-up name, though many clues lead me to believe that it was the countess's younger son, Alain de Pracomtal, who just a few years later would tumble into the mass grave of the First World War. And despite his pleas for her to break with tradition and marry him, the desperate Brinda couldn't summon the courage. 'I was not European enough to give up everything for love – my Indian training would not let me forget about my responsibilities so quickly.'

It was with a bleeding heart, then, that Brinda of Jubbal married her Sikh prince on 4 February 1911, before a throng of guests and curious onlookers who arrived by the thousands from all over India. And what a sight it must have been: 'A festivity in India brings not only invited guests but hordes of sightseers. From all over the country hundreds and thousands of beggars, holy men, would-be workers of miracles, and promoters of fertility began to arrive. They flocked into Kapurthala by train, on foot, by cart, and on every sort of beast. Nor were they unwelcome, for tradition decreed that they were every bit as important as the princes invited by His Highness.'

The bride's preparations began at dawn. The ceremony lasted six hours, after which there were two receptions, one at the women's quarters, where all the female Indian guests awaited the couple, and the other at the palace, where the newlyweds would be celebrated by the foreign guests and the Indian men. When it was all over, Brinda felt overwhelmed by exhaustion, and by the thought that the young man staring at her, sitting on a pillow in a corner of their nuptial chamber, was a complete stranger. 'There was no way for my wedding night to be a happy one. I was still only a child. Even his gentleness could not make up for my innocence.'

How mistaken Jagatjit Singh had been when he publicly lauded Louise de Pracomtal for instilling in Brinda 'the precious teachings of a modern education', which he himself had strongly encouraged, to prepare her for her future role as maharani. 'In the years to come we'll reap the benefits of this innovation,' he complimented himself. Brinda, however, would argue otherwise in her book.

For the women in particular, the privilege of a European education, conferred upon a few princesses of the Raj, like Brinda and later Amrit Kaur, was the equivalent of taking a spin on the carousel of modernity only to then be kicked back a few centuries.

And indeed, Brinda's memoirs – which at the time of their publication in 1954 enjoyed a certain popularity in the West, though they were banned in India – recount precisely that: a life lived in conflict between cultural traditions that were light years apart, paired with an extraordinary ability to adapt, thanks to champagne and the Charleston. For a young Rajput girl and strict adherent of the Hindu faith, the promise of marriage to a Sikh came as a shock in itself. 'Not only did they ask equality for women, both religious and legal,' she complained of the Sikhs, 'but they [. . .] refused to accept caste.' Nevertheless, her father, Rajkumar Gambhir Chand of Jubbal, had no choice in the matter. The marriage proposal arrived on the heels of a dynastic and governmental crisis that had driven Jubbal's prime minister to suicide. As a result, Brinda's father was expelled from his family's territories and exiled without the income of a sovereign grant to sustain him. Thinking back to those nightmarish days, Brinda turned her nose up at the prime minister's act, calling it an 'expensive suicide': he'd killed himself with a mixture of poison and ground-up diamonds.

Sita Devi of Kashipur, Amrit's other sister-in-law, completed her education in India; though even for her, only thirteen in 1928 when she married Jagatjit Singh's fourth son, Karamjit Singh of Kapurthala, such a premature marriage must have been disconcerting.

Like Brinda, Sita Devi came from a very traditional Rajput family, with the additional onus of having to observe *purdah* from the time she was seven – a practice requiring her to live in seclusion with other women and banning her from revealing her face in public. The day the young bride arrived by train in Kapurthala, however, the very first thing her hyper-modern father-in-law did was remove her *ghoonghat* – a veil worn by married women – and sweep her off, head uncovered, towards the crowds who'd flocked to greet her at the station. It's a wonder she didn't faint.

When I began my quest for Amrit Kaur, it came as no surprise that Sita Devi was the first Kapurthala to turn up: the portraits taken of her in Europe in the 1930s, by some of the greatest photographers of the day, had rendered her delicate features immortal. I found another Cecil Beaton portrait that shows her in profile, wearing a low-cut dress, a quill in hand and a stupendous diamond and emerald necklace covering nearly her entire décolletage. She was a muse for Man Ray. And Diana Vreeland, in the days when she was running *Harper's Bazaar*, declared her one of the most beautiful women in the world.

In Paris, Sita Devi's Eastern glamour influenced Elsa Schiaparelli's 'Indian' collection from 1935, and conquered other stars of the fashion world as well, such as Vionnet, Molyneux, Mainbocher and Lanvin; it inspired jewellery of the rarest and most exquisite quality, which her husband personally helped design with Cartier; and it enchanted Ira Gershwin, who wrote a tune after her for the Ziegfeld Follies in 1936:

*Even if you were just half as sweet,*
*It would still be like heaven to meet*
*Such a gay Maharanee . . .*
*Paris is at your feet!*

But it was the cultural historian Charlie Scheips who really gave me a glimpse into the world of Amrit's sister-in-law. His *Elsie de Wolfe's Paris*, a richly illustrated survey of the life and times of the lauded socialite and interior designer, recounts a lunch that Elsie de Wolfe, wife of the English diplomat Sir Charles Mendl, held in honour of Gertrude Stein in the spring of 1938 at her villa in Versailles – a bizarre occasion, since other than the fact that both were homosexual and American, the two women seemed to have almost nothing in common. And there, in the photographs depicting that sunny day, I found one of Stein and her companion Alice B. Toklas chatting with Prince Karam of Kapurthala; and another of his wife, Sita, sitting on the grass in a bright *tailleur* and a homburg, attracting the curious gaze of Douglas Fairbanks like a miniature mermaid. From that same book I also learned that Sita and her husband made the rather unwise decision of joining the German ambassador's lunch in honour of the Duke and Duchess of Windsor on 22 June 1939: an occasion that would go down in history as an outrageous scandal, given that England and Germany were on the cusp of war.

All of which left me wondering, yet again: how was it that Amrit Kaur appeared at exactly none of these well-documented events? Everywhere I turned I looked for her unmistakable features, to no avail. And yet these were her Paris years: from 1920 to 1940.

Perhaps a clue about Amrit's life, I told myself, lay hidden between the lines of Brinda's memoirs.

It wasn't such a hare-brained idea, really: after their wedding, Brinda and Paramjit Singh travelled regularly to Paris – ever since,

Lunch at Elsie de Wolfe's in honour of Gertrude Stein. From left to right: *Vogue* writer John McMullin, Gertrude Stein, Alice B. Toklas and Amrit's brother, Prince Karamjit Singh of Kapurthala, Versailles, spring 1938.

according to Brinda, Jagatjit Singh had told his son and heir to the throne of Kapurthala to keep his nose out of government affairs, leading Paramjit to grow bored at home. In Paris with Brinda, on the other hand, boredom was out of the question. So exuberant was his young wife, and so devoted to the gods of amusement, she inspired one of Cole Porter's most gleeful songs, 'Let's Misbehave'.

As I listened to Porter's ode to gaiety – which seemed the perfect encapsulation of that period and its cheerful recklessness – I took up my pencil and began circling the names of everyone Brinda mentioned in a memoir that covered two world wars and an age-defining financial crisis with the ease of a butterfly flitting happily above the three catastrophes. And I was all but convinced that there was nothing for me to find in those pages when my friend Priscilla asked to borrow Brinda's book and, upon returning it, remarked: 'I read that in Paris, when she was young, she lived with the

Pracomtals, who are family friends of ours. If you'd like, I can write to Louise de Pracomtal's granddaughter.'

And so, one spring afternoon, there I was, visiting an elderly lady whom I will call Geneviève Garnier, whose father, Guillaume de Pracomtal, was a childhood friend of Brinda's and whose grandmother, Louise, had not only looked after her during her school years but had accompanied her to India on her honeymoon as a surrogate mother.

Madame Garnier lived in an apartment in the sixteenth arrondissement; to call it beautiful would be an understatement, since it was something more. When a maid led me into the living room facing out on to the Musée d'Art Moderne de la Ville de Paris, my first thought was that it must have been recently redecorated. The bluish-green paint on the walls, the plush upholstery on the sofas and armchairs, the gouaches showing views of Vesuvius, the pale pink and fuchsia of the peonies in their vases: every detail seemed to evince a life of privilege, but also an uncommon degree of perfectionism. I couldn't have said why at the time, but something about that impeccable elegance, that admirable and yet predictable tastefulness, imbued me with an overwhelming sense of well-being.

Nor did the lady of the house fall short of expectations. Over the course of our conversation, Madame Garnier, slim and upright in grey trousers and sweater, proved to be very genial. She looked at least a decade younger than her ninety-two years, and seemed sincerely glad for the excuse to go digging into the distant past. While a maid in a blue uniform set down a tray with two teacups and a little silver Art Deco teapot, she told me that Brinda of Kapurthala had kept close ties with her family: with her father Guillaume; with her uncle Alain, whose death in the First World War had devastated the family; with her aunts Yolande and Béatrice. 'My grandmother Louise de Pracomtal was very beautiful, but she had no means, since we were not the family's main branch,' she explained. 'So instead of living in the seventh arrondissement she lived in Boulogne, where she took in paying guests. I don't recall how Brinda ended up with us, but I know we remained very fond of her.'

From my own research, I knew that Brinda and Paramjit Singh's marriage eventually gave way beneath the weight of his years-long affair with a dancer in the Folies Bergère – the ravishing and uninhibited Stella Mudge: in all likelihood, the only daughter of a tightrope walker ever to tie the knot with the heir to a monarchy. But Madame Garnier preferred to omit this eccentric detail, or else she simply wasn't aware of it. Instead she told me how Brinda and the Pracomtal family had kept close ties even after the separation, when she began spending part of her summers at their estate in Brittany, accompanied by her three daughters, Indira, Urmila and Sushila. 'We called her Aunt Brinda. She wasn't beautiful, she was a bit overweight, but always full of life and humour. When she came back after the war it was clear that her situation had changed.'

I stayed there chatting with Madame Garnier for nearly an hour, pleased to share her memories from that lost time, but learning

The three princesses of Kapurthala, daughters of Brinda and Tikka Paramjit Singh: Sushila, Indira and Urmila, *c.*1935.

nothing about Amrit Kaur that could be useful to me. Then I bid her goodbye, secretly wishing I'd end up like her if I ever made it into my nineties, and I walked on towards the Seine, still gripped with that same powerful sense of relief I'd felt inside her home: a feeling I couldn't explain, given that her apartment bore no resemblance to any of the houses I'd lived in, or had even wished to live in. And yet the mere sight of those volumes and symmetries, those shapes and colours, freed me from the sense of loss that had been following me like a dark cloud since the moment I had left Italy behind, along with the memory of my brother still alive, and my family still together. If only I had a life as reassuring as Madame Garnier's, I thought to myself, crossing the pont de l'Alma, the Seine glittering in the late-afternoon sun like crushed glass.

Priscilla was waiting for me at home, eager to know how things had gone. After my daughter had finished secondary school in Paris and left for university in London, I responded to her absence and to the recent financial crisis – which had dealt a terrible blow to my newspaper, and therefore to me – by packing all my things away in storage and moving into my friend 's large apartment on the floor beneath me, at least until I could get my life back in order. So there I was, sitting at the dinner table, in the middle of my story, when Priscilla froze with a plate in her hand and said, 'I told you what happened to Madame Garnier, didn't I?'

No, I didn't believe she had.

Madame Garnier and her husband, she explained, had been close friends with her parents. 'He was the French ambassador to Morocco and Spain. And their four daughters were our friends.' The four daughters, I thought, of course: I'd noticed their wedding photographs in the living room, in the customary silver frames. Priscilla carried on, telling me how the girl closest to her in age had married a boy who'd graduated from the École Polytechnique: a handsome young man who seemed to have it all. They had three children together, then the marriage began to crumble. Priscilla's friend decided they should get a divorce, despite how much it pained her as a devout Catholic. But her husband was opposed. Things dragged on that way for a while, until one evening he grabbed a hammer and a pistol and brutally murdered his wife and two of their children. 'Only the youngest daughter survived, because she'd managed to hide in a cupboard.'

It was like being slapped across the face.

How could I have been so mistaken before? How could I have felt such comfort in the home of a woman who'd walked through the flames of hell? How had Madame Garnier, who struck me as the picture of poise and measure, survived the murder of her daughter and two grandchildren? And what about my sense of awareness, my observation skills, that minimum amount of intuition we all possess – where had they been that whole time?

Then, amid all the questions swirling in my head, one thought pushed its way to the front. And I understood, or at least I thought I understood, that the harmony I'd sensed so acutely in her home, that calculated perfection I'd found so miraculously reassuring, was the glue holding together a world that had shattered into thousands of pieces: a bulwark against evil, a means of keeping brutal reality at bay.

# PART TWO

## *Voices*

# Our People Can Never Advance Unless Our Women Do So

It was just after my visit to Madame Garnier that I finally encountered Amrit Kaur's voice. That day, I came across a two-page spread from the *New York Herald Tribune*, dated October 1927, entirely dedicated to an interview with the rani conducted at her home in Mandi, a marble palace built in the 1800s in a tiny mountain state in northern India, a trading centre at the crossroads of two waterways. A backwoods region, worlds apart from the architectural and cultural ambitions of Kapurthala.

The interview came in response to the publication of an incendiary book, a bestseller that sparked an international controversy comparable only, in our day, to Salman Rushdie's *The Satanic Verses*. The book, written by the American white supremacist Katherine Mayo, was titled *Mother India* and was a dubious work of reportage denouncing India's poor living conditions, and plenty else: its cruelty towards animals, the humiliation suffered by the untouchables, its corrupt politicians and its undereducated elite. Above all, however, it attacked Hindu culture, for permitting child marriages, tolerating sex between minors, authorising unions between adult men and young slave girls and, until it was outlawed by the British, forcing widows to immolate themselves atop their husband's funeral pyre in the Hindu tradition of *suttee*.

Someone in New York must have thought that Amrit Kaur, then a young princess of twenty-three, would be the perfect person to weigh in on these accusations. And a journalist was invited to conduct the interview at her palace, beneath the icy crown of the Himalayas.

77

Mayo was a trained historian and researcher, adept at finding grist for her mill with just the right examples. But above all else she was politically motivated, and her mission was to defend colonialism and the supremacy of white Anglo-Saxons and Protestants over all, Catholics included. In her book she described Indian women as weak, ignorant and filthy, surpassed in their inanity only by the men, who, incapable of controlling their own sexual impulses, were perpetrators of rape and homosexuality and spreaders of venereal diseases contracted from prostitutes.

But Mayo reserved the most powerful condemnation in *Mother India* for the practice of giving young girls as brides to older men. These marriages, classified as 'child marriages' – the same term used for unions where both partners are minors – rendered the girls slaves to their husband's family, barred them from receiving an education, and exposed them to premature pregnancies and widowhood, from which they often emerged alone, illiterate and with no claim to an inheritance – condemned, almost always, to a life of prostitution.

Katherine Mayo wasn't lying. She didn't have to. One need only think of the brutal rapes still being reported in newspapers today, and of the wives and mothers who are being burned alive in daily kerosene 'accidents' in the kitchen, to understand that atrocities like these persist, even in an India racing headlong into the future – horrors to which we must now add targeted crimes, only feebly reprimanded by the authorities, if at all, such as the violence committed against Muslim women and girls, and more recently Dalits, otherwise known as 'untouchables', which led one passionate defender of the marginalised, the writer Arundhati Roy, to declare, 'In a country ruled by Hindu nationalists, it's safer to be a cow than a woman or a Muslim.'

Even if she wasn't lying, Mayo presented a cynical, manipulative and blatantly biased investigation. Having attacked America's 'negroes' in previous publications, arguing that their sexual aggression and lack of self-control were a threat to 'innocent white

Anglo-Saxon women', Mayo turned her attention to India in order to cast discredit on yet another population that didn't meet the supremacist requirement of being white and Protestant; and, more urgently, to convince American supporters of Indian independence that the British Empire was the only medicine capable of curing a country and culture in decay.

Amid the pandemonium of reactions to the book, the response from Gandhi – who had been naïve enough to concede an interview to Mayo – cut straight to the point. 'This book is cleverly and powerfully written. The carefully chosen quotations give it the false appearance of a truthful book,' he wrote in the weekly magazine *Young India*. 'But the impression it leaves on my mind, is that it is the report of a drain inspector sent out with the one purpose of opening and examining the drains of the country to be reported upon, or to give a graphic description of the stench exuded by the opened drains. If Miss Mayo had confessed that she had come to India merely to open out and examine the drains of India, there would perhaps be little to complain about her compilation. But she declared her abominable and patently wrong conclusion with a certain amount of triumph: "the drains are India".'

Just weeks after its publication, *Mother India* became a bestseller and the talk of the town across three continents. Newspapers published articles praising or panning the author's opinions; theatres held debates that fomented riots and protests; and Americans soaked up Mayo's skilfully delivered ideas. Meanwhile, the English gloated over the free propaganda and Indians protested in the streets of San Francisco, London and Calcutta, even burning copies of *Mother India* and the author's portrait in front of New York's Town Hall. Soon enough, some fifty essays and pamphlets were published in response to *Mother India*. Hollywood acquired the rights for a film adaptation, and Broadway turned it into a musical. Amid this climate of wounded dignities and rampant propaganda, the *New York Herald Tribune*'s interviewer 'Michael Pym', whose real name was Marie

Louise Pym, arrived in Punjab to interview a young princess with just the right background to act as a cultural bridge. But there was another reason, I discovered, for which Pym had set her sights on Amrit Kaur: her involvement in India's women's rights movement of the 1920s and 1930s.

Between 1926 and 1931, I came to learn, while her father was busy hobnobbing with scientists and politicians in Albert Kahn's rose garden, or courting the French aristocracy at the Pavillon de Kapurthala, his daughter Amrit was on the front lines in the battle for a woman's right to an education in India, and for raising the minimum marriageable age for girls. Her name appeared among the participants in several All India Women's Conferences, organised by the Irish suffragette Margaret Cousins to discuss the most urgent reforms for women on the subcontinent.

In 1928, just a year after she joined the viceroy and vicereine in posing for Kahn's autochrome at her father's jubilee, Amrit led a militant delegation to petition Viceroy Lord Irwin for the immediate abolition of child marriage; and in 1931, it was Amrit again who presided over the first All-Asian Women's Conference in Lahore, opening the proceedings with these words: 'It is not enough to have ideas or to cherish them in the abstract. Unless you make up your minds to make them as articles of faith, allow them to influence your daily lives and pursue them actively, your ideals, however laudable they may be, will be of no earthly use to you, or your countries.' Amid applause, she concluded her speech with a call to action: 'Let us discard the customs and traditions which have been strangling our domestic lives, and be an inspiring and noble influence in our households, in our countries and in the world at large.'

I was reading Amrit's interview in the *Tribune*, absorbing this new information, when Naheed, an Indian friend with a background in history and literature, came over to return a few books she'd borrowed. Noticing the article on my desk, she asked to have a look. A few seconds later she planted her finger on a sentence: 'Our people can never advance unless our women do so.'

'She was already out of the mould!' she exclaimed, after racing through the first few paragraphs, with an enthusiasm that only fuelled the fire of my own curiosity. 'What she says about child marriage reveals a modern woman, and someone more in contact with people than most rulers. Maybe because Mandi was such a small state. And look, here, when she says that our people cannot progress if women don't progress, she is nailing something that is still a problem today. And she says this in 1927!'

Naheed, too, is a woman I'd describe as 'out of the mould'. With her ardent spirit and her vibrant intelligence, she is a ferocious advocate for the powerless and the oppressed, qualities she inherited from her academic father and her mother, a reformist politician. A devoted, unorthodox Muslim descended from an eighteenth-century Sufi saint, she holds a doctorate from Oxford and worked as a researcher at the École des hautes études en sciences sociales (the School for Advanced Studies in Social Sciences) in Paris. She also married a prince, the humorous and courteous Hamid, a grandson of the Nawab of Surat. And because I had a vested interest in hearing the unmediated reaction of a highly educated Indian woman of her social standing, I decided to withhold my suspicion: which is that Amrit Kaur had adopted a strategy of evasion in her interview with the *Tribune*, deliberately avoiding a polemic with *Mother India*'s author ('On the whole, I think it will do some good,' she even said of the book) in order to promote her women's rights agenda. In other words, she'd taken advantage of the attention garnered by the controversy to advance her proto-feminist ideas – which, thanks to the unwitting white supremacist, now had international visibility.

When the interviewer asked Amrit if she thought that Indian women were moving away from the practice of *purdah*, she admitted that the North was lagging behind, but in the South, where the ports and commerce put the population in closer contact with Western culture, *purdah* was losing ground. 'But women will never come out of *purdah* until they make an effort and do it themselves,' she took care to point out. 'The men won't really do much to help them; that, I am afraid, is only political talk. It is for the women to try and get education for themselves and bring themselves to the level of men.'

She then used the topic of female segregation to argue that it was the job of the Raj's ruling houses to set an example and act first. 'Coming out of *purdah* can never be successful until the ruling houses set the example and give up plurial [*sic*] marriages. It is astonishing to me how many ruling princes who consider themselves modernised and advanced in every way are bigoted on this question. However,' she added, with the optimism of an activist, 'I do feel that very soon the time will come when the women of India will do something; not the men, unfortunately.'

Amrit Kaur of Mandi seemed like the ideal candidate for introducing the American public to the women's civil rights movement in India. She was young, knowledgeable, confident and beautiful in just the way that caught Westerners' attention. The kind of woman who walked around the Mandi palace in a gold-trimmed sari, as she did the day Pym arrived; or who wore French tennis outfits when she played her father's guests on the courts in Kapurthala, as Pym saw her do on another occasion. She seemed the embodiment of Curzon's ideal princess – dazzling in her Eastern costume while at the same time abiding by the rules of Western decorum. Which may explain why the *Tribune* journalist played along with her in the end, using her newspaper as a forum for spreading Amrit's ideas, which extended well beyond a few remarks on *Mother India*.

As I saw it, Amrit's strategy was a stroke of genius. Here she was, still so young, tucked away in the remotest of places, yet she'd clearly managed to keep up with the times. The more I read the interview, the more I began to suspect that hidden beneath her meticulously royal exterior was an atypical radical, determined to fight for the poorest and most marginalised women – determined as well to keep her distance from what she called 'the present tendency to extremism among educated women': in other words, from political activists such as Sarojini Naidu, the Bengalese poet who would stand with Gandhi in his civil disobedience movement, or Kamaladevi Chattopadhyay, the revolutionary socialist who'd spend her share of time behind bars but who also left her benevolent mark on India, spurring a renaissance of local handicrafts and hand weaving. For Amrit, universal access to public education was the one indispensable goal: 'You can't hope for proper upbringing of the children unless mothers are educated,' she repeated. 'That's a vital thing to-day.'

Offering a cigarette to the journalist – an emancipatory gesture that drew a chuckle from Naheed – Amrit lamented that India still had no adequate universities for women. And she invited all women of a certain social standing, who could afford to travel overseas, to broaden their horizons with a Grand Tour that included the United States.

'My greatest ambition is to visit your country,' she said to Pym, letting her emotional guard down for the first time. 'America appeals to me temperamentally. I admire American energy and the American outlook on life. Besides, it seems to me that America to-day is the greatest power in the world and it is the duty of every intelligent person, who possibly can manage to do so, to take an opportunity to study American methods and the American people first hand.'

At this remark, Naheed – who'd pulled a chair up beside me at my desk to read the interview – raised an eyebrow. 'Excluding her biased attitude towards America,' she commented, 'calling it the greatest world power when, let's face it, the British Empire was still around, I find her extraordinarily balanced. She is talking like a modern Indian woman, and this is an extraordinary fact. It's also unusual that she takes the responsibility to set an example, because it's something that didn't happen in the princely families, I assure you.' I couldn't help but wonder what role Amrit's international education at Clovelly-Kepplestone had played in such vocal admiration for American culture.

When Pym returned to the topics addressed in *Mother India*, like the humiliation of the untouchables and the rigid caste system, the rani, attacking one of her culture's major taboos, replied that the untouchables were human beings like everyone else, condemned to a miserable life through no fault of their own. And she added: 'India can never hope to become really progressive until the question and prejudice of caste has been modified or abandoned.' As I read this sentence, I shot a glance over at my friend, expecting a reaction: these were bold words. But there was a follow-up: 'A living religion and a great one such as ours, cannot be incapable of modification. There are many things we do to-day which we could not do one hundred years ago. Of course, basically, the institution of caste was completely justified by something you Americans ought to understand as well as we do – the necessity for racial purity. It has, I think, gone too far now and become too rigid and too subdivided, but without caste institution the best India can give, especially her Aryan element, would have been swamped long ago. On the other hand, no people which insists upon living wholly in the past can ever make any progress.'

This reflection on the Aryan race, though placed in its historical context and dismissed as a tradition to be overcome – and, in my view, expressed as a means of putting Katherine Mayo in her place – horrified Naheed. It was a true shame, 'a terrible shame', she insisted, staring me in the eye, for such a highly evolved woman to be filled with such racial pride. And yet, I asked Naheed, attempting to curb her disappointment, didn't it seem that Amrit's views on the caste system and women's liberation were truly ahead of their time – certainly more advanced than Gandhi, who in those days adhered to the status quo on both issues? And I pointed out a line towards the end of the interview: 'I detest his inconsistency,' Amrit said of Gandhi, in a flash of arrogance. 'He is a burst bubble, all hot air.'

Only later would I learn – from Sumita Mukherjee, a specialist in India's proto-feminist movements at the University of Bristol – that in those days it was quite common to be critical of India's liberator: 'As Gandhi saw it, women ought to stay home spinning and campaigning against alcohol. It was the men who should do the marching. He said that nationalism came first, and social reforms had to be postponed until after Independence. Some women agreed with this vision. Others said the two issues had to be dealt with at the same time.'

The problem with introducing reforms, Amrit explained, was that there wasn't just one India but a mosaic of different cultures, with different mentalities, religions, languages and next to nothing in common except being ruled by the British government. 'And what do you think India needs most?' Pym asked, before ending the interview. 'Oh, I should say a strong government. We need more men like the present Viceroy, Lord Irwin, a just, and simple, and honest gentleman,' Amrit replied – words that came as no surprise to me, since, with Indian nationalism on the rise, it was clear that the survival of her status depended on the Empire's stability.

'That, and more education among the women . . . because they are the only people who can really get at the evils Miss Mayo describes.'

And on that note, the interview came to a close. I again cast a curious glance at Naheed, whose expression betrayed conflicting emotions: admiration for this singular woman and her progressive, far-sighted thinking; condemnation for her racial pride, which she deemed as unpardonable.

But Naheed noted something else, too, which had slipped my attention: 'Clearly, there is a strong antipathy towards Indian men,' she said, with all the gravity of a judge issuing a sentence.

# Bubbles

A year and a half after the phone call in which Nirvana Devi of Bilkha had invited me to visit, I was ready to go to Pune.

Things had certainly changed since the 1970s, I thought, crossing the city by taxi, when a wave of Westerners in orange tunics, like so many lost sheep, came pouring in behind Bhagwan Shree Rajneesh, the spiritual leader who preached an eclectic doctrine of Eastern mysticism, individual devotion and sexual freedom. A few years later that controversial guru would change his name to Osho and move out to Oregon with his millions of dollars, his followers and his ninety-three Rolls-Royces.

Now Poona had become Pune. And in Pune, the roads lined with colonial barracks and enormous banyans that once lent the city its romantic allure were now overrun by internet joints, stores hawking garish saris, and ads for the Indian army. The latter, big as movie screens, depicted raging fires, explosions and soldiers in mid-air, launching attacks against who knows what, who knows where. 'Tough times never last, but tough men do,' read one of the slogans. Perched atop the billboards, and indifferent to the war scenes beneath their feet, crows enjoyed the traffic show from their privileged height.

It wasn't hard to see, from my taxi window, that this city once famed for its racehorse stud farms, its free-love ashram and its 'Iyengar yoga' school led by the illustrious yoga guru B. K. S. Iyengar, had become a giant industrial and university hub, teeming with students, call centre employees and IT workers. Even so, amid this frenetic urban landscape I did spot the occasional tunic, like an orchid in a

jungle – no longer orange but garnet, its plunging neckline revealing the snow-white cleavage of one meditation devotee or another,
flown in business-class from Brooklyn or Copenhagen for a week of
spiritual detox in Osho's former ashram. It was now known as the
International Meditation Resort, and visitors could only enter with
proof of a negative HIV test, and only if the test was taken that day.

Nirvana Devi of Bilkha had chosen the hotel where I was staying
as our meeting place. Petite, brown-skinned and silver-haired, more
than Amrit Kaur she resembled her grandfather Jagatjit Singh, from
whom she'd inherited her dark-circled eyes and the regal confidence
with which she wore her *churidar*, a simple but stylish cotton tunic
printed with white and orange geometric shapes. Around her neck
was a matching chiffon *dupatta*, a silk scarf that hung down, fluttering nearly to her ankles. After offering me her hand with a cheerful
'Hellooooo' and a few pleasantries, she informed me that no one
ever called her Nirvana, and that I, like everyone else, should refer
to her as 'Bubbles'.

We searched for a quiet corner in the lobby of the hyper-modern
hotel, overflowing with marble and surrounded by weeds, which
seemed to embody the new India – a country with one foot in capital-
ism and the other still planted on the earth – and set about chatting,
with the instinctive ease of two strangers who've discovered they
have a close friend in common. Right away I sensed that this elderly
woman, who moved with such aplomb, possessed a natural warmth,
along with another rare but distinguishable quality: the simplicity
born from an impeccable upbringing and from the awareness that
her social standing needed no emphasis. And she also giggled a lot,
like a little girl.

After telling her that I'd just come from Ajanta – where I marvelled at the frescoes in the city's famed Buddhist caves painted two
centuries before Christ – we turned our attention to the real reason
I'd come to Pune, and I asked her if I could record our conversation.

'Go ahead,' she said, making herself more comfortable in her velvet armchair, as if preparing for a talk show interview.

'Well,' I began, smiling to put her at ease and setting the recorder on the table between us. 'What can you tell me about your mother?'

Silence.

Bubbles stared back at me with a blank expression. Then she sprang to life and replied, with a touch of indignation, 'What can *you* tell me about my mother? I know *nothing* about my mother!'

Stunned, I leaned back in my chair to get a better look at her. Perhaps I'd missed something.

'I was only four when she left,' she explained, ignoring my bewilderment. 'My father was already married again. She was in touch with us, she would write letters, then in the middle, the war started . . .'

So she didn't just visit Paris in the 1930s. She left for good. She abandoned her family. Why hadn't her daughter told me?

A waiter approached holding a tray with mineral water, which Bubbles accepted with an air of surprise, as if the gesture had caught her off guard. She had slightly protruding teeth, and a wide mouth, painted pink with lipstick.

'My brother went to see her after the war, when she was very ill. But I never got a chance to go. She had already left Paris by then and she was living in London. But then, again, there was not very much news. I mean that they didn't talk about why she left. Maybe because she was ill. Very soon after my brother came back to India, she died.'

And this is what she had to offer in exchange for the 4,000 miles I'd travelled to accept her invitation.

Incredulous, but in a certain sense also awed, I decided to play along. Not that I had any options. After all, I'd done a little more research in the meantime, and there were indeed two or three things I could share about her mother. So I reached into my bag, drew out my notebook, and pulled back its elastic band.

'I visited a few archives in Europe. Unfortunately, in France I found very little, just the occasional article on your grandfather and on your aunts Brinda and Sita of Kapurthala. At the British Library, on the other hand, the India Office Records had a thick file on your mother, and I made some notes. If you'd like,' I said, her dark eyes fixed intently on me, 'we can take a look at them together.'

'I'm afraid you'll have to read them to me,' she replied, taking my words literally. 'I've lost my central vision. My eyes have a condition called macular degeneration. If I want to see you I have to look up,' she replied with a giggle, as if it were a laughing matter.

'Please, go ahead!' I encouraged her. And while this extraordinary woman turned her eyes towards the ceiling with the spontaneity of a child, I began flipping through the pages in my notebook.

'Did anyone ever speak to you about a friend of your grandfather's named Albert Kahn? He was a Jewish banker who lived in a kind of garden of wonders in Paris, not far from your grandfather's house. He visited often,' I said to her, imagining that Jagatjit Singh's friendship with a character like Kahn could not have gone unmentioned, even in such a well-connected family. But Bubbles merely shook her head.

'Never heard of him.'

All right then. A swing and a miss.

'How about the name Perrier, does that mean anything to you?'

I didn't know how much time I'd have with her, and in my uncertainty I decided it was best to focus on someone who, at the time, seemed like a key player in Amrit's story. This Perrier – I wasn't aware of his first name, nor was I even sure that Perrier was indeed his real last name – had signed a few of the documents I'd found at the British Library, and I had the sense that, if only I could uncover his identity, I'd be on my way to solving the entire puzzle.

'No, it doesn't ring a bell.'

Another strike then. OK.

'I believe that Perrier was a secret agent,' I explained to her. 'He was the one who sent a telegram to the Foreign Office informing them that Amrit Kaur of Kapurthala and Mandi had been arrested on 12 December 1940, in her apartment on the rue Keppler in Paris . . .'

Now, at last, the princess's face lit up. Perhaps a memory had surfaced?

'The day of my birthday!' she chirped, as if it were some happy coincidence.

'Excuse me,' I had to correct myself, 'I read that wrong, or wrote it wrong, rather. Your mother's arrest by the French police, acting on behalf of the Nazis, occurred on 8 December 1940, not the twelfth . . .' I was almost sorry to stamp out even that little spark of enthusiasm. 'Shortly after, they sent her to an internment camp in Besançon, in the east of France: a camp for civilian prisoners, where the Germans had locked up thousands of British citizens residing in France who, upon England's entry into the war, were classified as "alien enemies". Except that your mother was a special kind of prisoner. The fact that she was the daughter of a ruler of the Raj made her arrest a delicate issue for English diplomats. I found piles of letters exchanged between the British authorities in India and the Foreign Office on precisely this matter . . . Here, for example, I see that at one point she requested permission to go to Morocco. Any idea why Morocco?'

'No!'

By now it was clear that her answers tended to have a peremptory and somewhat indignant tone.

'In any case,' I proceeded, looking back down at my notes, 'each of your mother's requests spawned a flurry of correspondence. And the answer always came back *no*.'

Bubbles listened to me without saying a word. And meanwhile my hopes of stirring her memory grew dimmer and dimmer. Had I really come all the way to Pune for nothing?

'You see,' I tried insisting, 'this Perrier was in correspondence with your grandfather and father throughout the war. At one point he even gave them his address,' I said, flipping through my pages to find the relevant note. 'In fact, I see two addresses from two different times. The first in Vichy, which, as you know, was the capital of Marshal Pétain's collaborationist regime, after the Germans occupied Paris and northern France in 1940. The second, towards the end of the war, was in Chailly, a Swiss neighbourhood between Lausanne and Montreux, on Lake Geneva.'

But Bubbles chose to squash my hopes entirely, offering no chance to interpret my notes in the light of her memories: 'Everything you're saying now is completely new to me.'

What was I to do? Leave her there in peace, close my notebook on the mélange of novelistic characters I'd collected, all tied in their own way to Amrit Kaur's story, and head home? Or risk perplexing her even further, relating the tales of utopians, spies and explorers who'd all been ground up in the war's machinery?

'That's OK. I can fill you in a little myself,' I said, hoping to prepare her a bit for what was to come. 'Though your mother's life after she left India remains a mystery, all but impenetrable for the time being, a few of the people in her orbit left quite colourful records of their lives. First and foremost the banker I mentioned earlier, Albert Kahn. He was a major pioneer in photography, who sent a crew to document your grandfather's 1927 jubilee in Kapurthala. Don't write him off as just another rich banker – Kahn was a visionary, a utopian, a militant pacifist and a profoundly modern and cosmopolitan gentleman.'

'And you think he had something to do with my mother?'

'It's just a hypothesis. Kahn was a family friend, and he was Jewish. He found himself in serious financial difficulty at a time when Jews were not allowed to leave occupied France. It would make sense, if your mother had tried to help him.'

I then told her how my research on Perrier had led me down an odd path. 'When I looked to see if a Perrier had ever lived in the Swiss neighbourhood of Chailly, I did indeed find a man by that name, and from the right years. He was an important lawyer. And it seemed plausible to me that a lawyer, especially one from a neutral country like Switzerland, might have been tapped by your family or the Foreign Office to help with your mother. One thing is certain: Perrier didn't just keep an eye on Amrit Kaur on behalf of the English, he also loaned her money. You may not know this, but when the Germans invaded Paris, one of the first measures they took against alien enemies like your mother was to freeze their bank accounts. No subject of the British Empire could withdraw funds from their own account, nor receive any money from abroad. They were all left to starve. You can imagine how difficult it must have been to survive. In any case, Perrier loaned your mother a considerable sum . . .'

I cast her a hesitant glance

'Shall I keep going?'

'Oh yes, please don't stop.'

In the adrenaline rush of my research, I'd chased down every lead that seemed even vaguely related to Amrit Kaur. But it had taken entire days in the library and weeks of reading to absorb all that I was now pouring out in one breath to her daughter. For her, meanwhile, taking in this onrush of information – after so many years of silence – must have felt like spinning around on a speeding carousel.

'As I was saying, I unfortunately found very little on your mother's life in Paris, apart from the address where she was arrested, and a few letters in which she asked for financial help. The other letters held in London are mostly related to her pleas to leave France. It appears that she was dealing with serious health issues, that she was ill. The detention camp in Besançon had been harsh: food was scarce, there was no heat, the latrines were filthy. Both the Maharaja of Kapurthala and the Raja of Mandi did everything they could to extract her from that wretched place, but for five months nothing came of it.'

'Does that mean my father was in contact with her?' Bubbles asked, her eyes widening. Now she seemed stunned.

'I can tell you that he tried many times, and always in vain, to send her money through a third party. Even if the majority of the negotiations were carried out by your grandfather.'

'This comes as a big surprise to me. I've always thought my parents ceased all communications after she left India.'

'Well, I can assure you, that's not the case. The Raja of Mandi tried on several occasions to send her her private allowance. As rani, your mother was entitled to a state stipend, correct? I have written down here 2,000 rupees per month, the equivalent of around 150 pounds at the time. But, as I was saying, it was your grandfather who really went to great lengths, even writing to Marshal Pétain, the head of Vichy France. He knocked on every door he could. And in 1941 it seemed like he'd finally caught a break, when someone proposed an exchange of prisoners with a man named Filchner whom the Germans were eager to bring home. Does that ring any bells for you, the name Filchner? He was a Bavarian geographer and geologist, a pioneer in the exploration of Antarctica. As early as the 1900s he was working as a spy in India and Tibet. He participated in the Great Game, the diplomatic dispute between the British Empire and czarist Russia over control of Afghanistan, Central Asia and Tibet. An intelligence war.'

'A spy! Possibly.'

'I have it written here that the British arrested him in India in 1940, holding him and his daughter Erika at prisoner of war camps, one of which is not too far from here, in Satara. Frankly, I didn't get the sense that Filchner was too thrilled about going back to Germany. There's no question that he was a spy, he himself confessed it; but he was also a scientist, whose accomplishments were rather extraordinary. Imagine, at twenty he crossed the Pamir Mountains alone on horseback, and at twenty-three he made his first expedition in Tibet.'

Did any of this interest Bubbles? Maybe, maybe not. But it interested me, so I pressed on. 'He even led a geological expedition to Antarctica in 1911, rivalling Shackleton, Scott and Amundsen, which came to a dramatic end. His ship, I read, was trapped in the ice for months, leading to a series of unimaginable events. His first mate lost his mind and died of syphilis, after threatening to kill him; the second mate assumed command, but he too lost his head and Filchner was forced to challenge him to a duel; the third committed suicide; and one night, the shore base they'd constructed on the ice floated away on a detached berg, carrying with it nearly all of their scientific equipment. In short, a complete catastrophe.'

In the wake of this adventure, I wasn't surprised to learn that Wilhelm Filchner decided to return to his first love: Central Asia, Tibet and Nepal. And indeed, in 1939, as the war was breaking out, Filchner was off in Nepal doing geomagnetic research. 'It was around then that he fell ill with malaria,' I told Bubbles, 'and since there were no hospitals equipped to treat him, he was forced to head south, seeking treatment in British India. And naturally, the English arrested him.'

This was the man whom the Germans were proposing to swap for Amrit Kaur. But the Foreign Office was not interested. 'In fact, here it is, the cable that clarifies England's position,' I said to her, so pleased to have actually found it among my notes that I'd forgotten it was truly unpleasant.

' "I concur that the repatriation of Filchner and his daughter must be denied," the Representative of the Crown in India wrote to the Foreign Secretary. "Apart from other considerations, repatriation of the rani is not of sufficient political importance to justify such a breach of the rules. No counter-offer of exchange is therefore necessary." '

Bubbles sat in silence.

'Which means that, if your mother was released from Besançon, after nearly five months captive, as Perrier's telegrams indicate,' I said to her, setting my notebook down on my lap, 'it must have been for some other reason . . .'

I was running out of ammunition.

She cast me a pensive look. 'I heard about some general of the army. But then again, whether it is true . . .'

'I don't know. I'm sorry, but no one spoke of any generals in the documents I reviewed.'

Among my papers, I did have one note regarding a letter from Winston Churchill to the American ambassador in Paris, asking him to ensure that Amrit Kaur was treated properly and at least received the meagre monthly stipend given to all those interned at the camp – as if neither of these two things was already happening. And then there was the news of her release from Besançon, on 26 April 1941. In a letter dated one month later, Amrit pleaded with her father to do everything in his power to have her transferred temporarily to Morocco, where she could seek urgent medical care. In 1942 she again asked to be released for health-related reasons, along with her American lady-in-waiting.

'Does the name of this lady-in-waiting mean anything to you, Madame H. R. Hermesch?'

'Never heard it before.'

It was difficult for me to guess what effect the news I'd brought from Europe was having on this eighty-year-old orphan. Squalor, prison, sickness, spies, Nazis, and a mother forced to beg for her life. She was drinking in every word as if parched, though she also had the look of someone on the alert. And I couldn't tell if I was saying too much or not enough.

Whatever the case, I had little left to add at that point. The documents from 1944 only told of more anguish for Amrit after the war. I didn't want to distress her daughter, but there was no good news to speak of in my notebook. The day after the liberation of Paris, I told her, British authorities informed Jagatjit Singh that his daughter was well and in the care of a certain 'Countess Laubat' in Paris. But a month later the British Foreign Secretary wrote yet again of having to intervene to 'block the immediate seizure of the [Rani of Mandi's] properties by her creditors'.

'I'm guessing, Bubbles, that the name Countess Laubat doesn't ring a bell . . .'

The light was beginning to sink over the no-man's-land behind the hotel windows.

'How come you took this up?' she asked me suddenly.

The answer seemed obvious to me. 'It all started with that portrait of your mother, and the unresolved story on the exhibition label,' I replied.

And it was true; but there was more. Other factors had played a role: the sense of loss weighing on me that day in early March when I first chanced upon her; the unexpected longing I'd felt, a desire that caught me off guard in that dimly lit museum room; and the trace of hope I'd heard in Bubbles' voice over the phone in Paris.

It was nearly evening now. I closed my notebook and we stared across at each other.

'It's nice to know when you don't know,' she said, as a kind of thank you. Then she adjusted the silk *dupatta* around her shoulders and stood up.

Yes, I said to myself, watching her leave. But what was it I had said yes to?

# Losing the Past Is Like Losing a War

The next day, Bubbles invited me out to lunch. Her husband was sick and their cook was off-duty, she explained, so instead of having me at home she'd thought it best to reserve a table at the Turf Club, the old colonial club overlooking the racetrack.

On the drive over, she told me that her family had come to live in Pune in the 1960s, when her husband was running a racehorse stable. The story went like this: the Maharaja of Kashmir had an important stable up for sale, and the business magnate Suresh Mahindra had stepped forward to buy it. But the maharaja was opposed to ceding it to a 'commoner' like Mahindra, even though he'd married Baby, Bubbles' younger sister. So Bubbles' husband, the Raja of Bilkha, offered to act as mediator and run the stable on behalf of his brother-in-law, who lacked the requisite blue blood. They came to an agreement that allowed the Bilkhas to leave Gujarat and settle in Pune. For Bubbles, it meant she would again be close to her older brother Tibu, who had retired there after leaving the army. Now Tibu was gone, dead for several years.

In the car with Bubbles when she'd come to pick me up were her sweet-faced, ponytailed teenage granddaughter, Pooja, and the youngest of her four sons, a gregarious man in his fifties with a thick grey moustache, dressed like an American – jeans, polo shirt, sneakers – who greeted me with an energetic handshake and a hearty 'I'm Jack', though everyone called him Tiny, and his real name was Jagatshamsher Singh.

'This is a private club,' he began, acting as my host while Bubbles chatted with the doormen at the reception desk. 'You have to be a member. That's how my wife and I met one another, in a similar place called the Poona Club. Here, when the races are in, it's a fashion show. You have to understand that once Poona was the place where the maharajas had their holiday homes . . .'

While Tiny/Jack and his mother filled me in on how the city had changed after so many of its trees were felled and the temperatures began creeping up ('Once you didn't even need fans, and now you have to have AC!' Bubbles lamented), I observed the rather nervous haughtiness with which the staff led us to our table, out on the porch of the elegant, two-storey building overlooking the enormous oval of the racetrack. I couldn't help but note the contrast between the servants' obsequious behaviour and the oil stains on their bright lilac shirts. And I wondered what it counted for these days, in Indian society, to be royals without realms.

Meanwhile, Tiny was telling me how he only spent one month of the year in Pune. The rest of the time he lived in Chicago.

And what did he do in Chicago, I asked, embarking on the most predictable path of conversation.

'I'm a technician at Mercedes-Benz,' he replied, unfolding his napkin.

Technician. I didn't fully understand.

'What do you mean, technician?' I asked, flashing a routine smile.

'I mean that if you own a Mercedes and its air conditioning breaks down, you bring it to me and I fix it.'

Very well then, I thought. If Tiny's goal had been to derail me from my bourgeois prejudices, he'd succeeded. Whatever provincial, stereotypical ideas I'd had of India's former royal families, of their status and their privileges, he'd just dashed in a single stroke. Amrit Kaur's youngest grandson, the great-grandson of the last Maharaja of Kapurthala and descendant of the legendary Sardar Jassa Singh, made his living as a car mechanic.

'Had I stayed back in India, I would have done nothing. I would have married a princess and lived off her money. But I married a girl much smarter than I am. And since she was going to finish her studies in Chicago – she was studying graphic design, she is a very creative person – I followed her. She came from a family who worked from day one, and I came from a family that never worked!' he said, with a measure of bravado that seemed to betray a certain shyness, raising his hands as if in surrender.

At those words, Bubbles burst into one of her little giggling fits. Only then did I notice that the diamond stud in her left nostril was the sole piece of jewellery she was wearing. Her tunic and chiffon *dupatta* were identical to the ones she'd worn the day before, only in a different colour, with a yellow and white geometric print. Her elegance, again, was effortless.

'But her father didn't like the idea of his daughter marrying into royalty, so he sent people to Gujarat to find out about me. Her father was an engineer, and a managing director. It was another world . . .'

Tiny proceeded to tell me that his first job in Chicago was as a copy machine salesman, though he'd also worked as a plumber and a waiter. 'After, I worked for a printing shop. I used to do that and go to school, to study automotive. I've always been good with my hands, which was my luck. And at some point I asked myself: what do I really like? And the answer was: I like Mercedes. I wanted to work on cars and the best cars in the world were Mercedes-Benz, so I went there. But they wouldn't give me a job. Nobody would hire you because they wanted experience. And I never had experience in America. I certainly couldn't tell them that I used to repair my father's Rolls-Royce every time it broke down, which was almost every day, since I was twelve!'

It would appear that the Raja of Bilkha, who came daily to the Turf Club in his pearl and lilac Rolls convertible, had been forced to walk home nearly every other day.

'So they offered me to clean cars and to clean offices. And I did it,

I liked it. When you clean someone's car you get to meet the owner, you get to talk. And I liked to meet the people, even though some of them were a pain . . .

'After five or six months, when by then I knew everybody at the dealership, I asked again to be hired, but this time as an apprentice mechanic, as there was an opening. And so I started, twenty-five years ago.'

It was a good life, he said with satisfaction. The pay was good, and since he belonged to a union they respected his work schedule – from 7.30 a.m. to 4 p.m., five days a week. This left him time to spend with his children.

When I asked him if his employer knew that he was the Prince of Bilkha, I was almost embarrassed by the question's banality.

'Nooo. I didn't tell him!' he replied with emphasis. 'But there are a lot of Indians in Chicago. And one day, after fifteen years I'd been working there, two Indian businessmen who used to manage my father's money came to the dealership with a Mercedes to repair. And they started saying: but, do you know who he is? What is someone like him doing here? His father is . . . and his mother . . . And my co-workers were looking at me, saying, what's wrong with you, Jack? Are you crazy or what? Until the owner came, and he too asked me if I was out of my mind. So I told him: listen, now you know it, and you forget it. I want my job. And he understood. We never spoke about it again.'

It wasn't easy news to absorb, that a family who once owned emeralds the size of walnuts, palaces inspired by Versailles, vineyards in the Bois de Boulogne and golden tableware could have squandered all that wealth in a few dozen years – if this was indeed the conclusion to draw from Tiny's story.

Bubbles must have read my mind, since she stepped in to explain the effect that their private incomes, known as privy purses, had had on their lives – especially after they were abolished. In 1947, when

India declared its independence, her parents, like all of the Raj's princes, traded away state sovereignty, along with the Crown's lands and jewels, in exchange for a commensurate private income, which Viceroy Lord Mountbatten worked to install in the constitution as an inalienable right. And so it was – until 1971, when Indira Gandhi changed the constitution and abolished that right.

'And then everything went. Privileges, money . . .'

'Overnight!' Tiny chimed in. 'All of a sudden they also wanted you to pay wealth taxes on furniture, chandeliers, silver, estates . . . A lot of maharajas started melting silver and gold. Silver furniture, I mean, like my mother's bed,' he specified, just in case I was imagining a few forks and knives. 'If you didn't have the money to pay wealth taxes, they would take these things away. So they melted them.'

'The big rulers were not so seriously affected,' Bubbles picked up, in a much calmer tone. 'It was people like us who were affected badly. Because you didn't have any backing. You just had an income that suddenly stopped. It was hard to adjust, not to the change in general but to the financial change. Certain things we couldn't do any more . . . But we had to keep up a certain image – like today. If you don't keep up your image nobody will come to your door. That's how it is. Properties we didn't have very much. But whatever else . . . Then you sell things for a good cause, you know, the children being educated . . .'

The earth-shattering change she was describing was a phenomenon that affected only the smallest number of families, a sliver of India's sprawling population. Even so, its symbolic importance was striking. In a certain sense, the abolition of privy purses represented far more than the end of privileges for one particular caste: it was the nail in the coffin of a system that had been thousands of years in the making.

Thinking back to that vanished era, I turned to Bubbles – this woman for whom I'd felt an instinctive admiration and solidarity from the moment we met – and asked her what sort of power a family like hers had under the Raj.

'We could hang anyone,' she responded calmly.

For a moment I sat there breathless.

'Another example?'

'We printed our own money.'

Then she turned to examine her menu.

Once she'd ordered, and waited for everyone else to make their selections, Bubbles began telling me a bit about her childhood and adolescence – how she'd grown up in the royal palace of Mandi, and how at nine years old she was sent to study at Queen Mary, a prestigious boarding school in Lahore, a place which she described, laughing, as 'beautiful, but like a prison, with high, high walls you couldn't even peep out of! All girls, of course.' There she'd studied Hindi and English, but she'd also learned to play basketball, ping-pong, badminton, hockey, and especially tennis: 'There were five tennis courts. Tennis was very fashionable at that time. When my brother Bebu and I went to Kapurthala for the holidays, there were many uncles and cousins, and everybody played tennis. Tennis was the thing.'

I told her I'd found a newspaper article claiming that her mother, too, was an excellent player. Perhaps she had a few memories of that, I wondered.

'I don't have any,' she replied. 'But the people of Mandi were very fond of her. They said she was very sweet-hearted. That, again, is hearsay. That she would give, whenever asked, to the people. Very good to the people.'

'After she left,' Tiny cut in, 'the other wife of my grandfather made all pictures and souvenirs of Amrit Kaur disappear. She didn't want any memories of her around.'

'There were just one or two photographs that were left to us,' Bubbles confirmed.

It was now becoming clear. For a woman like Amrit Kaur – who'd taken a stand against polygamy and declared that it was up to the ruling houses to set a good example – the fact that her own husband had brought another wife into the home must have come as a crushing blow. With that marriage, the princess who'd arranged a conference on the need for Asian women to free themselves from the customs and traditions that were suffocating their domestic lives and become models for their country and the world, had been put in her place and humiliated in front of everyone.

Bubbles was five months old when her father took a second wife in 1931, meaning that Amrit had tolerated the situation for three years. Though, as unbearable as I knew it must have been, I myself, swayed by the mysterious and overwhelming force of maternal instinct, couldn't fully come to grips with an act as unnatural as abandoning two small children. And the war was no justification either, since seven years passed between Amrit's departure and the Second World War. What could have kept her away for so long?

But then I tried to step from the mother's shoes into the daughter's. And from the deepest recesses of my consciousness a memory emerged, of the intense attachment I'd felt towards my mother as a little girl: a most powerful feeling, in which unconditional trust in another human being fuses with love and the need for protection.

Bubbles must once again have read my mind, since she jumped in to add: 'My father's other wife was very good to me. In my childhood, I had no problem. She raised me and my younger brother – her son – exactly the same way.'

'But did your mother send news from Europe, in the meantime?'

'She wrote to me at school, and also at home.'

'And did she tell you something about her life?'

'Nothing at all.'

'You must have kept those letters, I imagine . . .'

'No. I have one, but I can't find it. We shifted once or twice, from Gujarat, and I can't find it. That one she wrote when I was getting married. The marriage was arranged by my father and his wife. She wrote: *I don't know who you are marrying, and I have no part in it at all. If anything goes wrong, don't blame me.* It was long ago. I got married in '46. That was the last letter I got. I was so furious that I wrote back that she was in no position to criticise. Where was she when I was growing up, when another mother was taking care of me?'

Clearly, the wound of her mother's abandonment was still raw: Bubbles had had her reasons for asking me to come to India, after all. And yet she still seemed at peace with herself. Almost as if her decision to accept the life she'd been dealt had been made long ago, and was beyond all argument.

Very well, then, I thought: since it was a tale of missing jewels that had led me to Pune, the time had come for me to give Bubbles something I'd brought from Paris: an auction catalogue from an antiquarian bookseller. The catalogue was for a jewellery auction, featuring several pieces that belonged to Amrit Kaur, which took place in New York at Parke-Bernet in December 1950, two years after her death. I hadn't been able to figure out who'd put them up for sale, or who was behind the name of the agents who'd purchased them. At Sotheby's, the auction house which had bought out Parke-Bernet in 1964, they informed me that too much time had passed to recover certain information. And when I insisted, they told me that the relevant archives had been lost in a fire.

There were nine pieces from the Rani of Mandi's 'estate' up for auction: an extravagantly beautiful Art Deco necklace, with several diamonds and an enormous sixteen-carat sapphire; a Cartier ring with an emerald-cut nine-carat diamond, flanked by two pentagonal diamonds; another diamond ring with a sixteen-carat rectangular diamond; and several diamond and sapphire bracelets.

'Look,' I said to Bubbles, flipping through the catalogue and completely forgetting that she'd lost her central vision. 'Some of your mother's jewellery is in here. Maybe you'll recognise it.'

'No!' she said, breaking into another of her giggling fits. 'I can't see, and, in any case, they disappeared. We got nothing and there were no jewels left in Mandi, that is certain! Or if there were, we never saw them. They are gone.' And since the case, for her, was closed, she handed the catalogue over to Tiny.

But then she must have reconsidered.

'After Mummy died, we went to America where we met a friend of hers called Louise. We went to this bank . . . I don't remember where; it could have been New York or Washington. There was a safe there, in the name of Louise, not Mummy, that's why we couldn't open it. So this Louise came to open the locker, but there was nothing much to talk about. And I couldn't take the jewels that were left to me, because my mother had a very heavy debt in London . . . What happened between Louise and the person who was looking after Mummy I don't know.'

I asked if she thought maybe Louise had been her mother's lady-in-waiting.

'I have no idea. But I think she was a friend. I only saw her once. She was old and she didn't talk very much. There was this famous sapphire . . . a big sapphire that belonged to a necklace. The necklace was not there but the sapphire was, and I remembered that they didn't want to give it to Mummy because there was a black spot in it, and they said it's not lucky. But she insisted and she got it. There was nothing else to talk about. There were some black pearls which had died and became powder in my hands. But she had a lot of jewellery, I was told.'

Perhaps it had been this Louise, then, who'd brought the jewels to America and put them up for auction after Amrit's death. But when I asked Bubbles for her full name she told me she couldn't remember, and there was no way of tracking her down because the person who'd put them in touch had died.

'Speaking of which,' I said – there was something I'd forgotten to tell her the day before – 'in the British archives I also found a letter that mentioned a lady-in-waiting of your mother's. But this one had a different name, she went by Swete. An American woman. Miss Dora Swete . . .'

'Is it not Louise?' Bubbles said, knitting her brow. 'Did I get the name wrong? Maybe I got the name wrong. The only companion of my mother I know about was named Louise. When we went to see the jewellery, everything was joint with Louise. Louise what, I don't remember. But now I think I may be wrong. Maybe she wasn't even called Louise . . .'

She must have felt she'd let me down. Raising her glass to her lips for a sip of water, she told me I should have come a few years earlier, when her memory was sharper.

A true shame, I thought to myself. And while two waiters busied themselves clearing away our plates, I turned my gaze above the immense dusty oval of the racetrack, where the city was silhouetted against a milky sky.

Perhaps the time had come to confront the matter that had brought us together in the first place. My hosts' genuine kindness, the complete trust they showed in sharing their family stories, had nearly distracted me from the very thing that had led me to Pune. So I turned my eyes once again towards the rani's own, still so remarkably lively despite their fading vision, and I told her that the Foreign Office was unable to explain why the Germans had treated Amrit Kaur so harshly – more harshly, it seems, than other 'alien enemies'.

'Maybe because she had helped the Jews . . .' Bubbles offered under her breath.

'Maybe,' I echoed. Though the tale of her selling jewellery to help Jews escape France during the occupation, despite my best efforts, remained just that: a tale, unconfirmed.

'In Paris I contacted Cartier, Boucheron and Mellerio, three of the historic jewellers who'd handled commissions for the Kapurthalas. It was reasonable to think that your mother might have sold her jewels back to the houses who'd made them. But I received neither confirmation nor denial. Cartier replied that during the war such transactions were done orally, to avoid leaving any trace. But then they refused to elaborate, since releasing information about clients goes against a jeweller's professional code of ethics.'

'Unfortunately, I don't remember how this story came to be told,' she said. 'I think the first time I heard about it was after I married. Then I asked, and an uncle of mine confirmed it. Grandpa we couldn't ask because he wasn't around. And I don't think we would have asked such a thing. That closeness wasn't there.'

She added that she'd been contacted by a Jewish association that wanted to include Amrit Kaur's name among the righteous. I knew that she was talking about the Jewish Foundation for the Righteous because I'd been there, in New York. And I also knew that their file on the Rani of Mandi was incomplete. They'd asked me to keep them posted, in case I came across any new information.

There was one thing, however, that someone had told me, though I was reluctant to share it because I wasn't sure how Bubbles would react. So I approached it in a roundabout way. 'Years ago a couple of friends and I visited a Baroque castle in Normandy, Champ de Bataille: a place filled with those kinds of rare objects you find in the home of a true aesthete. The castle's owner was a famous interior decorator by the name of Jacques Garcia, and he seemed to know the history of each and every one of those objects. For example, he showed us one of Louis XVI's parlour games, still in mint condition in its coloured cases. And an ivory handkerchief with black lilies, with which Marie Antoinette – according to our host – had dried her tears after the king lost his head to the guillotine. In short, this gentleman, outside of his passion for rare objects, was also a collector of histories. And it dawned on me that I should ask him if he'd ever heard anything about Amrit Kaur of Kapurthala or of Mandi, and of the jewels she'd sold in Paris during the war. I wouldn't have been surprised to hear that they'd fallen into the hands of someone he knew, at least indirectly. He replied, instead, that he only had a vague memory . . . of her being involved with a certain Jewish gentleman.'

'It's possible!' Bubbles exclaimed. This little rumour had struck a nerve, though she didn't seem scandalised. 'After all, she was young and beautiful . . . it would make sense.'

'Bubbles,' I said, hoping to jog her memory, 'could it be that your mother asked you to come see her in London after the war, as she did your brother Tibu?'

'No. But you have to understand that it was a very difficult time. The Partition happened just after my marriage. I was expecting my first son and I was deadly ill for three months. In those days we were not allowed to go to hospitals. If something went wrong, and you belonged to a princely family, they expected you to die in your bed! And we were having terrible troubles. In Punjab, there were riots. I was in Rajkot and couldn't even get in touch with Mandi, it was so bad. So, that was a very bad time. Me being so ill. Not getting through to my family. Then Mummy dying . . .'

I was touched by how truly sincere she was being with me, a person she barely knew. We'd begun the day following a rather formal script – her invitation, the chosen venue – but almost immediately our conversation took on a tone of polite intimacy. While Tiny studied the desserts and Bubbles gleefully ordered a cup of chocolate ice cream, I asked what the family she married into was like.

'Different from us,' she answered. 'Culturally different. We all are Rajputs, but then it depends what part of India you are from. I married into a big family, because there were four brothers, two sisters, the two parents and a lot of old ladies who were alive then . . .'

Which is to say, all of these people were living in the house she moved into.

'Imagine,' said Tiny, 'when she married she had to leave school and go live in a place many days away from home, and a very hot place: she, who had grown up in the snows of the North. She had to learn to read and write in Gujarati, everything.'

'It's true that you didn't know what you were getting into,' Bubbles said. 'Although then, you were groomed to adjust to whatever it was. Sit and stand. Maybe now I wouldn't be able to adjust. But in those days I was so young.'

'What she went through . . .' Tiny continued, shaking his head in disapproval. 'She never enforced the same thing on our wives. They never forced us to marry in our caste. All of us brothers had love marriages.'

That was when I tried asking her: 'But Bubbles, do you ever regret—'

'No!' she exclaimed, with such fervour that we jumped back in our seats. She hadn't even let me finish my sentence.

'No. Not really. I think it is a good thing to have been a part of a certain era. At least we can look back and talk about it. Our children can't, as they don't really know what it was, they haven't lived through it. But I have no regrets: if you start regretting, you can't go on. We were young enough to adjust, that is the main thing. But for the older generation it was sad. Because it's the past you've lost. And losing the past is like losing a war!' she said, breaking again into her giggles.

The following afternoon she invited me to her home, an apartment building in the residential area of Koregaon Park. She wanted me to meet her husband, whose severe diabetes kept him confined to an armchair. Afterwards, she told me, we'd go out just the two of us for a cup of tea.

When I entered the living room, the first thing I noticed was just how long her husband's legs were, stretching out endlessly over the ottoman. In his immensity – even though disease had worn him thin – Jashwant Singh of Bilkha looked like a Jonathan Swift character, stuck in a room much too small for him. His cheeks were sunken, the skin stretched tight around his cheekbones, and he had pitch-black eyes, which were now darting around the room with an alarmed curiosity.

While Bubbles searched for something in her bedroom I scanned my surroundings, noticing the lush Malabar chestnut just outside the main window that gave the room a certain charm. The simple furnishings made the family photographs on the walls appear all the more lavish. I recognised Anita Delgado in the opulent odalisque seated on a rug in front of a silver coffer; Bubbles' husband as a young man, his cheeks full, a *sarpech* with diamonds and feathers affixed to his turban. I paused to admire a young Tibu in his military uniform, with all the charm of an Indian Tyrone Power, but with a shyness and gentleness about him. And I read the dedication on another portrait, a giant image, dominating the room from its position above the sofa.

It showed the face of a beautiful woman, her eyebrows in a perfect arch, her gaze muted, one end of her organza sari pulled up over her hair, wearing long diamond and pearl earrings. The dedication read: 'For my darling Bubbles, all my love, from your mother.'

# 'Why?'

'You see, Livia, when you hear about my mother's nature, I don't think she would have accepted another woman in the house. Look at Grandfather: he had a trail of wives, and they used to all live together. It was a different way of thinking.'

When Amrit arrived in Mandi – a journey that required one long leg by train, then another on horseback, and another on a palanquin, up through the mountains – she'd gone from a court life filled with brothers, in-laws, nieces and nephews, stepmothers and foreign visitors to the company of just two people: her husband, who'd had a much more traditional upbringing than hers, and his stepmother, a kind but uneducated woman. It was a life filled with solitude, and just as much bitterness. Whoever arranged that marriage never took the cultural differences into account.

'After she left, Mummy didn't have any relationship with my grandfather any more. She was very angry. I don't know why. I think that Grandpa wanted her to stay in India. He said I'll get you a place in Delhi, but it didn't work out.'

Bubbles and I were sitting in a café near her house. The doors were open, but Bubbles seemed indifferent to the hum of the scooters and voices in the street. Maybe she was used to it, or maybe her thoughts were drifting elsewhere. She hadn't been back to Kapurthala since one of her uncles or cousins – she couldn't remember any more – had sold the royal palace, which was now a military school. But as children she and Bebu had spent their Easter holiday there every year, feeling like two fish out of water, because everyone, even the servants, spoke in French. She said this with a comic emphasis on their inadequacy, adding one of her giddy exclamation points. They were permitted to see their grandfather only in the morning, over English breakfast; and after toast, eggs and porridge he'd take them for exercise in the garden. One day they'd go riding around the park on bicycles, amid peacocks and parrots and other exotic birds. The next they'd take a ride in a one-horse carriage – a very special carriage, since it was pulled by a zebra, not a horse. The loop around the park was a bore, but for the zebra they were glad to be up early.

'But I was never close to his wives. I just met them. He had four or five. The only one I knew well and remember was the French one. You mean she was actually Czech? Really? I thought she was French. She was very nice, very sweet. Tall. Not beautiful, but very nice-looking. She and her mother were in Kapurthala for a long time. She was called Nina, although when he married her she changed her name to Tara. But then, after I married, I never saw them again. I was surprised when she committed suicide. Because when I knew her they got on quite well . . .'

After Amrit left, it was her father's second wife, Kusum, who looked after her and Bebu, the son she'd had in the meantime with Joginder. Bubbles and Bebu were nearly the same age, and they were inseparable. It was a point on which Bubbles insisted, that Kusum treated them as if they were her own children. But her relationship with Amrit's firstborn, the handsome Tibu, was less agreeable. Maybe she didn't like him, Bubbles admitted, before giving her stepmother the benefit of the doubt, adding: I wouldn't know. I thought back to the story Tiny had told me: about how Kusum had done away with the photographs of Amrit as soon as she left, along with any other trace of her memory. Some even claimed that she took certain liberties with regard to the inheritance.

'Yet, she never ill-treated any of us. Maybe material-wise, yes. But as I tell my children: material means nothing to me. If you are to get it, you get it; if you are not to get it, you don't. Finished. That's the

Bubbles with her brother Tibu *c.*1933, the year when their mother left.

way I feel. It may not be right, but I see it that way. It doesn't come from my religion. It's the way I think. My children get angry with me, but when my father died, I told them: I can't. Especially with my second mother: she gave me a beautiful childhood, I will never do anything against her. Just for something material? No. My husband knew I was like that, so he didn't press the point very much.'

The palace in Mandi had a separate wing for the nannies and children, and Tibu, Bubbles and Bebu (Baby was born about ten years later) were taken to see their parents every morning and again after tea, but they only lunched with them on Sundays. Before they left for boarding school, the governess, Betty, was in charge of educating the two youngest – a strict and affectionate woman, generous with the castor oil. Tibu, meanwhile, was left to the instruction of one Mr Gilmore. And he got out as soon as he could, enlisting in Mandi's army and finding a bride, with a wedding worthy of a future raja.

'You asked me about my arranged marriage. Well, there were these men who made the rounds of the princely states, with photos of all the eligible boys and girls. They would hand up this huge package, from one ruler to another. Mummy showed me three or four photos. Some of the other boys were nice. But it wasn't up to me to pick my husband. He was picked for me! We were introduced in Delhi, in a tea room at the Imperial Hotel. At the time the Imperial was the thing. And that was all: the parents decided. No, I don't remember how I felt in that tea room. You were brainwashed for that. I was also very young. Duty meant you did what you had to do. One didn't give it a second thought. It's not like you think: I wasn't nervous or excited when I met my future husband. It was just something that had to be done.'

The wedding followed quickly – there was no time to finish the school year. Her grandfather, who'd attended the month-long festivities in honour of Tibu's marriage, didn't show up for Bubbles' wedding. She wore red for the ceremony, as was traditional. Then she boarded a train with six servants, and after five days she arrived in Bilkha, in the heart of India, where a surprise awaited her.

'When I arrived at the train station I was whisked away because there were these people sitting in trees with rifles in their hands, who wanted to kill me! Now it feels like a joke, but at that time it was terrifying. I thought I had landed among the barbarians! You see, in Gujarat we have the Kathi tribe. In the old days they were warriors. Every time they won, they would get land. So a part of Gujarat was known as Kathiawar. They are Rajputs like we are, but they only intermarry. And I wasn't accepted because I wasn't of their clan.'

The groom's family welcomed her warmly, but his mother proved very strict. She gave her orders. To protect Bubbles from the outraged community – every night the local gang leader and his men showed up outside their residence and yelled at the young bride, firing a few shots – she kept her under house arrest for nearly a year.

Then, when tensions refused to die down, it was decided that the newlyweds would move to Rajkot, where the Bilkhas owned a residence. Things couldn't have got off to a worse start – and yet, despite the alienation and fear, the young couple managed to establish a strong relationship.

'Marrying so young meant that we grew up together. I was seventeen and so was he, but I was far more advanced than he was. Maybe because I was in a boarding school. Boarding school toughens you up a bit. It makes you independent. We grew up like friends. It was companionship, more than anything. It takes time, but you expect it because you don't know the person at all.'

It was their shared love of sports that brought them closer. Tennis, hunting, target-shooting, cricket. In Rajkot they could at last go out into the world together, and attending sporting events became a shared passion. I imagined Bubbles sitting up in the stands of a stadium, small and bursting with energy beside that giant with a gentle smile.

'Loving music and reading and travelling also helped me to adjust. Of course, now I can't read any more. And a lot of books were lost in the floods in Bilkha. But I loved reading and we loved dancing. You have seen my husband, he is very tall, and then he was also rather heavy. But he danced like a feather! We loved modern music – of that time, of course. We listened to Elvis Presley, Dean Martin, Frank Sinatra . . . Nat King Cole . . . Sammy Davis Junior . . . I loved them so much! And every year we would sail to England on the *Queen Mary* and spend two or three months at the Savoy Hotel in London. We were both fun-loving people, so we went to lots of parties. We visited Paris, Florence, Capri, London, Lake Como. Oh, and once, in Italy, we met Frank Sinatra. I nearly went overboard! I couldn't believe it. We met him in Rome, at a party. That was a great day!'

Later, when they moved to Pune to manage her brother-in-law's stables, they ended up staying there for their children's schooling. Two of them, Billy and Sunny, went to university, but then Indira Gandhi abolished all privy purses. So Billy moved to Germany, where he found work at an accounting firm, and never returned. Over time he became the financial director of a large clothing company. Sunny, meanwhile, was hired by the automobile manufacturer Mahindra, which had its own cricket team; he made his career as a manager and competed at national level.

'My eldest son, Lalji, remained in Bilkha, where he managed for us what was left. But a few years ago he died suddenly of a heart attack. And we discovered he had mismanaged our fortune. Totally. We were wiped clean. He had power of attorney. He gave away a lot of land. It was a great shock to my husband. He'd cleaned us out, and the kids too. We still can't understand why, because he didn't have an expensive lifestyle at all. No womanising, no drinking, no smoking . . . His wife stayed back there, and their three daughters – you have met Pooja; the others are called Kookie and Priya – came to live with us. He and his wife were partners in crime, I think. But what happened with him was our fault also. We should have gone to Bilkha more often. Should have asked.'

Bubbles' children were never very close to their father; maybe because as parents they were travelling abroad too much, she allowed. But the kids were close to her. That much she knew.

'In the end, Sunny has done well, Billy has done extremely well, Tiny is all right. But then he is not a person who wants to climb right to the top. His nature is very like mine: he takes it as it comes. It has helped him to pull through. You know Tiny. Tiny is happy-go-lucky.'

Just then a growing crowd of people formed across from the café, as if there had been some minor accident, and for a while we were distracted. Then a shadow swept over her face and she changed the subject.

'Sometimes I think that if Papa hadn't married again, maybe we would have learned why Mummy left, you know? Because she was never discussed. So we never knew. Never, never. My father didn't talk about her. And my second mother wouldn't either. Never, never. Not to me, and I don't think to my elder brother. Otherwise he would have mentioned it.'

I wondered if that thick layer of silence had been heavy enough to bury her memories too. Did she truly not remember her mother?

'My brother used to remember her. I don't.'

This time, though, she was willing to contradict herself.

'I only remember one incident. She was lying in bed, and I got up on the head of the bed, and she told me: get down. And you know how children are. I didn't listen, I fell and I broke these teeth.' With her finger she pointed out her two slightly protruding incisors.

'But other things I don't remember. Maybe I blocked it out, and went on with my life. But now, afterwards, I think: why? What had we done? I mean, we were kids. What had we done?'

# Eagles, Diamonds and Peacocks

In the summer of 1901, while England was still mourning the death of Queen Victoria, Queen Alexandra summoned the French jeweller Pierre Cartier to Buckingham Palace. Her wish was to commission a spectacular 'Indian' necklace, using stones the empress had received as gifts from Raj princes. The resulting piece comprised pearl, emerald and ruby cabochons, with two large, rectangular emerald talismans that paid homage to Mughal tastes as well as to Hindu tradition, which held that precious stones had the power to absorb and emit cosmic energies.

Talisman jewellery had been an interest of mine ever since, years earlier, I was gifted the Navaratna that now sits on my right-hand ring finger as I type these words: a gold ring with small gems arrayed in an oval, which in Indian culture is considered a powerful – if not the most powerful – antidote against curses and bad luck. Whether oval, square or round, the Navaratna bears a precise design: a diamond, a pearl, a sapphire, an emerald, a topaz, a cat's eye, a coral and a red zircon must orbit like satellites around a ruby representing the sun. In the Hindu tradition that assigns each gem a specific meaning and cosmic power, some of the gems bring good, others evil, and, in order to enhance or neutralise the powers of the various stones, it is crucial that they always be worn together, in this precise order.

From my Navaratna I learned that Indians associate each precious stone with a celestial body: ruby with the sun, pearl with the moon and diamond with Venus. Sapphire, given its bond with shady Saturn, was considered a jinx – assuming that whoever wore it lacked the proper astrological profile to neutralise the poison dart of that vivid-blue stone, extracted from the mines in Kashmir.

Back at my desk in Paris, I set about studying Amrit's Lafayette portrait, wondering if it had been an astrologer who'd given her the authority to flaunt such huge sapphires, thus daring bad luck to strike; or if her predilection for a stone that any jeweller would have considered unadvisable for an Indian client was yet another sign of her penchant for swimming against the current. Amrit's jewellery collection included not only the enormous sapphire with a black spot that Bubbles had found in an American safe – and which she'd rid herself of as soon as possible, as she told me. On her right hand that day, when the twenty-year-old Amrit Kaur posed in Lafayette's studio, was the sapphire I already knew well: the sixteen-carat stone that went up for auction two years after her death, at Parke-Bernet in New York, while the ring on her left-hand ring finger was very clearly the emerald-cut Cartier diamond listed in that same auction. In December 1950, the sale of the estate of the Rani of Mandi caught the attention of the press, which is how I discovered that the auction had brought in $75,000, today's equivalent of nearly $800,000.

The other jewels Amrit Kaur wore for the portrait, with her gold-threaded silk sari that refracted the light like the surface of a lake – known as a 'tissue sari' according to my friend Naheed, who called it the 'uniform of a certain social class' and, in a stroke of generosity, gifted me a gold-and-sand-coloured one she no longer used – had a decidedly Indian feel. In her left hand, the young Amrit held the ends of two long strings of pearls, with a gold and pearl medallion; on her wrists were pearl bracelets; on her ears, long diamond earrings; and a spectacular necklace, with antique-cut diamonds and three large pear pearls, covered her collarbone.

The prevalence of diamonds and pearls was in line with Indian tradition. At the time, the principal market for natural pearls found in the Persian Gulf was Bombay, where princes vied for them. At the Lafayette exhibition, nearly every maharaja wore multiple strings of pearls around his neck. As for diamonds, up until the second half of the nineteenth century the Transvaal mines that had made the young Albert Kahn's fortune had yet to be discovered – nor had Brazil's, on the other side of the globe. Diamonds were an Indian monopoly for thousands of years. As early as 2000 BCE there's mention of diamonds in river beds throughout the Indus Valley, spewed from volcanoes together with stones and other sediment, and then carried along on the water, over the course of millennia, to their resting place. And what a place! I thought, when I first dug into the history of the Golconda mines, on the southern end of Deccan, in what is now Andhra Pradesh.

Word of the mines began to spread in the thirteenth century, when the Venetian merchant Marco Polo visited the Mutfili kingdom, now believed to have been Telangana, north-east of Hyderabad. Several years after his return to Italy, Polo was taken prisoner by the Genoans in a battle between the maritime republics of Genoa and Venice. And, as fate would have it, his cellmate was a writer named Rustichello da Pisa. To pass the time, the Venetian recounted his adventures to the Pisan, who transcribed them in what would become a classic of Italian literature, *The Travels of Marco Polo*. So it was by sheer coincidence that the two prisoners passed on this miraculous journey, which took Marco, his father and his uncle from Venice all the way to the court of the first Chinese emperor, Kublai Khan.

To Rustichello Polo described his arrival in Golconda, where he discovered that the rains during the monsoon seasons would knock the diamonds free from the riverbanks and drag them along the beds. After the monsoons, the shallows glimmered like a starry sky. But the stones remained inaccessible – surrounded by thousands of snakes.

Marco Polo had likely embellished his tale a bit, drawing on the ancient Arab story-cycle *Sinbad the Sailor*, in which Sinbad, clinging to a giant bird of prey, manages to escape the desert island where he and his crew have been abandoned. The bird then drops him in a valley rife with diamonds, all surrounded by snakes big enough to swallow an elephant whole. This tall tale would later be adopted by the *One Thousand and One Nights*, as well as by Hollywood. Just as it had worked its magic on Rustichello, it would capture the imaginations of Cecil B. DeMille and Steven Spielberg.

But the most fascinating part of Marco Polo's tale was yet to unfold. To recover the diamonds, the Venetian merchant explained to his ghostwriter, the locals developed a system in which they threw pieces of raw meat down into the base of the valley. Bald eagles, which were plentiful in and around Golconda, would dart down to grab the meat and carry it back to the surrounding rocky hills, where they'd dig in. Just then, men would charge forward and chase the eagles off, seizing the pieces of meat – which, from the impact of their fall, were littered with grains of dirt and diamonds.

There was yet another way of fetching diamonds: with ox meat. This consisted of raiding the bald eagles' nests and digging through their excrement for the diamonds they'd swallowed along with their food. A third method involved catching the eagle, opening up its stomach and seizing the spoils.

As it turns out, the story of using eagles to fetch diamonds in inaccessible valleys was already known to the Greeks and Romans. And it likely derived from Hindu mythology, in which Garuda, the eagle god, was the mortal enemy of the Nāgas – the sacred serpents who watched over the earth's treasures. Other travellers after Marco Polo attested to this custom as well. One of them was the Venetian doctor Niccolao Manucci, who arrived in Golconda in the late 1600s. It wasn't until three centuries after the publication of Polo's *Travels* that the diamond-hunting-with-eagles business was officially labelled a myth by William Methwold, an employee of the East India Company with little patience for such fanciful tales. Visiting Golconda in 1626, Methwold confronted the spectacle of 30,000 slaves – men, women and children – immersed in the muck of the Krishna River, passing buckets of mud along the surface. The mud was then dried in the sun by other slaves and sifted for diamonds. Two and a half centuries later, when the French photographer Louis Rousselet arrived in Golconda, the extraction method was exactly the same.

One thing, in any case, was certain, at least according to Amin Jaffer, the expert at Christie's whom I'd consulted on the first of what would be many occasions: the diamonds, sapphires and pearls that Amrit was wearing in the portrait that sent me down my research rabbit hole were all wedding gifts. And this, in the sequence of events that brought her to Europe in the 1930s, was an important detail.

With Indian brides whose backgrounds permit such extravagance, it's common practice for their own or the groom's family to present them with jewellery. These jewels are their *stridhan*, meaning 'a woman's wealth', and, unlike the dowry that becomes the husband's property, it belongs exclusively to the bride, who's free to use it as she pleases. As a consequence, the *stridhan* (which today can encompass other assets) functioned for centuries as a kind of insurance policy. And I like to imagine that this is why Indian women, regardless of social status, almost always have a little gold on them, even when they're cleaning out drainage ditches or splitting stones on the side of the street.

Since giving 'used' jewels was considered a bad omen, as Amin Jaffer explained to me, when it came to weddings the great families of the Raj ordered new settings for all the gems destined for the bride. Often their commissions fell to the Parisian jewellers on the rue de la Paix or thereabouts, like the place Vendôme or the rue des Pyramides – which is to say they turned to Cartier, and to Mellerio, Vever, Marret, Boucheron, Chaumet and Van Cleef & Arpels.

The Kapurthalas had a reputation as good clients of the rue de la Paix, though without going overboard. Perhaps because he wasn't as rich as the Western press liked to depict him, Amrit's father was always judicious about his purchases. Years later, when a journalist investigated the family's wealth, the incomparable Paramjit, the Maharaja's firstborn, felt the need to specify: 'You can write that I'm a millionaire, just leave out the "multi".'

While in Le Touquet the *femme fatale* Indira Devi of Cooch Behar was flinging her chips down at the casino, fiddling with her live tortoise on the green felt, its shell decked with three rows of rubies, diamonds and emeralds, in Paris the Maharaja of Kapurthala nearly always ordered jewels that had a representative function. In this regard one might almost call him sober. He had no taste for bejewelled tortoises or other wildly eccentric jewellery, like the glasses Emperor Shah Jahan commissioned after he'd ruined his vision by crying too hard over the death of his beloved wife Mumtaz: one pair with diamond lenses, one with emerald.

Amrit's father's diaries speak of his fascination for the great Parisian jewellers even before 1900, though his conversion to Western tastes could be said to have occurred at a precise place and time: the 1903 Delhi Durbar, when Lord Curzon threw the most spectacular of imperial pageants to celebrate the succession of Edward VII and Alexandra of Denmark as Emperor and Empress of India.

Like everyone there, Jagatjit Singh was awestruck by Lady Curzon's entrance. After the Nizam of Hyderabad and the Maharaja of Mysore opened the festivities with a parade of elephants, the beautiful, cultivated and strikingly tall American heiress Mary Leiter, now the vicereine, kicked off the dancing in a Worth gown embroidered top to bottom with gold and silver thread in a peacock-feather motif. The Peacock Dress would go down in fashion history for its extravagant embroidery, and because Worth had sewn beetle wings over the eye of each feather, which everyone took to be emeralds. Atop her gathered mass of brown hair the young vicereine wore a Boucheron tiara of platinum with diamonds in a delicate lily pattern. Two years later Jagatjit Singh would approach Boucheron with a handful of diamonds and ask him to make a *sarpech* – a turban ornament – in the ribbon-and-garland Louis XVI style so in vogue at the time. The fact that Boucheron had chosen to use platinum for the *sarpech* – a precious metal as yet unknown in India, where gold was sacred and silver was used, if at all, for the feet and ankles only – was evidence of the young maharaja's willingness to embrace the new, to boldly adopt the latest trend, passed down to the great French jewellers by the Russian aristocracy.

But the Maharaja of Kapurthala did not stop at Boucheron. In 1905, as he was preparing for a trip to Madrid to attend the marriage of Alfonso XIII of Spain and Princess Victoria Eugenie of Battenberg, Amrit's father paid a visit to Mellerio, the jeweller favoured by France's queens, and acquired a spectacular yellow-gold, diamond and enamel brooch in the shape of a peacock: a fashionable choice, though one of particular significance for an Indian. The peacock, in India, heralds the monsoon season, and therefore prosperity, and in Hindu symbology is tied to Krishna, the supreme god from whom all others descend. That peacock, however, which would become one of the most celebrated pieces ever made by the enterprising jeweller, would not stay for long on the maharaja's turban. When Jagatjit Singh fell in love with the young Anita Delgado he gave her his Mellerio peacock, saying '*tu seras toujours mon petit oiseau des îles*' (you'll always be my little bird of the islands): a prophecy that, despite their separation twenty years later, seems to have largely come true. In any case, after arriving in Kapurthala as maharani number five and adopting the name Prem Kaur, Anita noticed a half-moon-shaped emerald of the most radiant green on the forehead of her husband's oldest elephant, and asked if she could have it. Jagatjit Singh agreed, but on one condition: she had to learn Hindi. And so it was – the bright young girl held up her end of the bargain, coming away with the emerald talisman, which she'd later embellish with diamonds and begin wearing on her own, unwrinkled forehead, not so differently from the elephant.

But apart from these occasional forays to Boucheron or Mellerio, it was clear that the Kapurthalas' jewellers of choice were the Cartier brothers, Pierre, Louis and Jacques, who in 1899 had opened their luxurious boutique on 13 rue de la Paix, having come a long way from their grandfather Louis-François' humble beginnings.

Of the three brothers, Louis was the one who best knew the ins and outs of the business, but he was also an aesthete with a passion for eighteenth-century French art and an in-depth knowledge of Indian and Persian miniatures, through which he came to study Mughal jewellery.

Pierre, on the other hand, had diplomatic ambitions, though he was forced to sideline them to open the Maison Cartier in New York, which he launched to enormous success with America's upper classes and Hollywood, thanks in part to a wealthy and well-connected American wife. Jacques, the youngest and most introverted, revealed himself to be no less entrepreneurial than his siblings. It was to Jacques that the brothers left the task of opening a London branch, and therefore, over the years, of dealing with the maharajas who'd made London their second home.

It was no doubt as a direct result of these circumstances that Jacques Cartier became the first of the great French jewellers to travel to India, taking advantage of the 1911 durbar, when, to celebrate the crowning of George V, hundreds of Raj princes accompanied by servants and bodyguards set up camp in Delhi to pledge their allegiance to the new sovereign. I found it hard to believe that, in the early twentieth century, a week of ceremonies, military parades, garden parties, tiger hunts and polo games could draw 200,000 people, all gathered in the shade of the Red Fort.

For Jacques Cartier, who went so far as to learn Hindustani and sit Indian-style on the ground to bargain with local gem dealers, the last great Imperial Durbar was an opportunity not to be missed – a chance to introduce himself to the maharajas and sound out their interest in Western-style jewellery After disembarking in Bombay with his cargo of platinum jewellery and timepieces, he soon discovered that the most in-demand item was the pocket watch, which was all the rage in Europe.

Jacques Cartier was most likely unaware of the fact that, thanks to the East India Company, watches, grandfather clocks and automatons had existed and been collected in India since the eighteenth century. 'Tipu Sahib, the feared Sultan of Mysore from 1782 to 1799, was said to have commissioned a life-size automaton of a tiger which, to musical accompaniment, savaged a European, from a French clockmaker,' wrote the Maison Cartier historian Hans Nadelhoffer. Jacques Cartier had no human-hunting beasts to offer his clients, but he succeeded all the same in selling a number of watches. The Nizam of Hyderabad chose a gold one; the Maharaja of Nawanagar platinum; the Aga Khan wanted his studded with diamonds; and the Maharaja of Kapurthala preferred a more modest blue enamel watch, even though he'd go on to collect another 250 of them.

Jacques Cartier examines gem merchants' wares in India, 1911.

Travelling through India in those days – especially with precious cargo, as did Jacques Cartier when, after the durbar, he paid a visit to the Maharaja of Kapurthala, as well as to the Maharajas of Nawanagar and Baroda, the Aga Khan, the Nizam of Hyderabad and the Nawab of Rampur – was not for the faint of heart: the distances were enormous, as were the cultural differences. When, in 1888, the goldsmith Federick Emery, of P.Orr & Sons of Madras, travelled to Hyderabad at the nizam's invitation, he sent his mother a rather apprehensive letter, reporting that he'd been set up in a luxurious apartment. The problem, however, was his extreme isolation. 'I am situated right in the heart of the city . . . surrounded by walls at least 20 feet high . . . and not another European as far as I know anywhere in the vicinity. I thought when the Nizam's barber was shaving me this morning how easy it would be for him to cut my throat and dispose of me and nobody be any the wiser. The Nizam even asked if I was not afraid to stay there all alone.'

Jacques Cartier himself, when he visited the Maharaja of Baroda in 1911 at his 500-room palace in Gujarat and landed the job of resetting his entire jewellery collection in platinum, was forced to flee for fear that the local jewellers would seek their revenge.

No such fate awaited him in Kapurthala, where, as we know, Cartier even found himself attended by a crew of French-speaking servants. Between the most French of Indian princes and the most Indian of French jewellers it was only natural that a lasting bond would form – which in 1926 resulted in one of the inter-war period's most celebrated pieces of jewellery: a pagoda-shaped tiara with a row of eleven massive emeralds, topped by a 177-carat hexagonal emerald, which was itself topped by three more emeralds – one hexagonal, one crescent-shaped and, at the top, one teardrop emerald cabochon.

Cartier would take out a full-page ad in the magazine *Spur* to feature Jagatjit Singh's tiara. 'The Maharajah,' went the copy, 'like most other Indian potentates, has faith in the increasing value of pearls and precious stones and regularly devotes a portion of his annual income to increasing his collection. The Hindu princes look upon gems as a permanent investment to pass from generation to generation.' With all due respect to the Cartier brothers' marketing intentions, whatever happened to the tiara, I knew that not a single one of its emeralds had made its way from 'generation to generation' down to Bubbles.

But beyond the salesmen's adventures, the clients' extravagant tastes, the bejewelled turtles and the rakish fingers that toyed with them while the ball spun on the roulette wheel, the encounter between the rue de la Paix and the princes of India marked a turning point in twentieth-century tastes that lifted French jewellery to new heights. It was a true aesthetic revolution, bringing the colours of Mughal enamels to the Cartier palette, paired boldly with the oranges, blues and emerald-greens of Diaghilev's *Schéhérazade*, the ballet that had caused a sensation at Paris's Théâtre de l'Opéra in 1910. The combined influences of Mughal culture and the Ballets Russes freed the Cartier brothers from the bows and garlands of Louis XVI style, of which their father Alfred had become such a master, inspiring a new approach situated between modernism and orientalism that to this day represents one of the high points of Art Deco.

'All of Paris is now dressing in Oriental attire,' the set and costume designer Léon Bakst wrote to his wife, with a touch of exaggeration. All of Paris, perhaps not, but the fortunate few who could afford Paul Poiret's odalisque-style pants, his turbans with feathered *aigrettes* and his kimono-coats that put an end to Worth's whalebone corsets and strangled waistlines, yes. Even the token necklace of the 1920s – that long string of pearls, fluttering in ballrooms to the rhythm of the Charleston – was a reinterpretation of the *mala*, a traditional Hindu rosary.

And yet India and Russia were not the only influences on the rue de la Paix's Art Deco creations. When, in November 1922, the English archaeologist Howard Carter and Lord Carnarvon opened the first of the secret doors that led to the pharaoh Tutankhamen's tomb, the worlds of art, literature, fashion and cinema were swept up in an Egyptian craze, broadening Cartier's palette, which by the end of the 1800s had already included lotus flower designs and depictions of the goddess Isis.

No surprise, then, when I discovered that in July 1931 Amrit Kaur bought an 'Egyptian' vanity case from Cartier: a black-enamel powder and lipstick carrier with a thin border of diamonds and, in the centre, a portrait of the goddess Maat in profile, outlined by a stream of brilliant-cut diamonds. It was an exquisite object, with Art Deco's geometrical influence adding a touch of elegance to the Egyptian original, which showed a goddess with dark brown skin and a leonine profile, her right hand clutching the *wa* sceptre – a symbol of power – and her left hand the *ankh*, the symbol of eternal life.

After a little more research on Maat and her role in Ancient Egyptian religion, I discovered that she was the goddess of truth, balance, order, morality, law, harmony and justice – all qualities, as I'd discover, that had little or nothing to do with Amrit's life. From her marriage on, it was all disorder, disharmony, injustice.

# The Coldest Winter Anyone Could Remember

One December night in 1940, Lieutenant Gillet was sleeping in the Vauban barracks in Besançon when he was woken with an order to report immediately to the gates.

Medical officer Gillet was one of the French soldiers whom the Germans had captured in their advance across France six months earlier, which culminated in the humiliating armistice signed by Marshal Pétain. Of these prisoners, 20,000 were sent to the Vauban barracks and from there, not long before that freezing December night, transferred to Germany on foot. Only 100 or so French soldiers would remain in Besançon, along with a few English stragglers who didn't make it to the Dunkirk beaches in time.

Hence the scene that Gillet encountered when he arrived at the barracks entrance after midnight: 500 women, plagued by cold, hunger and thirst, walking through the heavy snow towards the immense Napoleonic structure of the barracks, dogs nipping at their heels and German soldiers prodding them with their rifles. They were British women, or the wives of Britons, citizens of the Commonwealth or the Empire – many accompanied by young children or ageing relatives in need of assistance. That terrible scene represented just one of the many dark pages in the history of the German occupation of France: nearly 4,000 'alien enemies', across all of France, were arrested in one week and deported to wretched barracks in the north-east, with no heat, no bathrooms and scarcely any food, in the middle of one of the century's coldest winters. Gillet would soon discover that they hadn't had anything to eat or drink in three days. He and the other medical officers had to set to work immediately.

Amrit was among those arrested that week. As I had told Bubbles, she was seized by the *gendarmerie* from her apartment in the sixteenth arrondissement on 8 December. However, when I began researching the internment camp where she was held prisoner for five months, I realised that none of the people I asked – friends, writers, historians, journalists or diplomats – had ever heard of that prison camp where hundreds of people had lost their lives in the first month alone. Even Besançon's Museum of the Resistance and Deportation didn't have any record of Amrit Kaur. And yet, eyewitness accounts published by survivors in England, and documents held at London's Imperial War Museum, could not be any clearer: the French *gendarmerie* had arrested them on behalf of the Nazis. The only person in Paris who seemed to have any real knowledge about it was Jimmy Fox, the former editor-in-chief of the photography agency Magnum, whom I contacted after hearing that he'd made it his life's mission to collect the testimonies of all the survivors of the Besançon internment camp named by the Germans 'Frontstalag 142'.

Strangely, I found no trace of Amrit Kaur's arrest in the Paris Police Prefecture archives. The prefect and the secret service seemed more interested in her father's peccadilloes. An entire folder was dedicated to Jagatjit Singh's comings and goings from the Ritz or Le Meurice, with his retinue of eight or nine attendants. There were several reports on his car accidents and his social outings, one of which, dated 1900, stated that the British government had 'taken umbrage' at the maharaja's relations with the French government, and especially with the Duke of Orléans, whose reputation was less than glowing. As a consequence, the British ordered a certain Colonel Marshall to tail the maharaja wherever he went. Viceroy Lord Curzon's fingerprints were all over this attempt to put Jagatjit Singh on a leash. But the plan failed spectacularly: 'It appears that the zeal with which the colonel is carrying out his assignment is at times most embarrassing and indiscreet,' read the report.

Another report in the Kapurthala dossier, dated 1918, reads more like one of those three-line movie plots: 'Jane Renouardt is the Maharaja of Kapurthala's *maîtresse*. At the present moment she's being entertained by a Belgian lieutenant. She's seeing the maharaja and a Russian captain at the same time.'

Jane Renouardt was a silent-film actress with curly brown hair and dark, droopy eyes who cast her charm in the films of Max Linder, the French comic actor, director and dandy who served as an influence on Charlie Chaplin and the Marx Brothers. With the arrival of talkies in the late 1910s, she'd stepped away from the big screen and reinvented herself as a theatre director, assembling a group of generous friends, one of whom was Amrit's father.

Among the Prefecture's records I found other traces of the maharaja's lovers, mostly French women of less notable backgrounds than Jane Renouardt's. But there were only a few items mentioning Amrit Kaur, stating that she lived in the sixteenth arrondissement and that she'd registered with her neighbourhood precinct.

After a first, frustrating glance at those files, I turned to an employee for help: 'Bonjour, Monsieur, these are the general police archives, correct?'

'Bonjour, Madame, yes.'

'And if someone is arrested in Paris, this is where I would find the files on that arrest?'

'Yes, Madame.'

'Would you be so kind, then, as to explain why this woman's record isn't here?'

'I wouldn't know. Perhaps you wrote her name down wrong.'

'I don't think so. I checked. I have the right name. And the right date. That week in Paris, in December 1940, the police arrested nearly 2,000 women with British passports. How could this not be on record?'

'I wouldn't know, Madame.'

When I asked to speak with the archive's director, a woman with a patient air about her kindly suggested that 'perhaps there'd been a fire'.

According to the files at the India Office Records, Amrit was in Brussels when the war broke out. From there, in May 1940, she attempted to travel to the United States, only making it as far as Paris, where it was impossible to receive funds from abroad. This much was clear at the Mémorial de la Shoah, whose archives held countless testimonies of how the Germans had starved Jews and 'alien enemies'. However, there was another, unexpected emotion awaiting me there in the Prefecture archives – and I'm not referring to the heartbreaking compassion one feels when reading the pleas of people trying to salvage something for their children and grandchildren. I'm talking about a photograph that was hanging on the bulletin board in the reading room: an old, wartime class photo, with young boys from a school on Île Saint-Louis lined up in two rows. Beside the photo was a note that read: 'If you recognise any of the children, call this number immediately.' Perhaps it was just a scholar working on a book who'd posted the request, though the urgency of the tone suggested that, after seventy years, there were still people out there searching for those missing. If I needed proof that the wound of the Holocaust was still open in Paris, there it was, in the grey faces of those schoolchildren with their backs to the wall.

The Paris that Amrit Kaur encountered on her flight from Belgium was a city suspended between fear and its denial. 'Unless something unexpected happens within the next ten days, 1939 will be remembered in France as the year that began in uncertainty and ended in mild boredom,' wrote the *New Yorker* correspondent A. J. Liebling. 'Many of the same people who three months ago were ready to pop into their cellars like prairie dogs at the first purring of an aeroplane motor, expecting Paris to be expunged between dark and dawn, are complaining now because the restaurants do not serve beefsteak on Mondays, Tuesdays, and Fridays, and because the season has produced no new plays worth seeing.'

I've always admired the humour and deep humanity of the work of Liebling, a man who made the most improbable of war correspondents – poor eyesight, overweight, clumsy and dressed completely wrong for the occasion. The *New Yorker* sent him to Paris because he was a top-notch reporter, and because he was extraordinarily well versed in French literature and cuisine. Between his hearty meals at the city's bistros, Liebling wrote that the anticipation of war in the early months of 1940 had ground Paris to a near-halt. And so, one spring day, while Hitler was seizing Maastricht and attacking Rotterdam, he decided to check out the scene at the Auteuil Hippodrome. There he discovered that what mattered most to the racing crowd, as the Netherlands was falling to German forces, were the latest trends in racehorses and in women's fashion. 'The advertising department of the Magasins du Louvre discovered another duty for France,' he wrote wryly. 'The store slogan was "Madame, it is your duty to be elegant!" "They shall not pass" was considered *vieux jeu* and hysterical. The optimistic do-nothingism of the Chamberlain and Daladier regimes was, for millions of people, the new patriotism.'

Naturally, this didn't last. On 15 May, the fall of Sedan unleashed the fear that had been lurking beneath the French population's feigned indifference. Paris began to see the arrival of those like Amrit, in flight from a besieged Belgium. 'The great, sleek cars of the deluxe refugees came first,' Liebling noted. 'The bicycle refugees arrived soon after. Slick-haired, sullen young men wearing pullover sweaters shot out of the darkness with terrifying, silent speed. They had the air of conquerors rather than of fugitives. Many of them undoubtedly were German spies. Ordinary destitute refugees arrived later by train and as extra riders on trucks. Nothing else happened at first to change the daily life of the town.'

But then it did, and quickly. Following the surrender of the Netherlands and Belgium, in the early days of June 1940 the majority of Parisians fled west in search of safety, in a massive, lumbering, motorised exodus that would leave thousands dead on the road. 'Anything that had four wheels and an engine was pressed into service, no matter what the state of decrepitude,' the American journalist Virginia Cowles wrote in *Looking for Trouble* (1941). 'There were taxicabs, ice-trucks, bakery vans, perfume wagons, sports roadsters and Paris buses, all of them packed with human beings. I even saw a hearse full of children.'

Refugees leaving Paris after the fall of France, 1940.

Not everyone in Paris with a British passport decided to run, however. Amrit Kaur did not, nor did Sofka Skipwith, a young Russian aristocrat who'd married an RAF officer. Her granddaughter and biographer Sofka Zinovieff tells us that, on 11 June, Skipwith phoned the English ambassador to see if she should leave Paris and was advised to wait: the newspapers would be the best source for updates. Meanwhile, word was spreading that London was planning to organise transport for British citizens. Like many other Parisians, however, all Skipwith had to do was step out of her house to have a sense of the situation's gravity. In her diary, the account of that day is marked by a staccato rhythm: 'Montparnasse, people of all ages sitting on streets, backs against walls of houses, filling doorways. Round the station itself they are about 10–15 rows thick, all with their bundles and suitcases. A soldier was handing out wafers from a huge basket. The station is closed with iron gates and police cordons to keep the crowd from storming them. People fainting, people ill, children screaming, women sobbing, girls giggling, others reading, sleeping, eating, just staring. People, people, people . . . the stench defies description . . .'

With German tanks at the gates, on 10 June the government fled Paris, and on the 22nd Marshal Pétain signed an armistice that would hand over nearly two-thirds of French territory to the Germans. A German-friendly government, headed by the eighty-four-year-old Pétain, would govern 'free' France from its new capital in Vichy.

It was then that Amrit Kaur's fate was decided. One of the Germans' first actions was to round up all British men between the ages of sixteen and sixty-five and send them to the Saint-Denis barracks near Paris, to Fort Romainville, or directly to Germany. But no one imagined that they'd arrest the women and children too. For a time, these two groups were merely required to sign a registry each day at the various police stations to confirm their presence, as I knew Amrit had done. But then things began to take a sinister turn. On

20 October the Kommandantur ordered the French to report the names and movements of any British citizens to whom they rented an apartment, or to whom they'd given refuge in their own homes. Violators would be shot.

Those women who were already registered with the police were easy to round up when the time came. In the testimonies Jimmy Fox had so generously made available to me, the arrests all followed the same script. The gendarmes came to the door when it was still dark, around five or six in the morning. By torchlight, they ordered whoever answered to quickly get dressed and grab the bare necessities for one night away. Nicholas Shakespeare, who recounted his aunt's experience during the war in France in his book *Priscilla*, describes the scene of her arrest: 'The blackout was still in force and she followed the beam of the gendarme's torch down the stairs to a waiting car. She could make out people watching in silence from windows and balconies.' Like all the other women, the blonde and debonair Priscilla Mais was hauled to the police station and then to her neighbourhood's *mairie*. No one said a word to her about where she was going or why.

Another particularly vivid account was written by Elizabeth Hales, an elderly woman who, along with Amrit Kaur and Priscilla Mais, was detained in Frontstalag 142's Bâtiment A. Early one morning, Hales heard someone pounding on her door, followed by the voice of her concierge explaining that the police had come to arrest her and her husband. 'We filled a sack with clothes and food stuffs were put in a suitcase. The policeman grumbled and said I was slow but when I gave him half a pound of coffee he became sweet and said if questioned he would say I was out when he called and had to wait on me. My jewels and some dresses went into Mme Faugeras's safe keeping. Meanwhile we ate a hurried breakfast and I put on my best fur coat etc and a good hat – warm things as the police said we were going to a very cold place . . .'

Awaiting them in the chaos of the fourteenth arrondissement's *mairie* were many of their friends and acquaintances. The contrast between the happy couples depicted in the grand eighteenth-century paintings that hung in the *Salle de Mariage* and that distressed throng of captives was almost surreal.

I found many more accounts of that tragic day, and reading them between the protective walls of my apartment I began to grow fond of a few of their authors. Rosemary Say, for one, was only twenty years old and worked as an au pair for a family in the seventh arrondissement. When they arrived at Gare de l'Est, she wrote, they found an alarming number of desperate souls wandering aimlessly around the station, clinging to their belongings. 'The noise was deafening with people shouting and protesting. German soldiers were everywhere but they were having a hard job keeping the crowd under control.'

Among the crowd were children, the elderly and infirm, and most of all women – of every age and background. Only a quarter of them had been born in England; the others had married Englishmen or were from the Commonwealth or other countries of the Empire, as well as from Palestine, where the British Mandate was still in effect. Among the Englishwomen, several had been raised in India, the daughters of officers or functionaries for the Raj. There were nurses, seamstresses, nuns, nannies, housekeepers and jockeys' wives; there were dancers from the Folies Bergère and ladies in fur coats and leopard-skin hats, looking like something out of a P. G. Wodehouse novel; there were prostitutes rounded up from the *maisons closes* and the ports along the English Channel. And as one witness recounted to Nicholas Shakespeare, there was 'the daughter of an Indian maharajah, who had boarded the train dressed in a veil and a sable coat'.

The trip was long and excruciatingly uncomfortable. Rosemary Say tells of how the train they'd stuck her on had neither toilets nor running water, and how the compartments lacked electric light and heating. 'After two days the lavatory situation was unimaginable. We managed as best we could at any stop when we were allowed down beside the tracks. It was an extraordinary sight to see women of all sorts and ages openly relieving themselves in front of the guards.' Many of these women were nuns, some of whom had spent their lives in cloisters and hadn't seen the outside world for decades. Awaiting them in Besançon was medical officer Gillet and thirty inches of snow.

There was a reason why a trip that should have lasted mere hours took two or possibly even three days: the game of political arm-wrestling under way between the German and English governments. During the train ride, word spread among the deportees that they were being sent to work in an ammunition factory in Germany or to a concentration camp. And the fact that they'd departed from the Gare de l'Est seemed to confirm that rumour. But then the trains began to zigzag, making long stops, changing direction. Only later did they learn what was happening: Churchill had sent word to the Nazis, through the Red Cross, that if they transported those women into Germany he'd transfer the whole lot of his German prisoners to the tundra of northern Canada.

That small French town, not far from the German border, had therefore been a last-minute solution. Which was why, just a day before the women arrived, thousands of prisoners of war were cleared out of the Vauban barracks, leaving them completely unready. 'Wait and see how clean your room is!' one of the French soldiers jeered at Rosemary Say as she approached the building, huddled with a group of girls she'd met on the train. The Vauban barracks, now razed to the ground to make way for a 'sustainable model district', consisted of three main buildings referred to as Bâtiments A, B and C. When Rosemary reached the fourth floor of Bâtiment A, where Amrit would spend five months, the scene before her eyes left her 'dazed and dismayed'. The floor and pallet beds were soaked, snow was pouring in through a massive hole in the ceiling, and 'there was an overpowering stench of urine'.

Of the 20,000 prisoners who'd occupied the barracks before them, 100 or so had been ordered to clean the dorms. First they burned the infected garbage, but then they dumped buckets of water over the floor with no concern for the straw mattresses, covering everything in a layer of muddy grime. For the first few days the detainees were forced to eat from large communal pots or else make do with abandoned helmets, plucked from the mounds of trash. Bowls and spoons would not arrive until the second week. There were no sheets, blankets or towels, never mind pillows, just wooden cots with sunken frames. As protection against the cold, the Germans handed out French army coats they'd found in one of the storerooms, dating back to the First World War. 'It was a very sad thing to see children of five or six years old, often without shoes, dressed in overcoats of French soldiers,' lamented one nun from the Marianites of Holy Cross. A few of the coats were still covered in bloodstains.

Through all of December and a good part of January, the temperature in the dorms remained below zero. Chilling winds curled up the stairs. Each floor, with more than 100 occupants, had to make do with one toilet, which was immediately clogged. The only alternative was the outdoor latrines, built above a large drainage ditch. The *tinettes*, as the prisoners called them, were a series of planks with holes in them, above which you had to squat in plain sight of the others. There were twenty for 3,900 prisoners, and to direct traffic they'd assigned a former jockey from Chantilly who was nicknamed 'Mr Bottom' and who claimed never to have seen so many backsides in his life. Rats as large as rabbits leaped from that open sewer and made straight for the kitchens.

Samuel Hales, Elizabeth Hales's seventy-two-year-old husband from New Zealand, slept on the floor for his first eight nights at Frontstalag 142. While the snow kept coming down outside, the heater didn't work for the entire month, and he survived thanks only to a heavy-duty coat, though others were less fortunate. Prisoners, he wrote, had to walk fifty yards through the snow to reach the latrines, and the elderly who collapsed along the way at night were found frozen the next morning. 'During the three and a half months we were there, about 600 died!'

Prisoners contracted bronchitis and pneumonia. The flu was rampant. Nearly every woman's menstrual cycle came to a halt (which many considered a blessing). The most common afflictions were stomach problems and gastrointestinal diseases, and the most virulent epidemic struck Bâtiment A, where Amrit Kaur, Elizabeth Hales, Rosemary Say and Sofka Skipwith were staying. The more I read about the green, mouldy bread that gave you colic if it wasn't heated on the stove and the repulsive slop they were forced to eat, the more I understood why Amrit felt the way she did after Besançon, and why she pleaded so many times to leave France for medical treatment. Whatever it was she contracted in that internment camp, she seems never to have recovered.

Despite it all, the survival instinct prevailed, and as the days passed the detainees' lives took on a semblance of routine. First thing in the morning, the youngest would descend and bring breakfast up to the others – some kind of coffee concoction and a spoonful of rancid lard per person. At one they were served a watered-down soup, with a few thawing chunks of potato and shreds of horse meat drawn from the carcasses hanging in the courtyard. In the evening, more lard, another 'coffee', and on good days a bit of cheese squeezed from a tube and a spoonful of jam. And because each meal meant queueing for hours, to divvy up the labour the younger women took care of the food and wood, while the elderly swept the floor and kept the fire burning. 'We did our best to heat pans of water on the stove in our room,' Rosemary Say wrote. 'But in that cold winter it was difficult to carry up enough water for cleaning yourself and washing your

A sketch of daily life in Frontstalag 142 by Mabel Fanny Twemlow, Katherine Lack's aunt, 1941.

clothes. Water that was spilt on the steps and in the corridors would soon turn to ice, making any passage treacherous.'

Throughout the entire first month there was no soap at all; after that, one bar per twenty prisoners, distributed once every two weeks. Only then did the Germans install twenty rudimentary showers, but with so many detainees, each could only expect two quick showers a month. Astutely, Sofka Skipwith managed to secure herself the position of shower manager, which meant she could clean herself every night.

For the young women who'd spent their early years at English boarding schools like Amrit Kaur, Rosemary Say and Priscilla Mais, that routine reminded them of their schooldays. The same regimented schedule, the same war against insects (except here the fleas, bedbugs, lice and cockroaches put up more of a fight), the same need to carve out a measure of private emotional and physical space for oneself and to become self-sufficient. The more bookish prisoners used their free afternoons for reading; the more active, for teaching or playing sports. One former gym teacher, a long-legged lesbian whom everyone referred to as Stanley, organised volleyball tournaments and folk-dancing lessons. Another woman assembled a Welsh choir. A Professor Eccles, from Oxford, began teaching a French literature course, and one Miss Owen followed his example, offering a course in Babylonian history. To discover that these women, in such miserable conditions, were studying Mesopotamian civilisation was like seeing lilies sprout in the desert sand.

This spirit of resilience, as the captive sought refuge in knowledge, seems to have caught on with Frontstalag 142's British women and children. The people of Besançon began sending schoolbooks to the prisoners. And as the women there used them to teach the children English, Latin and maths, the Vauban barracks soon earned itself the nickname Lycée Vauban. Everyone looked for ways to keep themselves busy. Artists drew scenes of life in the dormitories. A beautician offered up her services. And the prostitutes went back to work: two nights in the German quarters for a pack of cigarettes. Rosemary Say recalled: 'One particular brothel-owner from Boulogne with bright red hair and heavy make-up would sit in the courtyard and sum up the rest of us as we walked by: "Good legs. Could use her." Marie-Ange, her daughter, would nod quietly.'

But there were those who never found a way to adapt. In Amrit's Bâtiment A, one such woman passed her time crying on the stairs. Others spent the entire day curled up in the foetal position on their bed. One woman leaped to her death from a window. And an Indian woman was about to set fire to herself and her three children when her eldest daughter, eight years old at the time, ran to a nun and begged her to reason with her mother.

I'd spent several days reading these testimonies, the facts always the same but the spirit of each so different – the younger the author, the greater her resistance to depression and her ability to adapt –

when I received an email from Jimmy Fox: 'You're in luck!' he wrote. 'The document I'm sending you speaks of your "relative". Something having to do with a jazz band that formed in Besançon.'

Jimmy Fox must have indeed read this information somewhere, since he had no way of knowing that Amrit had led a jazz band as a young boarding-school student in Sussex. But the document that the ninety-year-old researcher had attached to his email was incomplete and, in any case, damaged. And my attempts to obtain a full copy from that kind soul, hampered by his old age, came to nothing. Only ten or so pages of the document were legible, in a sprawling diary that someone had plucked from a bookshelf. In it were the musings of a White Russian by the name of Vera Timoteieff, the daughter of an Orthodox archpriest who'd escaped the Bolsheviks with his family; she too was interned at Frontstalag 142. 'Teenager stuff, à la Françoise Sagan,' Jimmy Fox had defined it, adding, 'A gem.' But the pages in front of me said nothing about jazz in Besançon; rather, they conjured the shock of Paris's first bombardment with a teenager's fondness for exclamation points ('Whistles, explosions, cannon fire, the roar of airplanes, without pause, without end!'); they attested to young Vera's anti-Semitism ('Paris, if you're suffering, it's thanks to the Jews!'); and they even revealed her crush on a young blue-eyed German soldier.

And yet, as abominable as the situation was for those 3,900 civilians, just two weeks after their arrival they managed to celebrate Christmas. In one dorm, someone organised a play for the children. In another, the French soldiers who were permitted to purchase goods in the city scraped together a dinner of meat, cheese and wine, to which they invited a few English girls. Sisters Sonia and Stella Gumuchian repaired an old piano and sat down at the keys. And when the crowd began to dance, a pair of Bluebell Girls, the statuesque dancers of the Lido de Paris theatre, struck up a performance, spinning their legs in the air in unison. Then a girl stood up on a

HH Rani Shri Amrit Kaur Sahib, daughter of the Maharaja of Kapurthala, wife of Raja Joginder Sen Bahadur of Mandi, London, 1924.

Maharaja Jagatjit Singh of Kapurthala's golden jubilee, Kapurthala, December 1927; Amrit is sitting at the far right in an orange sari.

Princess Brinda of Kapurthala.

Princess Sita Devi
of Kapurthala, 1934.

Maharani Indira Devi
of Cooch Behar, 1928.

Princess Indira of Kapurthala,
Brinda and Paramjit's eldest
daughter, Delhi, mid-1930s.

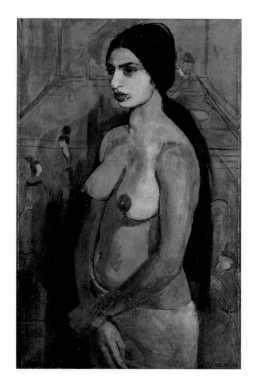

The Hungarian
Indian artist
Amrita Sher-Gil,
*Self-Portrait as
a Tahitian*, 1934.

Portrait of
Amrita
Sher-Gil,
1936.

Maharaja Jagatjit
Singh of Kapurthala
in full regalia,
wearing Cartier's
emerald tiara, 1933.

Cartier's
emerald tiara for
the Maharaja of
Kapurthala, 1926.

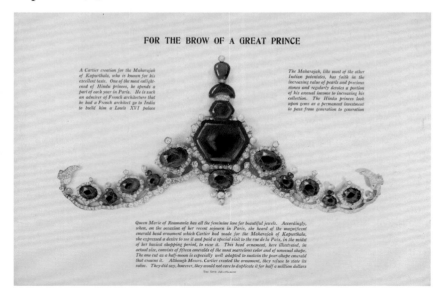

Anita Delgado's
half-moon emerald.

Anita Delgado, Maharani Prem Kaur of Kapurthala,
Amrit's stepmother and dear friend, London, 1912.

Cartier's 'Egyptian'
vanity case, bought
by Amrit in 1931.

Boucheron's platinum
and diamond turban
*sarpech* for the Maharaja
of Kapurthala, 1913.

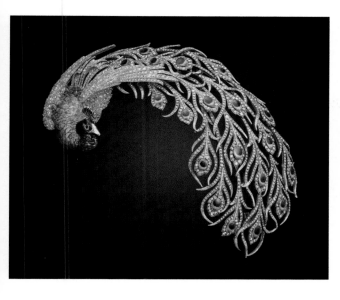

Mellerio's famous peacock brooch, bought by the maharaja and offered to Anita Delgado.

Kapurthala's treasure.

The rani's
library
bookplate.

A lovely portrait
of Rani Amrit
Kaur of Mandi,
dedicated to her
'darling Bubbles'.

chair and sang 'It's a Long Way to Tipperary', after which everyone rose to their feet for a rendition of 'God Save the King'. The French soldiers concluded the evening with 'La Marseillaise'. Meanwhile, in another large room, the Germans celebrated Christmas Eve with a bout of heavy drinking.

'Inevitably, no one took notice of the time,' wrote Rosemary Say. Which is why, at midnight, 'The doors suddenly opened and a procession of nuns and their congregation tried to enter for Mass. For a while there was complete chaos as soldiers, nuns, dancers, and worshippers struggled to carry out their own particular form of celebration. Elderly ladies were whirled around the floor by drunken French soldiers and the priest had to fight his way up to the makeshift bandstand.'

News that a bacchanal was under way quickly reached the Kommandant, who came storming over to restore order. With the room cleared, the nuns were able to enter and begin Mass. Some 600 of them, from ninety different orders, had been held prisoner at the barracks. One, from the Marianites of Holy Cross, reported that a few of the less drunk German soldiers had helped her build an altar, using a wooden plank and two workbenches, a bedsheet and a paper cradle. No Mary, Joseph, oxen or donkeys. It was enough that they'd managed to procure a baby Jesus. After running through the Mass several times, to accommodate the flood of prisoners, they closed the evening by singing the Polish national anthem, 'for those who no longer had a homeland'.

Even so, the day after that heartbreakingly sad affair the survival instinct that so many of the prisoners had felt at the beginning before succumbing to depression came rushing back and the mood changed. 'It was great fun,' said Sister Gauley, quoted in Katherine Lack's *Frontstalag 142* (2010). Behind such a mood shift was an oversight by the Germans, who'd retired to their quarters for Christmas lunch forgetting they'd left the coal room open. 'Everybody filling their buckets over and over again and hiding it under our beds. It was awful, really . . . We also stole potatoes when possible. My companions started having scruples so I went to confession and said "Father, I've been stealing potatoes!" and he answered *"Très bien, ma soeur, continuez!"* '

But there were other, bolder transgressions. At midnight on 31 December 1940, the 'red princess' Sofka Skipwith walked completely naked into the dorm she shared with Rosemary Say and the other girls on the top floor of Bâtiment A, reciting Pushkin's poetry with a glass of wine in hand. No one could figure out how she'd got the wine, or the glass for that matter, but one of the girls grabbed a piece of paper and sketched her in the act, *à poile*, in the midst of giving a little theatrical bow, her hands behind her back and her long hair cascading over her breasts.

The real Christmas gift, however, would not come until the end of January, when the first Red Cross packages arrived.

Most of the prisoners were able to make small purchases now and then at the storeroom, as long as they were willing to queue for hours in the snow. But not Amrit, who never managed to obtain even the few pounds that all prisoners were entitled to each month. Why the Germans chose to treat her more harshly than the others, I was never able to determine. Even the employees at the Foreign Office were puzzled. One of them guessed that they'd taken her for a Roma, because of her brown skin.

These packages from the Red Cross, which saved so many lives, most certainly saved hers. But along with the Red Cross came an unpleasant surprise. The delegation that made its first visit to the Vauban barracks, towards the end of January 1941, included the wife of the commander-in-chief of Germany's armed forces, Hitler loyalist Hermann Göring. It was ironic, to say the least, that Emmy Göring – the blonde and buttery ex-actress considered to be the First Lady of the Third Reich, since she so often accompanied the Führer at official functions – was placed in charge of the German Red Cross. It was her visit to Besançon that would inspire the Kommandant to install showers.

Those month-late Christmas gifts changed everything. Every prisoner received one. Canada sent powdered milk and maple syrup; Australia canned meat; England jam, kidney pies and cigarettes. There was sugar, butter, sweets, tea and even a little Christmas pudding. There was a portrait of the king and queen, posing with their daughters Elizabeth and Margaret, and a greeting card from Queen Mary, along with a reply postcard that could be mailed through the Red Cross. Fifteen-year-old Mona J. Maka-Cockrell recalled the day's excitement: women running like little girls from room to room, trading sweets and other gifts. In a cruel attempt to spoil the party, the Germans officially announced the death of Queen Mary, the king's mother, though the lie was soon exposed.

One thing struck me about these stories: each of the women who bore witness to that prison, in diaries and in interviews published in England after the war, stuck to a mere recounting of the facts. Not a single one dared broach the subject of emotions – perhaps because their memories were gathered too many years afterwards, typically by one of their grandchildren.

Instinctively, however, something told me that Amrit Kaur must have held up well. She was a woman of character, in the prime of her life, and whatever health issues she may have suffered, I couldn't imagine her letting herself go.

All the while, her father and husband were writing to the Crown representative in India and to the Foreign Office in an attempt to get her out. As a result of their efforts, Sir Harold Satow from the Prisoners of War Department contacted the American embassy in Paris. The embassy replied by telegram: 'Von Roeder, Chief of Internment in France, was approached informally concerning [the release of the

Rani of Mandi] and expressed the opinion that no grounds exist.' The only valid reason for obtaining the rani's release, according to the German officer concerned, would be if she were over sixty years old. In his reply to Satow, Colonel Gordon Neale, renowned for his service in India, expressed his doubt that the Rani of Mandi was older than sixty (she was thirty-six). However, in a surge of optimism he ventured to add that 'it is perhaps relevant to point out that the disabilities of age overtake Indian ladies much sooner than in the case of European women'.

In any case, with the arrival of spring the Germans decided to transfer the prisoners to Vittel, a spa town whose deserted hotels could serve as lodging, and negotiations fell through. The relocation was a PR move, mostly likely facilitated by the Red Cross. But before departing, the detainees were forced to suffer one last indignity: to strip naked and descend to the courtyard wrapped in blankets to be disinfected. The nuns' humiliation incited a protest.

'We left Besançon a couple of days later,' Rosemary Say wrote. 'It was a warm day in early May. What a sight we must have been: thousands of female tramps laden down with all sorts of clothes, bags and other possessions. One woman clutched two saucepans made from cans, another next to me had three old forks carefully tied up under her belt. It was a very different group from that tired but orthodox-looking collection of women who had arrived a few months before. Our time in Besançon had taught us that even the most despised piece of rubbish could have value.'

Amrit Kaur was released six days before the transfer.

Perhaps, as Bubbles speculated, someone had managed to secure a prisoner exchange. Or perhaps someone had paid someone else off.

# PART THREE
## *Road Trip*

# The Dinner Party

How many months or years had passed since I'd stepped into this time machine? By now I'd got used to living with the heap of papers in the corner of my studio, the books on the Raj claiming more and more space on my shelves, the scattered photographs of that lost world, whose sumptuousness I found in turns fascinating and cloying – a world I was studying as if it were a new language, though I barely knew the alphabet.

Bubbles had gifted me an official portrait of her wedding ceremony: an ensemble of the most improbable colours – the gold of the couple's clothing fading into a dark, mustardy hue, and the lily-coloured background blurring around their silhouettes like a kind of giant halo. I'd hung it in my home mostly out of my deep sympathy for her, since the bright and spirited Bubbles I'd met in Pune had almost nothing in common with the melancholy young woman posing in the picture, for a photographer who was by no means Lafayette.

On the back, she'd scrawled a caption in red pen about the 'good old days' in which the photo was taken (May 1946), and added a generous thought: 'wishing you success in all you do'. Rereading it now, I wonder if she understood that I was taking a step back at that point. After the bankers lost their massive bet on families deluded into thinking they could afford a house in one corner of America or another, thus embroiling the rest of the world in their fraud, I was forced to rearrange my priorities and turn my attention to projects of a much more concrete nature.

Nevertheless, Bubbles kept in touch. Shortly after my visit to Pune

Wedding portrait of Nirvana Devi – Bubbles – and
Jashwant Singh of Bilkha, 1946.

I received an envelope with an orange seal, in which the letters B and
D of 'Bilkha Darbar' (meaning Princely State of Bilkha) were flanked
by two rearing, Ferrari-like horses. In big, slanting calligraphy she
thanked me for giving her 'so much news' about her mother, who
for her had been 'a closed chapter'. And she begged me to ignore
any errors in the letter, since her vision was going from bad to worse
and she hadn't been able to read over it. 'I hope to see you when you
will come to India. I will keep in touch,' she wrote, before signing off
with a formal 'Sincerely yours, Nirvana'. And she stayed true to her
word. For Christmas she sent me a warm-hearted greeting card. And
a year later she mailed a pale-green aerogram with a few updates:
'Dear Livia, no news since you left Pune – hope all is well at home.
Tiny has left for the USA – always sad when he leaves because at my
age one wonders if one will see him again. We tried to call you but
could not get through.' Then she apologised again for her errors,
which were non-existent, and signed, 'With my love, Bubbles'.

A year later came another aerogram, this one with news of her husband's death. 'As you know he was bedridden for eight months. He drifted away peacefully from us – no pain – we were married for 65 years, a long time, & he has left an enormous emptiness and homelessness, but life has to go on.'

After that, each and every December I continued to receive her Christmas wishes, on the same card with the orange seal, which I always kept, propping them in the picture frames around my studio. 'Keep in touch,' she wrote each time before signing off. Though I must not have been so good about holding up my end of the bargain, since after a certain point she switched to 'Don't forget us'.

I don't know what kind of special powers this woman had, but I do know that after convincing me to go all the way to Pune with a simple 'Come to see me' it had once again taken her only a few words – 'Don't forget us' – to beam me back into her orbit.

Not that I'd forgotten her in the meantime. And even though the circumstances that had kept me away from India were inescapable, that 'Don't forget us' became a thorn that slowly worked its way towards the centre of my body – I could tell you the exact point – and formed itself a permanent home. Of course I hadn't forgotten her. But in order for me to dive back into my research, I needed to tie it to a real project. Would she give me her blessing, if I were to write such a book? When she said yes, I took care to warn her up front: neither of us had any way of knowing what I'd turn up. Was she willing to run such a risk?

'First of all, you'll need to go see my cousins,' she said, her thoughts already clear, as if she'd known all along that my return was only a matter of time. 'They know many things, and will certainly be able to help you. And my son too, who lives in Mumbai. In Kapurthala, though, there's no one left. But if you're thinking of going to Mandi you can stay with my brother Bebu, who turned our guest house into a hotel.'

True to his mother's word, Sunny – Bubbles' third-oldest, whom she described using the adjective 'suave', the prince-turned-cricket-star-turned-manager – sent an email around to various people in their family's orbit, introducing me and asking them to give me a hand. And I hopped on a plane.

I had no idea what to expect from the trip, which was probably its greatest allure: it was a dust cloud of possibilities, tiny particles destined to swirl together and drift apart, forming who knows what nebula of feelings and motivations. My itinerary began in Delhi, then on to Punjab and the Himalayas, then back to Mumbai via Simla and Chandigarh, and finally to Pune and Bubbles. Though I also left some room for chance.

Unfortunately, however, the first cousin Bubbles suggested claimed to be unavailable. The second wrote to tell me that we couldn't get together since he was 'busy all winter'. And a third cousin agreed to show me the jewellery, beautiful as it was, that he himself had designed, but when I asked him about the Kapurthalas' collection he suddenly clammed up, saying that they were 'a very private family'. Which is why, when I received a reply from the final relative on my list, who graciously invited me to dinner the next evening, I felt a wave of relief that I hadn't completely wasted my time and resources.

Though I'd arrived on time, I had to wait half an hour – in a living room that, were it not for the imperial-age paintings and exotic photographs on the walls, would have fitted in the bourgeois environs of Neuilly-sur-Seine.

With all that extra time to observe my surroundings, I soon discovered that I wasn't to be the only guest: at the back of the room was a buffet for fifteen or so, laid out on a magnificent *phulkari*, a traditional Punjabi cloth, embroidered with golden-yellow and fuchsia silk, of a quality rarely seen.

When he made his entrance, the master of the house approached me with an air of resolve and, after shaking my hand and inviting me to take a seat, addressed me without preamble: 'Let me be direct and get right to the point.

'I've met dozens like you before. People coming to me asking for help, saying they're going to write a book on the history of the Sikhs, no less! On the gurus from our history! And who instead end up publishing a bunch of rubbish about the Maharaja of Kapurthala and his wives. The maharaja! Who's dead and can't even defend himself! They wrote that he had 200 wives, can you believe that? They invented schemes, heinous crimes, sexual scandals, all to sell books. You journalists and writers see us only as puppets to use to invent stories and make money!!'

Jagatjit Singh had indeed inspired a few books, typically rather imaginative ones, serving up a dish of his spiciest exploits for their readers. And among them a few did achieve commercial success, beginning with the first, *Maharaja*, in which one of his aides-de-camp, Diwan Jarmani Dass, the son of a government minister in Kapurthala, wove together the family's less admirable achievements with the thread of his own class hatred and misogyny.

Confronted with such bewildering hostility, my first thought, which I quickly discarded, was to respond in kind. My second was to stand up and walk out of the door. But this solution, too, seemed preposterous: what sense did it make to have come all the way to his house, at his invitation, only to sit there while he insulted me, and then walk out of the door without saying a word? And so, as he rattled on, I decided to follow the voice in my head whispering, 'You are a writer. So stay and listen. Because this is interesting.' And indeed, as his invective gained steam, he passed from 'you wretched journalists and writers' to 'you disgusting Westerners' to 'you Europeans, now down on your knees, forced to watch as the great nation of India takes its place in the economy of the entrepreneurial world!'.

He continued with his invective even when the door opened and a spindly, dandyish man with delicate features cautiously entered the room, trailed by a sporty younger woman in black trousers, with big, intelligent eyes and a mass of dark brown hair. Not only was the host undeterred by their arrival, he seemed to embrace them as an audience. And one by one, as other guests made their entrance – each introduced to me with a fanfare of princely titles that had been stripped of their power since 1972, while I was entitled only to my first name – they took their place among the rest of the perplexed and captive audience.

Then, when at last the host ran out of breath, an electric silence took hold of the room. And finally I had the chance to tell him, seeing that he'd yet to ask, who I was and why I was there.

I spoke about my earlier trip to Mumbai, and the Vikram Chandra novel that had introduced me to that city, about my stop at the museum, the portrait of the Rani of Mandi who may or may not have saved lives during the war, all the way up to my meeting with Bubbles in Pune. And when I arrived at the climax – explaining how, over time, my desire to discover whether or not Amrit Kaur had truly helped Jews escape to safety had merged with a second, no less urgent desire, to help an eighty-year-old daughter reconnect with her mother – I saw a wave of relief wash away the embarrassment of everyone listening, and a smile form on the faces of all but one. 'It's marvellous!' one woman said, her voice filled with naïve enthusiasm. And to my utter astonishment, I found that I'd passed from the villain of the evening to its improbable main attraction.

'I've never understood why Jagatjit Singh, who was in Paris at the time, returned to India in 1939 without his daughter,' one woman started in – an elegant lady in Western-style clothes, her handsome features undiminished by age. 'Really?' I prodded her. I was unaware that Jagatjit Singh had been in Paris on the eve of the war, and indeed it was strange that he'd return to India without Amrit at such a time. 'Poor thing, they arranged her a terrible marriage. A woman like her,' she continued, raising a bejewelled hand towards the ceiling, 'married to a man like him,' and her hand dropped to the level of an imaginary poodle. 'So young, a woman with such personality, tall, beautiful – and her brother too, he was such a handsome man, her brother – married off to someone so . . . so weak . . . A terrible, terrible match. It couldn't possibly have worked.'

Meanwhile, the woman with the thick mane of hair who'd entered first was telling me how her grandfather had been a close friend of Amrit's, and if I gave her my business card she'd look into it and get back to me.

Later, plate in hand, I took a seat next to the dandy in the camel-coloured *achkan* and we spoke of his homeland, a state much further to the north, to which he extended me a polite and seemingly genuine invitation. In the meantime, the elegant lady who'd chimed in first came over and took a seat across from us. Speaking under her breath, she informed me that Amrit Kaur had left her husband in the throes of passion; everyone knew that she'd found someone else in Paris. 'That's the way it is, isn't it? People are always splitting up when they find someone else,' she mused philosophically, prodding a piece of tandoori chicken with her fork. And she once again remarked on how handsome Amrit's brother had been, and how Amrit was a strong-willed girl, prone to rash decisions. 'I heard that she died of tuberculosis, probably contracted at the internment camp. Or maybe it was cancer,' she said with a sigh, lowering her gaze to what was left on her plate.

When I went back up to the buffet to get a drink, I stopped to chat with the guest who'd earlier asked me for my business card. She told me she'd been the first woman to earn a doctorate in a very special field of wildlife conservation, and that she'd spent years living in a shack in the jungle. But her Oxford PhD had attracted the press, and the fame she garnered had sparked strong feelings of envy in her family. Which was why, now that she was getting a divorce, she'd decided to take a year's sabbatical and try her hand at underwater photography. She was a lively person, intriguing and independent. When she saw the host coming towards us, she turned and asked him if he would like to join her on a trip to a place in north-east India, where every October one million migrating hawks passed through.

It was then that he – treating me with the utmost courtesy – formally invited me to have a seat on a small sofa beside a young-looking, cat-eyed woman, who greeted me with a beaming smile. She was beautiful in the way that certain Indian women are, with a grace that spreads to every movement, and she'd been the last to arrive, along with her husband, who was currently talking horses with a small group a few feet away from us. And since she seemed so invested in her role as royalty, I readied myself for one of those polite conversations where neither party ends up saying anything at all. But I was wrong. And she must have read my mind, since she wasted no time in proving herself to be curious and, within the confines of her position, even open-minded, at least regarding her children's education.

After her wedding, she told me – a marriage that, I didn't need to be reminded, represented the union of two great bloodlines – she went to live with her husband's family, as Bubbles had done in her day, obeying tradition. But she seemed to adapt well to the role and tried to approach it without prejudice. She and her husband – a handsome man with a lean, athletic physique – divided their time between Delhi and an estate in the North. She never mentioned that the militarisation of her husband's former principality had rendered it too dangerous to live there, nor did she discourage me when I told her that I'd always wanted to see its jade-coloured lakes, surrounded by eternal snows. She seemed so young that I could hardly believe it when she told me they'd married in 1987.

'What about you?' she asked, attempting, I think, to find some common ground.

'A year earlier.'

'Ah!' Her face brightened. 'Was it a beautiful wedding?'

'Well, I got married very far from home.'

'Really? With many guests?'

'One. A friend who was travelling with us and acted as our witness. You?'

'We had 40,000,' she smiled.

Later on, the princess-turned-wildlife-conservationist offered me a ride home. And as she drove down the brightly lit avenues, she confessed that at the beginning of the evening, when she arrived with the dandy in the camel-coloured *achkan*, they were so intimidated by the host's tantrum that they'd stood outside the door debating whether or not to come in.

A few days later, I wrote emails to every kind person I'd met that evening who offered to help me find out more about Amrit Kaur.

No one replied.

# Mandi

*Béni Soit L'Heureux Couple*

Amrit Kaur and Joginder Sen were married in Kapurthala on 5 February 1923, at the height of spring, when the Punjab Plain was a sea of wheat. The photos in the wedding album I found in New Delhi – an album that had gone missing and was later recovered from a second-hand dealer by the Alkazi Foundation, dedicated to the preservation of India's cultural history – showed two dumbfounded young adults beneath layers and layers of embroidered fabric: she

Wedding portrait: Amrit Kaur and Joginder Sen of Mandi under layers of embroidery, Kapurthala, 1923.

seated, slumping forward with an almost painfully demure expression; he by her side, small and ill at ease.

The celebrations persisted for three days, following the same routine as Brinda and Tikka Paramjit Singh's nuptials twelve years earlier. White tents were arrayed in the garden for guests, the maharaja's orchestra opened the parade through the city, soldiers marched in their white and blue uniforms, elephants filing in behind them, decked in silver. There was a banquet for 150 with Viceroy Lord Irwin seated in the place of honour, followed by torches, fireworks, dancing and formal photographs. At night, a cheerful string of lights decorated the royal palace's façade, spelling out 'BÉNI SOIT L'HEUREUX COUPLE' (Blessed be the happy couple).

A few English-language newspapers carried news of the wedding, but it was André de Fouquières, in his role as reporter-courtesan, who spread the word to French readers in the paper *Le Gaulois*. 'The Raja of Mandi,' he wrote, 'only nineteen years old, an excellent athlete, the recipient of an exceptional education, descendant of the lunar race, will become, on the completion of his twentieth year, the de facto ruler of his state situated to the west of Simla, the summer residence of India's viceroys.' As for Amrit Kaur, he noted her charm, her French education, and the 'noble sentiments' that made her a 'highly desirable' bride.

In the days leading up to the wedding, nearly 100 miles to the east, the festively clad citizens of Mandi sang and danced and prayed in the temples, before accompanying the young prince to the train festooned with flowers that would bring him to Kapurthala. And the welcoming ceremony for the couple two months later was just as joyous, when men, women and children lined up along the street flanking the Beas River and tossed flowers to the newlyweds.

Amrit Kaur and Joginder Sen settled into the royal palace constructed by the groom's grandfather, a building later remodelled by

Amrit's portrait from her lost wedding album, Kapurthala, 1923.

Walter Sykes George, the gifted English architect who, after working with Edwin Lutyens on the imperial project in New Delhi, stayed behind to enjoy the colony he'd helped to glorify. A year later – just enough time to provide an heir to the throne, Yuvraj Yashodhan Singh, Bubbles' older brother, whom everyone called Tibu – the couple departed for an extended stay in Europe.

The prince of that little sub-Himalayan state, measuring just over 1,200 square miles, had studied at Queen Mary's College, one of Lahore's elite schools, though he'd never been abroad, and this needed fixing. Their first stop was London, where George V and Queen Mary received the Prince and Princess of Mandi at Buckingham Palace, and where Amrit sat for Lafayette, in the filtered air of his studio on Bond Street. After that the young couple set off for the Somme and Verdun battlefields, to pay homage at the tombs of Mandi's soldiers who had died while serving the Empire in the

Group picture with the Prince of Wales sitting at the centre, between Brinda of Kapurthala and Amrit, Kapurthala, 1922.

First World War. And then on to Luxembourg, Belgium, Cologne, Zurich, the Alps, Venice, Florence, Rome, Vienna, Budapest, Lausanne, Geneva and, finally, Marseilles, from where in October 1924 they set sail for Bombay, returning home after five months away.

Mandi was smaller than Kapurthala, and there was decidedly nothing French about it. The tiny capital that welcomed Amrit Kaur as its new queen was a market town situated 2,600 feet above sea level at the confluence of the Beas and Sukheti Khad Rivers – which at that altitude were little more than hearty streams. In the late 1920s, the art collector and historian J. C. French described it as an austere little town with a burbling river, a ring of towering mountains and steep, narrow streets surrounding a market with medieval charm. 'The river front of Mandi is a miniature Benares, temples, old houses, long flights of steps.'

The reason for all those temples was that one of Joginder Sen's ancestors had hoped to turn Mandi into a kind of Benares – the city,

View of Mandi houses and Victoria Bridge at about the time
Amrit Kaur lived there.

now known as Varanasi, that Hindus consider to be their spiritual
capital. Nevertheless, Bubbles told me, 'Religion wasn't forced on us.
My family's attitude to religion was always moderate. Not too much,
not too little. But because we had important temples in Mandi, you
had to follow. You had to do certain things. And in some you believed,
and in some you didn't.'

The city of Mandi, founded by Raja Ajbar Sen in 1526, featured
houses with simple slate roofs. Its oldest temples were classic, mitre-
shaped stone structures with vibrantly painted sacred bulls at their
entrances. Deeper in the valley, along the jade-coloured ribbon of the
Beas that descended from the snowy Himalayas, tufts of palm trees
blended with ferns and pines, giving the landscape a sub-tropical
feel. But closer to the city, where the Beas was still dark and rocky,
the forests were made up mostly of firs and oaks, along with cedars,
sycamores and walnut and chestnut trees. Further to the north, above
Manali, along the snow-covered strip of the Rohtang Pass, a sign-
board enticed explorers' imaginations with the words, 'The end of

the habitable world'. From those snows to Mandi and beyond, lions were extinct, but bears and leopards still made their home, pheasants and wild boar abounded, and so did trout. Falconry was popular, and hunters who lived further from the city crossed the river using inflated buffalo pelts, just as Alexander the Great had done when crossing the Indus in 326 BCE.

In Amrit's day, the Upper Beas Valley was famed for being one of India's most alluring landscapes, and seeing it today the valley seems to have retained its untamed beauty – a beauty and a fertility that were central to the refined school of painting which flourished after the decline of the Mughal Empire, at the time when artists who had trained in the Mughal style migrated to the Himalayan foothills in the late eighteenth century. When I travelled there after leaving Amritsar, my driver, Boni – who'd ferried me safely past hairpin turns along the edges of harrowing cliffs – told me through his laughter that: 'Up there, above Manali, they grew the best cannabis in the world.' Which, along with the luxuriant landscape, helped explain why such a place had become a favourite destination for hippies from the 1960s on.

The Englishmen who ventured into the Upper Beas Valley in the latter half of the 1800s found a paradise awaiting them. When the First Anglo-Sikh War came to a close in 1846 with the Treaty of Lahore, the Raja of Mandi was forced to cede partial control of his state to England, and it was then that the Crown sent British functionaries to aid with local administration. A few of these men, once they'd completed their mission, had no interest in returning home or accepting a transfer, and set about planting orchards in the area above Mandi.

These Englishmen sold their apples, pears, cherries, plums and apricots in Simla, about sixty miles south-west, where the cream of the Raj's crop gathered in the summer at the viceroy's residence, and where Amrit made a name for herself on the tennis courts and at tea parties. The Indians, meanwhile, tended buffalos and goats, grew wheat, tobacco, poppies and barley under a sharecropping system, and worked in the iron and salt mines that stood for centuries as Mandi's principal source of wealth: a hereditary job, paid half in rupees and half in salt. Then, as now, Hindus in the capital wore turbans, though the further up one went the more Tibetan the shepherds appeared, with felt caps and shawls.

For a modern woman and a champion of women's rights like Amrit Kaur, to suddenly find herself in a place still dominated by ignorance and superstition must have come as a shock. And yet, as I'd discover, Mandi was not the most backward of kingdoms. In fact, it and nearby Kullu were the only kingdoms in India whose regulations allowed for *dum*, a general strike: a right exercised not so much to protest against the raja, whose authority was unquestionable, but against his corrupt and incapable administrators.

Moreover, unlike in other areas of Punjab, in Mandi the punishment for adultery did not include hacking off the adulterer's nose. This widespread practice was literary in origin. In a passage in the Hindu epic *Ramayana*, the giantess Surpanakha – after a failed attempt to seduce the god Rama and gulp down his wife Sita – is punished by Lakshman, Rama's stepbrother, with just such a brutal mutilation. In Mandi, however, adulterers were subject to a much more practical form of punishment: betrayed husbands could free themselves of their unfaithful wives by selling them to another man, a transaction on which, up until recent times, Mandi's rajas collected a 20 per cent tax. It was a system that came with certain advantages. One man could have several wives, but one woman could also have several husbands, and it was rare for an elderly woman to end up alone. John Maynard, an English functionary who left for Mandi in 1889 to spend three years as Raja Bijai Sen's assistant commissioner, reported that elopements were the order of the day, though reconciliations 'once the spree was over' were no less commonplace. Women in these territories, especially women from the lower classes, were most certainly freer than in many other areas of India. There was even a popular saying: 'Go to Mandi and become a *randi*' – a widow, in other words, though also, by crude extension, a promiscuous woman.

In *A History of the Mandi State* (1930), which the newly married Joginder Sen commissioned from a historian named Man Mohan, I read that the first European to set foot in Mandi was the explorer and horse expert William Moorcroft. While crossing through the district in 1820, Moorcroft was stopped by a party of men armed with bows, arrows and swords, who ordered him to obtain a signed travel permit from the raja or else return home. Moorcroft, who was on his way to Tibet to find horses for the East India Company, obeyed their command and requested a hearing with Raja Ishwari Sen.

The raja, whom Moorcroft described as 'a short stout man, about thirty-five, of limited understanding and extreme timidity', nevertheless proved accommodating, and the Englishman was permitted to continue on towards the highlands above Mandi – where, as it turned out, he was hoping to discover something far more valuable than a healthy breed of horses.

There are two mountain chains in Mandi, and they run nearly parallel. The first is known as Gohar ka Dhâr, a woody stretch of land with fertile soil and plenty of wild game. Here, too, are the salt mines that long provided Joginder Sen's realm with the majority of its revenue. And it's also the place where, according to popular belief, every year on 3 September demons, wizards and witches gather from all over India for a spectacular rave, which J. C. French described as a battle between demons and witches. It's not a day you want to go out wandering, lest a flying stone catch you on the skull. 'On the night of the battle the graziers move their cattle away from the ridge where the rival hosts meet, and the peasants are careful not to go out after nightfall. The doors are bolted, thorn branches placed before them, charms nailed on the lintels, and mustard seeds sprinkled on the fields and round the houses and cattlesheds. That night you should sleep on the left side, for otherwise a witch may snatch one's heart.' If on that night the demons emerged victorious, there would be little sickness that year, but the harvest would be scarce; if the witches prevailed, there'd be an abundant harvest, but also much death.

Mandi, however, was not only a playground for wizards and witches. It was also an area filled with hot springs, which fostered a whole series of legends. My favourite involves the goddess Parvati: travelling with her husband, the god Shiva, through a valley north-west of Mandi, Parvati found the region so enchanting that she decided to linger a while. At some point during her 1,100-year sojourn, before bathing in a brook Parvati removed her earrings and set them down on a rock. But when she emerged from the water they were gone. Shiva flew into a rage, rounding up a host of lesser gods to track down the earrings and return them. This crew went searching in Patala, the underground realm ruled by Shesha the serpent. When Shiva's emissaries interrogated Shesha about the theft, the serpent grew so furious that he released a powerful gust of air from his nostrils, accidentally expelling the earrings he'd been concealing. And so the jewels were returned to Parvati's ears, protruding from the earth directly in the spots where piping-hot water surges forth.

Mandi's second mountain chain, Sikandar ka Dhâr, instead derives its name from Alexander the Great, since it was here that Alexander, his soldiers at the point of exhaustion, was forced to bring his campaign of Asian conquest to an end. And it's said that here, on the left bank of the Beas River, chosen by Alexander as the furthest stretch of his immense empire, the general erected twelve gigantic towers dedicated to the most important Olympian gods, one of which bore the inscription: 'Here stopped Alexander'.

What became of the Altars of Alexander no one really knows. To this day, it's unclear if they crumbled during an earthquake, were top-pled by the river when it shifted course, or if they were dismantled and used as parts for fortresses – Mandi once boasted 360 of them, of which only ten remained in Amrit's day. Nevertheless, Moorcroft was surprised to discover that even in the world's most far-flung places people seemed to know the name of Alexander.

Someone showed him the purported site of the general's encamp-ment. And when Moorcroft travelled there he found a low stone wall in the shape of a rectangle, with one end opening out on to a cliff's edge. Within the rectangle's perimeter were signs of destroyed hab-itations, which may indeed have been ancient, though they may also have been the remains of an abandoned fort. To the Englishman, this was not sufficient proof to claim that the Macedonian had made camp there. But even though he was underwhelmed by the results of his search, there was still room for surprise: while the village of Hatli's inhabitants, under the cover of dark, were busy bringing out a staggering number of the crippled, blind, asthmatic and leprous for a breath of fresh air, one villager responded to his queries about Alexan-der by showing him a handful of copper coins with Kufic characters.

Not twenty years later, in 1839, an English gentleman traveller and writer named Godfrey Vigne visited Mandi and claimed to have discovered the altars' remains in an old Rajput fort, though exactly which fort no one could say. In the disheartened words of Sir Mor-timer Wheeler – the stern, erudite and racist archeologist who from 1944 to 1948 led the new Archaeological Survey of India that suc-ceeded Lord Curzon's: 'And yet it is astonishing how very little actual trace we have of [Alexander's] passing . . . his material presence has eluded us. It is as though a disembodied idea had come and gone as a mighty spiritual force with little immediate tangibility.'

So here Amrit Kaur was, at this new juncture, a woman who'd read Flaubert and played jazz, living in a town that combined a fascinating distant past with a long history of mostly dull rajas, admitting a few exceptions. In the fourteenth century, for example, we find one raja who was a cannibal. His name was Mangal Sen and he had a habit of eating a little fresh game each day, hunted down by his bevy of servants. One particularly rainy morning, his servants failed to catch anything. But rather than confess their failure, they carved some flesh from a recently dead man and served it to the raja – who, unwittingly, found it rather appetising. When he learned of their trick, the raja was at first horrified, but then decided to go on eating human flesh for the next 100 days, since this would allow him to aspire to the position of *Abhdut*, a kind of enlightened figure. As the days passed, however, his servants grew tired of sacrificing a human every morning and decided to rebel: demonstrating an admirable sense of equanimity, they set a trap for the raja in the woods and sacrificed their own king.

More poetic was the story of Sidh Sen. Between the seventeenth and eighteenth centuries, this prince proved himself so astute in battle and so capable in the management of his kingdom that his subjects believed he had the power to fly. It was said that Sidh Sen possessed a book of spells, with which he was able to control Mandi's demons and yoke them into submission. Every morning he'd leave to bathe in the Ganges and return in time for lunch, since all he had to do was put that little book in his mouth and, *voilà*, he took off flying. When he sensed his death approaching, Sidh Sen began to fear that someone would use his book for evil and decided to throw it into one of the deepest stretches of the Beas. His precious talisman was forever lost.

But apart from its more forward-thinking qualities, like the right to strike and its relative leniency towards adulterers, Mandi did remain a land of ignorance and superstition, where an attempt to vaccinate the population against smallpox – an evil administered by the terrifying goddess Shitala Devi – gave rise to a mass revolt that had to be squashed by force.

In the late 1800s, the British functionary John Maynard told of his troubles in assisting Raja Bijai Sen, who refused to make decisions without the advice of his astrologers and brahmins. Bijai Sen was the prince responsible for constructing the palace where Amrit and Joginder were to take up residence as young newlyweds and was considered to be Joginder's grandfather – even though that wasn't technically the case. Lacking any male heirs, Bijai Sen adopted a young relative, who in turn failed to produce any male heirs, leading him to adopt yet another family member, Joginder. John Maynard didn't know whether to be shocked or amused by the advice the astrologers and brahmins gave to the raja, and which the raja took literally. Their counsel ranged from the amount of cow dung the excommunicated should eat before being allowed back into their caste, to which spells were best for combatting a disease affecting the local buffalo.

Whenever Bijai Sen wanted to travel, it was up to his interpreters of magical thinking to determine the date and time of his departure. Moving 341 camp-followers, of whom fifty were tasked solely with transporting the kitchen utensils, was not a feat to be undertaken without the blessing of sorcerers, witches and the stars.

I don't know where Joginder's grandfather was off to with such a formidable retinue, but the lot of them parading out of his court and into that valley of firs and sycamores must have been a sight to see.

# Balzac, Dostoevsky and the Audacious Amrita Sher-Gil

There's little doubt that Amrit Kaur was unhappy in Mandi. And she wasn't the only woman in her position to have suffered there, in that place so tied to its own traditions and superstitions.

Sub-Himalayan legends are rife with desperate princesses. And signs of the dreadful conditions that women faced there were visible right at the capital's entrance, where, carved into the pillars and blocks of stone, alongside the figures of the successive rajas throughout the centuries, were those of their wives, burned alive atop their pyres – and not just one or two, but up to thirty at a time.

Godfrey Vigne, the explorer who claimed to have seen the remains of the Altars of Alexander in 1839, left us with a description of that atrocious ceremony: 'One morning my *Munshi* came to me, and told me that a *suttee*, or widow who was going to burn herself on the funeral pyre of her husband, was about to pass by the garden gate. I hastened to obtain a sight of her. She was dressed in the gayest attire, a large crowd of persons followed her, as she walked forward with a hurried and faltering step like that of a person about to faint. A Brahmin supported her on either side and these as well as many around were calling loudly and almost fiercely upon the different Hindu deities . . . Her countenance had assumed a sickly and ghastly appearance, which was partly owed to internal agitation, and partly, so I was informed, to the effect of opium and bhang and other narcotics, with which she had been previously drugged in order to render her less awake to the misery of her situation . . . In about half an hour the preparations were completed. She was regularly thatched in upon the top of the pile, whilst her husband's body yet lay outside. It was finally lifted up to her; the head, as usual, and which is the most interesting part of the ceremony, was received upon her lap; the fire was applied in different parts and all was so quickly enveloped in a shroud of mingled flame and smoke that I believe her sufferings to have been of very short duration, as she must almost immediately have been suffocated.'

Upon assuming power in 1846 with the Treaty of Lahore, the English took measures to ban the rite of *suttee*. And to their list of severely punishable practices they added female infanticide, slavery and the persecution of lepers, who had otherwise been drowned or burned to death. Even after the sacrifice of widows was banned, however, people continued to fear the spirits of these unfortunate ranis.

North of Mandi, in the village of Naggar, is a fifteenth-century cedar and stone castle tied to a legend that's still in circulation. That castle, it's said, has been haunted ever since an itinerant troupe of actors knocked on its doors and asked to perform for the raja and his family. At the end of their enrapturing show, the raja turned to the youngest of his ranis and asked her to point out the actor she liked best. And once she'd chosen, the raja had him decapitated on the spot. So horrified was the princess that she ran out on to the veranda and threw herself into a ravine.

From that day on, visitor after visitor – including, in 1930, a respected collector and connoisseur of Himalayan art such as J. C. French – claimed that they'd witnessed a spirit in Naggar Castle, moving through its halls like a bone-chilling wind. 'I slept in the western room of the castle,' French wrote in *Himalayan Art*, 'and shortly before midnight I awoke with a sense of uneasiness and oppression . . . The fear was absolutely interior, and I instinctively felt without any possibility of mistake that it was useless to search with stick or gun for the Thing which was causing it.'

When I asked Bubbles if she'd heard of the legend, she gave me a slightly different version. 'The story is that she was a princess, and I don't know what really happened, but I know that one day she jumped out of the window and died. They say that on that particular day or night when she committed suicide, they see her coming and going out of the window,' she reported with a chuckle.

Only later, in Mandi, speaking to Ashokpal Sen – Bubbles' step-brother Bebu – did I learn that Naggar had been an important place in Amrit's life as well.

When I paid Bebu a visit – travelling along a road that flanked the canyon carved out by the Beas, where monkeys walked hand in hand like happy families on a Sunday afternoon – I found him with his daughter Kiboo in the garden of the only palace they still owned, which in the late 1970s they'd converted into a hotel.

Rather than an actual palace, in truth, the Raj Mahal Palace Hotel was the guest house of the Mandis' former royal residence. Located just past the market square, it had the look of a colonial lodge, whose oldest section, where Bebu lived with his daughter, was done in wood with lace-like fretwork and painted white. The hotel seemed a little the worse for wear, with an enormous, half-empty restaurant and a bar that did possess a certain elegance, though it was closed, and bore the rather un-Himalayan name of Copacabana. The private apartments where Bebu and his daughter lived had been fashioned in a long, narrow wing that, like the rest of the hotel, was much in need of a freshening up. But for precisely this reason – with its walls painted a spring-green, its portraits from the days of the Raj and its sofas hanging like swings – it had its own charm, which time and use had rendered even more alluring.

When I stepped out of the car and asked respectfully to see 'Raja Ashkopal Sen' I was pointed towards a man in his eighties wearing a grey windbreaker, zipped all the way up to his neck, and a pink, orange and gold embroidered cap, sitting in silence at the outdoor bar, beside a middle-aged woman bundled in a red overcoat, wearing coarse wool stockings and a pair of gold sandals.

Bubbles' stepbrother was a man with liquid eyes, a pleasantly symmetrical face, and a temperament that was neither welcoming nor standoffish, mostly indifferent to what was happening around him. And he was laconic. When at one point, after exchanging pleasantries, I asked him if he could recommend a hotel in Manali – well known as a tourist destination – his response was, 'I wouldn't know. I haven't been there in ages.'

That evening I dined with father and daughter in the TV room, on the top floor of their wing, the television on but muted, ordering à la carte from the hotel menu and eating in an armchair, the plate balanced on my knees. Here, too, the master of the house proved a man of few words, indifferent to the long and rather awkward moments of silence. And when I told him of my plans to visit the library the next day, where Bubbles had suggested I might find photo albums and other documents, he replied that it was impossible because the library was locked. Only when I insisted – I hadn't just travelled thousands of miles to surrender at the first obstacle – he explained that the keys to the ground-floor rooms were kept by the man who looked after the garden temple dedicated to the goddess Durga, and that the library doors could be opened only when this man wasn't at the temple. Which was never.

The next morning, after I'd refused to give in, that 'never' shifted to an 'almost never', and the man in question, with an almost cartoonishly evil look about him, came to remove the library's padlock, casting what seemed to be genuinely threatening glances; luckily he took his leave once the door was open, leaving me alone in that poorly lit room with its dust-covered Sino-Tibetan-style furniture, where I had ample time to explore.

Once my eyes had adjusted to the dimness, I discovered that Amrit and Joginder had compiled a not inconsiderable collection of books, ranging from Rousseau's *Confessions* to *The Letters of Sacco and Van-zetti.* Whoever had lived in this house, or in the houses that preceded it and from which these volumes rebound in red, blue and green had come, seemed to have read all of Flaubert, Balzac, Dostoevsky, Anatole France, H. G. Wells and of course Dickens, as well as the Bible and the *Mahabharata*, the philosopher and Indian nationalist Sri Aurobindo, *The Montessori Method*, *Mein Kampf* and *The Truth about Dreyfus*, the biographies of George Bernard Shaw and the Marquis de Sade, and Gertrude Bell's letters.

In that abandoned room, where no one had set foot in who knows how many years, a curious reader could have spent months without peeking their head outside, like Patrick Leigh Fermor in the snow-bound castles of Romania, where he'd stayed in the 1930s; one could lose all track of time reading the history of China or of the Jesuits, or the ten volumes of the *Kathāsaritsāgara*, the immense collection of Indian fables and legends that predated the *One Thousand and One Nights*, and which C. H. Tawney and N. M. Penzer had translated into English under the title *The Ocean of Story*.

The photographs Bubbles had told me to search for were there, on a ledge half hidden behind a sofa, in old, fraying albums. And even though the raja's second wife had erased all traces of Amrit, including the wedding album I'd turned up in Delhi, I managed to find her all the same, in one of the photos that must have escaped her rival's attention. It was a snapshot someone had taken in a garden, picturing Tibu, Amrit and a nanny in a white nurse's uniform carrying a kind of rolled-up rug. Beneath the rug, with her arms raised in the air as if to prop it up, was a chubby little curly-haired girl of about three years old, wearing a white dress with ruffled knickers. It was a sweet photo, with Tibu, who must have been around eight or nine, gazing tenderly into the camera; while Amrit, on the other side of the rug, looked down at Bubbles, her head tilted affectionately, almost completely obscuring her face.

It took another day of convincing for Bebu to grant me access to the rest of the house, since the dining room and the ground-floor lounge were also kept under the sinister attendant's lock and key. My guess is that Bebu never used them at all – and admittedly, they were more formal and less inviting than his apartment on the floor above, where the walls were graced with portraits of enchantresses like Indira of Cooch Behar, ethereal vicereines like Edwina Mountbatten, and Jackie Kennedy-esque beauties like Baby, Bubbles' younger half-sister, their allure and elegance bursting from the frames, even in black and white. Nevertheless, a surprise or two still awaited me in those charmless, dust-covered rooms.

I'm speaking not only of the miniatures from the extraordinary Kangra Valley painting school, Hindu in spirit and Mughal in style, that flourished in Himachal Pradesh in the eighteenth century, of which the Mandi family held a notable collection; nor of the niches filled with Lalique vases; nor of the silver elephant harnesses now hanging on the walls as decoration. What really caught my attention were two paintings that seemed out of context: a scene of daily life in a poverty-stricken Indian village; and another canvas done by the same hand, showing three female figures with deep brown skin and a shawl covering their heads – most likely a mother and her two daughters – which reminded me of certain Renaissance Madonnas.

Both canvases depicted figures from the lowest rung of society, and both were done by Amrita Sher-Gil, a post-impressionist painter who became the first star of twentieth-century Indian art, and whose work I'd come across at Delhi's National Gallery of Modern Art. 'My father and Amrit Kaur knew Amrita Sher-Gil well, my mother no,' Bebu told me when I asked how those paintings had ended up in Mandi. 'They saw each other in Lahore, before it was Pakistan, and in Delhi. They may have met abroad. She was already a famous painter at twenty. She died at twenty-eight.'

This young woman whom Amrit Kaur and her husband befriended

was a daring artist in her day, as evidenced by her most famous painting, *Young Girls*, which I'd admired in Delhi. In it, an Indian woman with elegant features (her sister Indira) sits in a boudoir beside another young woman, semi-nude, with pale white skin and long blonde hair falling over her breast. The painting won her the Gold Medal at the 1933 Grand Salon in Paris. One year later, in her most celebrated self-portrait, *Self-Portrait as a Tahitian*, Amrita painted herself nude down to the waist, her large breasts exposed in three-quarter view and her *jeune fille* expression still absorbed in the world of adolescence. It was a bold subject for an Indian artist: an homage to Gauguin and a powerful reclamation of her own femininity. Observing these two paintings, it struck me as paradoxical that this Tracey Emin of her day was now the namesake of one of the streets in New Delhi's most luxurious residential areas.

Amrit and Amrita seemed to have had more in common than just their names, even if one was a princess who appeared to have stayed in her lane and the other an unconventional woman and provocateur. Both hailed from Punjab's aristocracy and both had received a cosmopolitan upbringing, while nonetheless maintaining a strong connection to India. But were they really friends? I wondered. They were nine years apart in age: while Amrit was busy honing her tennis game in Kapurthala, Amrita was born in Budapest, in 1913, to a family one could hardly call ordinary.

Her father, Umrao Singh, was an aristocrat, a scholar, a Sanskritist, a philosopher and a risqué photographer who loved to take self-portraits – clothed or semi-nude – or to point the lens at the bedazzling physiques of his beautiful adolescent daughters. Their mother, Marie-Antoinette, came instead from a family in Hungary's affluent bourgeoisie, and was a lover of music, art and high society. The two had met in Lahore and moved to Budapest soon after marrying in 1912.

Amrita had already lived three lives before painting the village scene I saw in Mandi. In the first, she was a child of mixed background, half-Indian, half-Magyar, with a few drops of Jewish blood, in a Hungary plagued by the First World War. In the second, when her family fled to India, she distinguished herself as a young prodigy at music school in Simla. In the third, from the age of sixteen on, she was an art student in Paris, first at the prestigious Académie de la Grande Chaumière and then at the École des Beaux-Arts. And at the end of this highly unusual path she matured into an ambitious, insolent, courageous and frustrated painter, set on making a name for herself in India at all costs – since, as she claimed, 'Europe belongs to Picasso, Matisse, Braque and many others. India belongs only to me.'

Her teachers in Paris were Cézanne, Gauguin and Modigliani. But when she decided to return to India at the age of twenty-three, she declared that even just one of the Buddhist frescoes in the Caves of Ajanta was worth all of the Renaissance combined. It was one of her many provocations, since the truth was that she loved those Renaissance painters, ever since her mother had followed an Italian lover to Florence and enrolled her daughters in boarding school at Poggio Imperiale, outside the city – until the flame of that passion consumed itself and mother and daughters returned to Simla and to Umrao Singh.

Judging from her letters, Amrita at last found her true home in the bohemian Paris of the 1930s, where her parents brought her at sixteen to test her talents. In a photograph from that period, we find her on the *terrasse* of a Parisian café amid a group of young artists, all men, with the exception of one other girl whose figure is entirely eclipsed by the young painter's commanding presence.

It was during those Parisian years that Amrita Sher-Gil discovered sexual freedom and began leading a promiscuous life. When her mother attempted to rein her in, by enticing her with a rich Muslim husband from a good family, things took a turn for the worse. Before he stopped coming round, the young man left her pregnant and with a venereal disease, and Amrita, enraged, turned to a Hungarian cousin who was studying medicine for treatment and an abortion. Perhaps because she was unable to live off the proceeds of her art, she married that penniless cousin, whose name was Victor Egan, destroying her mother's hopes of ever cashing in on the investment the family had made in her.

In photographs, Victor and Amrita made for a curious pair: he European, tall, with an arrogant wisp of blond hair; she small and shapely in a bathing suit, or else ravishingly elegant in a black sari with gold trim. In the early years of their marriage they lived a modest life in Budapest, but then they moved to Saraya, in Uttar Pradesh, to one of her uncle's feudal residences, where the main activities were elitist sports like horse riding and tiger-hunting, and there was no trace of intellectual life.

In that luxurious and claustrophobic place, surrounded by the poverty of rural India, Amrita painted the village scene I'd come across in Mandi. Then, in 1941, she and Victor moved to Lahore, where he planned to open his own medical practice. According to the author-journalist Khushwant Singh, by the time the young painter arrived in Lahore rumours of her sexual prowess had already spread, along with the news that India's future prime minister, Jawaharlal Nehru, was among her lovers. Even in that highly conservative city, though, Amrita managed to find a group of like-minded, progressive students, and began to reveal her enthusiasm for Gandhi's nationalist efforts. Over the next three months she took an active role in the city's cultural life, began work on new paintings, met new people, and was invited to speak on the radio. Then she found out she was pregnant again.

She'd always said she never wanted children, that she wanted to be free. The cause of her death at twenty-eight was a botched abortion performed by her own husband.

# Artists, Settlers, Gurus and Spies

In the days when Amrit Kaur first arrived in Mandi, the road came to an end just above the royal palace, and the only way up was on the back of a horse or a mule. Sheep were used to transport salt, and cowbells echoed through the valley.

I, on the other hand, had the privilege of travelling to Naggar by car, a dense cloud of exhaust enveloping us the entire way up to that fourteenth-century castle, which resembled an enormous mountain chalet. There, I holed up in a restaurant with wood-panelled walls that reminded me of a Swiss *Stubetta*, filled with travellers like me, in search of a warm bite to eat and shelter from a violent downpour. I wondered if the path that led from Naggar to Manali, famed as one of the world's most beautiful hikes, would ever be free of the fumes from the beaten-up diesel trucks I saw crawling up and down the mountain like lines of ants along the pine-flanked road. Above the brick or wood villages, above the terraced landscape, the streams, the waterfalls, the woods I'd admired on the road in, the massive ice wall of the Himalayas obscured the horizon line with thick white and grey brushstrokes. The women had Tibetan features and walked around cloaked in marvellous *puttoos*: tweed cloths with classic geometric designs, but with brightly coloured hems in orange, red and fuchsia, which brought to mind mandala patterns.

That morning I asked Boni, my driver, to accompany me to Naggar, since I knew that there was a road not far from the castle leading to a chalet that once belonged to Amrit Kaur. 'It was the house they sent her to during her pregnancies,' Bebu had told me as we basked in the sun in his hotel garden. And then, to my surprise, he added, 'She had two children there, both of whom died.'

This is how I discovered that Amrit Kaur had actually given birth to four children. In between Tibu and Bubbles, their young mother had had one stillborn baby and another who died in its first few months of life. Repulsed by the home where these events had taken place, Amrit demanded that it be sold. Its purchaser wasn't just one of the many English settlers who'd come to live in the valley: the man who stepped forward was a White Russian, a well-known and much-gossiped-about artist by the name of Nicholas Roerich.

Roerich was a figure with ties to Tibet and its environs who'd begun his own multifaceted career as an archaeologist; he'd served as a set designer for Diaghilev in the early years of the Ballets Russes; he'd collaborated with Nijinsky and Stravinsky on their extraordinarily successful *Rite of Spring*; he'd painted thousands of Himalayan land-scapes; he'd conducted an important exploratory mission in Punjab, Sikkim and Tibet, which he followed up with another in North China and Manchuria.

Before retiring to Naggar in 1927 at the age of fifty-three, he'd also managed to take on the mantle of spiritual leader, founding his own philosophy: a blend of Buddhism, Hinduism and Orthodox Christian-ity whose influence spread all the way to Roosevelt's America. In this role, he was able to establish a steady correspondence with powerful figures across half the world and keep in contact with the Kremlin, all the while seated at a desk in a chalet overlooking not the Hudson or the Thames but the much less accessible waters of the Beas. His work as a symbolist painter had a folkloric bent, harking back to Russian fables. While in Mandi, in one of the rooms under lock and key, I'd seen a painting of his that could well have been an illustration of the *One Thousand and One Nights:* a mysterious figure, shrouded in a bluish haze, makes his way into a building by the light of three oil lamps.

★

When I arrived, rain-soaked, at the chalet that Roerich had purchased from the Mandis, it looked as if time had ground to a halt in the days when he still lived there, with his wife Helena and his sons: not only the furniture, but even the dinnerware, inherited from Amrit and Joginder, was still in its place, laid out on the table. There were Indian and Persian rugs, wooden dressers and desks with no pretence of elegance, colonial armchairs, Tibetan *thangkas* and icons on the walls. Nonetheless, the Roerichs knew how to welcome their guests in grand fashion. In his memoir *The Way to the Labyrinth*, the French Indologist Alain Daniélou tells of the trip he made there in 1939 with his companion, the Swiss photographer Raymond Burnier. To receive them, the Roerichs sent two horses rigged with tooled-leather saddles and silver stirrups. Having forded the river and ascended the other shore, Daniélou and Burnier climbed their way on horseback to the property walls, where two young Tibetan guards clad in red blew a ram's horn to announce their arrival. 'Madame Roerich was a grand matron with her hair done up in the shape of a crown, a wimple, a corset. She might have stepped out of a book from 1900 on the Tsar's court . . . The painter arrived later on, wearing Tibetan dress. He put on the airs of a prophet.' At dinner, they were joined by his sons George and Svetoslav, aged thirty and twenty-five. Daniélou describes the dining room as dark, lit only by candles, with a lace tablecloth, fine crystal glasses, antique silverware, Russian cuisine and caviar. Two young Russian girls aided the house staff in serving the guests. 'Madame Roerich explained to me that she'd brought them on for the express purpose of satisfying her sons' sexual needs, until they were able to find wives of good standing', a detail that led the renowned French Indologist to remark, 'It was truly in the great tradition.'

The Hall, as that chalet had been so grandly baptised, was built in the 1880s by a Colonel Rennick, one of the British settlers who'd

Nicholas Roerich standing beside a live leopard in Naggar, 1937.

put down roots in the Upper Beas Valley when there were no more than a dozen of these Simla/Surrey-style estates.

It was an extraordinary world apart, this realm of the settlers who'd come to Mandi when it entered the British orbit after 1846: a band of hedonistic pioneers living out their Indian romance, enjoying the temperate valley climate, fishing for trout and a freshwater fish called *mahseer*, playing tennis and polo, hunting pheasants and deer and the occasional bear or leopard. They made a living through their orchards and by growing tea and tobacco. And when one of them fell in love with a local girl, there being no churches to get married in, he signed a contract for a certain number of years or for life, following the local custom – rebranded by the English as 'stamp marriages'. As for the baptism of their eventual children, an American missionary would travel in for the occasion from the nearby district of Kangra.

In *Kulu* [*sic*], the travel book recounting her ascent by mule through Kullu, Mandi and Naggar in the early 1960s, Penelope Chet-wode gathered information on these settlers from two ageing English sisters, the last survivors of a world that had dissolved along with the Empire. And in Barbara and Hilary Donald's stories I found an extraordinary portrait of that world, which left a long trail of memories in its wake.

There was an English widower, one General Osborne, who bickered with Colonel Rennick over matters of women and water in the rice season, and who always kept a brahmin with him to carry his water pipe. There was an eccentric English painter named Mrs Budd, who travelled up and down the valleys using a large dog equipped with a saddle to carry her paints, canvases and brushes. There was the Donald family, of Scottish stock, to which the sisters Barbara and Hilary belonged; their brother Robin, a linguist specialising in dialects of the north-west border, served as the inspiration for Kipling's character Strickland in *Plain Tales from the Hills*. There was even a man of mystery, the very wealthy Mr Theodore, who wove his own tweed like the women from the Solang Valley, was conversant in the local dialect and fluent in German, and was rumoured to be a Habsburg grand duke who'd fled Vienna. And to round out the group there was the clandestine Mr and Mrs Tyacke, who'd met in Malta: she, seeking refuge from her violent husband, was a pip of a woman who cared for all animals except for bears, which she hunted mercilessly in her nineteenth-century get-up, a long skirt and jacket cinched at the waist over a red corset; he was a colonel, unmarried. To escape the rumour mill, they fled as far as possible from the Mediterranean and lived as lovers in Naggar until old age intervened, one dying a week before the other.

These settlers kept in close contact with the Rajas of Kullu and Mandi, and it's easy to imagine them luring Amrit Kaur away as a diversion from courtly life. Among them, the most eye-catching was Colonel Rennick, who in the 1870s took advantage of the Kulu [sic]

Valley Tea Company's liquidation to amass a large quantity of land. It was then that he built the chalet at Naggar, which passed from him to the Mandis, and from the Mandis to Roerich. The colonel, it appears, made such a good cider that when his guests returned home they swore they'd seen the spirit of the rani who'd leaped from the castle veranda.

In a valley brimming with such legends, the colonel's tale seems more like something out of an English colonial novel. It appears that Rennick, who married a Persian princess, was a well-known philanderer. His wife kept a lady-in-waiting who was faithful to her for many years. When this woman fell sick and died, she was replaced by an English widow who turned out to be an opportunist. The people of Naggar called her Midge. And when, not long after Midge's arrival, Rennick's wife died, too, word spread that this newcomer had poisoned her.

Apparently, the colonel was deaf to all gossip, or perhaps he was the kind of man who liked to be taken advantage of by women – or both, given that the two often go together like martinis and olives – because immediately after his wife's death, at nearly seventy years old, he married Midge. And it was a disaster from the outset. They fought incessantly, and at the end of such scenes the colonel would gallop off to one of his distant properties. The tale that the elderly Hilary Donald told to Penelope Chetwode, and which I read by the warmth of a fireplace at a hotel in Manali, seemed almost like a comedy from the silent-film era. 'About an hour later down would come Midge in her rickshaw with all the bells tinkling and the *janpannis* running as fast as they could. "Have you seen Bob?" she would ask us. "He's not up at the Hall, he must have gone to Bajaura. I can't have it. I can't have it!" And off she'd go again. By the time she got there the colonel was just starting to ride back to Naggar, but the poor *janpannis* were dead-beat and refused to go another yard so Midge was stuck down until the next day and the colonel had a little peace. It was quite like a musical comedy and happened again and again.'

In the end, Midge convinced Rennick to return to Europe, which was when he sold the house to Amrit Kaur and Joginder Sen. The Rennicks packed their bags and took up residence in the Florentine hills, where it seems Midge burned through all their money. Before long, the colonel was found dying on a street in Florence, just a few coins in his pockets, and no *janpanni* in sight to take him to the hospital.

In Mandi, Tibet's proximity was tangible, and not only in people's facial features. At Bebu's house I noticed several pieces of Tibetan furniture and a photograph signed by the twenty-year-old Dalai Lama, his expression of youthful wonder still intact despite his tragic flight from Lhasa in 1959, when the occupying Chinese army brutally repressed his people's rebellion. 'It was my father who granted him political asylum after he fled Tibet, and who allowed him to settle in Dharamsala. He was three years younger than me,' Bebu said, beginning and ending the discussion there. After Independence, Joginder Sen had served as a member of India's Parliament from 1957 to 1962, and likely did possess such power.

Mandi's short distance from Tibet, just a few hundred miles, must have been an enticing factor for Nicholas Roerich as well. Two years prior to his encounter with Amrit and Joginder, Roerich embarked on an expedition that began in Punjab and proceeded through Kashmir and Ladakh, then on through the Karakorum Range and the Altai Mountains, with a final stop in the Gobi Desert. His movements were alarming enough to attract the attention of the English, American, Japanese and Soviet secret services, and criss-crossing suspicions of potential spy activity: a completely plausible, if secondary, motive, since Roerich's main priority was to look for traces of the mythical kingdom of Shambhala, the earthly paradise of Tibetan Buddhism.

It was then that Roerich made his way to the Upper Beas Valley. 'Someone sent them up to Mandi, to meet the ruler there, my father,' Bubbles told me, 'and ask him for the property in Naggar. And that's how they got this place. I used to go with Papa. I called him Uncle Roerich. His wife never left the house, that I remember. She came to the gate and that's all. She was very psychic, she followed spirits. They were in Russia when they had – not the Mutiny . . . the Revolution, correct? She had told her husband we have to go to India, *before* the Revolution.'

Following that 1925 expedition, documented in numerous paintings, writings and photographs – Roerich was a true pioneer in the art of communication – came a second, sponsored by Roosevelt's agricultural minister, which took him through Mongolia, Manchuria and China in 1934 and 1935. The mission's official purpose was to gather the seeds of a plant resistant to desert climates and therefore capable of surviving in the dried-out prairies of America's Dust Bowl, though for Roerich and his wife, at least, the true aim was to search for something much more significant: traces of the Second Coming. But things didn't work out as they'd hoped. The expedition was a failure and became an embarrassing diplomatic debacle for Agricultural Minister Henry A. Wallace, with the Soviets taking Roerich for a Japanese spy, the Japanese taking him for a Soviet spy, and the Chinese convinced he was an American spy. Wallace would later find himself in trouble when his correspondence with Roerich surfaced, making it clear that he'd been duped by a guru-charlatan.

Yet again, I was left astonished by just how many outlandish characters had found their way into Amrit's orbit – it felt like looking at an unusually lively group portrait in which the central figure had been cut out. And Roerich the White Russian, who'd hoped to persuade the Kremlin to revive the spiritual life in Russia that had been stripped away by socialism, was without doubt one of those characters, along with his wife Helena, the one whom Bubbles had called a 'psychic'.

Both Roerichs were members of the Theosophical Society led by Helena Blavatsky, the irrepressible Russian spiritualist who formulated her own metaphysical philosophy, aimed at discovering a spiritual unity between human beings, religion and nature. Around the turn of the century, Blavatsky's theosophy attracted a range of artists, and it's no coincidence that famous members like Kandinsky, Mondrian, Kupka and Malevich who, like Roerich, had begun their careers as symbolists, found in theosophy an inspiration for abstract art.

As I dug further into Roerich's past, wanting to know more about this man who'd been so close to Amrit Kaur's family, I learned that he came from a long line of notaries and lawyers, and that his wife Helena Ivanovna Shaposhnikova was the great-granddaughter of Kutuzov, the general whose retreat from Moscow brought Napoleon to his knees. Helena was also related to the Putyatin princes and to Modest Mussorgsky; and in Saint Petersburg, where she was born and raised, she studied music and art, and was a passionate reader of Tagore and Indian philosophy.

With Roerich, whom she married against her parents' wishes, Helena shared the idea that art must be a mystical experience and that the preservation of churches, archeological sites, museums and architectural monuments was fundamental to humanity's survival. The writer and noted India expert Côme Carpentier de Gourdon told me that, in Naggar, the Roerichs stood as a rare example of encyclopedic knowledge and aristocratic grandeur. They refrained from consorting with the English settlers and received only important guests, like Nehru and his young daughter Indira Gandhi, and of course the Raja and Rani of Mandi. In the evenings Wagner's music echoed from the Roerich chalet, wafting through the valley and setting loose the nymphs, Nibelungs and Valkyries in Naggar's forests.

I confess that my curiosity about the Roerichs did not lie in the theosophical doctrine they followed as a sect of Madame Blavatsky, which blended elements of Tibetan Buddhism, Hinduism and theosophy, and to which they gave the name Agni Yoga; nor in their conviction that the Second Coming had occurred in Mongolia; nor even in the years they spent searching for the mythical, lotus-flower-shaped Buddhist kingdom of Shambhala, hidden from the world by a crown of snow-covered mountains. More concretely, more prosaically, I found it extraordinary that even in a place like Naggar they were able to cultivate powerful relationships with such a large number of the world's most influential people.

Like Albert Kahn in the days of the Societé Autour du Monde, Nicholas Roerich was a *fin-de-siècle* idealist and pacifist set on using art and culture as a means of guarding humanity against all barbarism. In 1935, he managed to convince the United States to sign a treaty stating that, in the event of war, all nations would refrain from bombing museums, scientific institutions, churches and hospitals. The Roerich Pact declared that all protected areas must be marked by a Peace Flag that Roerich himself had designed – a red circle surrounded by three spheres, against a white background. The fact that this flag had absolutely no effect during the Second World War did nothing to keep it from flying on a Soviet Mir orbital station in 1990, or at the North Pole, as it does today.

All of this earned Roerich a nomination for the Nobel Peace Prize, along with a highly monetisable notoriety that far outstripped his fame as a symbolist artist or a set designer for Diaghilev. 'From The Hall estate on Naggar which he bought from the Raja of Mandi, he wrote regularly to his followers in New York who, in return for his greatly sought-after spiritual advice, sent him handsome monthly payments so that he was relieved of all financial worries for the rest of his days,' Penelope Chetwode noted ironically on her arrival in Naggar by mule in 1963.

'Do you know Nicholas Roerich?' I asked a Russian friend of mine, a television producer.

'Of course I do, he's the one who wrote to Stalin offering to serve as a mediator between him and God,' he replied.

It was a trip to New York in the early 1920s that earned Roerich the title of spiritual leader. His paintings of the Himalayas at dawn or dusk – glaciers and peaks in green and orange, or indigo and yellow, or even purple and pink – were given their first important exhibition in Manhattan. And the American financier Louis L. Horch fell so in love with them that he became convinced the paintings possessed thaumaturgic properties.

Horch was one of Roerich's most passionate supporters. And when the idea for a museum dedicated to his work began to circulate, it was Horch who took care of the financial end, allowing for the construction of the first skyscraper on Riverside Drive in 1928. The Roerich Museum, blessed with more than 1,000 paintings by this Russian artist who called India home, half of which were completed during his expeditions in Central Asia, was one of New York City's very first museums of contemporary art.

Their joint venture, however, came to an end after only ten years, when Roerich and Horch began to squabble over money. Horch retook possession of his skyscraper, and the IRS placed Roerich under investigation for tax fraud. So it was that his technicolour mountains were packed up and moved to a much more modest brownstone on West 107th Street. When I went to visit, under one of those heavy, February snows you often see in places like New York and Saint Petersburg, I felt I was entering the dacha of one of his initiates: where everyone spoke Russian and the elderly woman taking tickets looked like she knew a thing or two about Shambhala and its mysteries.

The cosy atmosphere in that small museum – where I saw sketches for the backdrops that would set Paris ablaze at the premiere of Stravinsky's *The Rite of Spring* – could not have been further from the bare, cold building in Naggar, in the garden of Amrit Kaur's chalet, that now functioned as the local Roerich museum. There to greet me, on that inclement winter day, was a woman wrapped in a green wool *puttoo* with a bright, flower-print handkerchief tied around her head. She was lost in thought, sitting beside an electric heater, entirely indifferent to the spectacular photograph above her head, picturing Nicholas Roerich on the boundless plain of Mongolia: a photograph that looked like it had been staged by a master of framing like Erich von Stroheim, for the express purpose of enchanting the press and Hollywood – and certainly not the rare visitor to that modest and lonely room where it now gathered dust.

What I'd have liked to ask this woman, her skin hardened by the mountain air, was what memory the villagers held of that pair of eccentric Russians; and if they knew that one of the solar system's minor planets now bore their name.

But our exchange was limited to just a few gestures: with a toothless smile, she informed me that, unless I felt like getting ill, I should probably remove the shawl covering my head and shoulders and lay it out to dry by the heater. And I, thanking her, had no choice but to keep my questions to myself.

# Sunny and Lina

That coarse cashmere shawl, which I'd bought at the market in Mandi – a sort of rope-coloured blanket, thick and furry, the kind a shepherd would wear – would soon find its way to the bottom of my suitcase, only to reemerge, in all its incongruity, on the rue du Bac. The time had indeed come to leave India and return to Paris. However, at the end of a journey that still left so many questions unanswered, I was to meet Bubbles' thirdborn son. Sunny Bilkha had invited me to spend a weekend with him and his wife Lina at their home in Alibaug, a resort town about sixty miles south of Mumbai, where the grand beach houses of India's nouveaux riches stand side by side with the rundown peasant homes that preceded them and that now, in all likelihood, were also worth a fortune.

It was hot and sticky the day I arrived by car. And the first thing I noticed was that the couple there to greet me, in the airy and modern villa at the end of a dirt road, were quite unike any other couple I'd met before on this trip. Sunny and Lina Bilkha were beautiful, still full of youth in their fifties, with a lovely home surrounded by a neatly arranged garden. Its variety of spaces – a shady corner with an umbrella, an open-air terrace, a small meadow – seemed intentionally designed to offer maximum pleasure, following the shade at different points in the day. It felt almost like a set design, through which my hosts moved with all the ease of two veteran actors running through a familiar play.

Lina was an executive coach for businesswomen. Sunny had left his glory days as a cricket star behind him and was now close to retirement. Together they welcomed me with the polished self-assurance of two worldly hosts – even arranging for an impeccable Italian lunch, served in the garden, to make me feel at home.

Later that afternoon, when the sun had fallen behind a thick veil of mist, we left for a long walk, crossing the grey, duneless, deserted beach that stretched towards the faint profile of Mumbai as far as the eye could see. Their marriage, I learned, represented a union between an upper-middle-class woman and a man who – in the eyes of Lina's banker father and very conservative mother – bore the double flaw of being a cricket player and a descendant of the Raj's decadent line of princes. The obstacles were not negligible. But, judging by Lina's radiant face, her long hair tumbling youthfully down to her waist, and by Sunny's smiling contentedness, the gamble had paid off.

Part of that contentedness, I felt, was attributable to a successful career, despite, or maybe thanks to, a rocky start. It had been a shock to hear his father say: the privy purses are gone, the privileges are gone, now you are commoners, go and work and make your life. 'We were thrown out. From one day to the next, there was nothing. When I think of it, in Mummy's place I would have been a mental wreck. I would have just kept talking about all that I had lost, what I was, what I've been reduced to, and who I am today. I wouldn't be able to live with it . . . What I love about my mother is her temperament.'

Even after Independence, the Bilkhas maintained the behaviours they'd inherited from the days of the Raj, one of which was to send their children to the boarding schools the Empire had established to teach the princes English values and habits. Which was why, at four and a half years old, Sunny was sent to Rajkumar College in Dehradun, even though it was a four-day trip from their house.

'With our father, we didn't really have much of a relationship. He wouldn't write to you, he wouldn't call you on your birthdays. You had to ring him up to say it's my birthday, so he could say happy birthday . . . When I came back from school for the holidays, the first question would be: how did you do in your cricket match? Studies, OK, but it was not so important. In college I went straight to play cricket at the state level. I was part of the national team four times, from 1977 to 1980. World Cup too. In the very first match I played for India – against England in 1977 – I got two world records. One of those records was broken after nearly thirty-eight years: the maximum catches. But the innings record is still there. And I kept on doing well when I joined Mahindra's car company, which had a cricket team. You could actually balance work and cricket: that was India in the old times. It was a different world. Even though, to me, some things are only new in appearance. Think about it. The online dating sites, for instance: they are quite like the catalogues used for our parents at their time. What I find ironic is that when I started working I had to hide the fact that I was a prince, while today they want to be like us.'

As we walked through what seemed to be the Indian version of the Hamptons, with grotesquely lavish villas looming behind walls of lush palms and banana trees, Sunny asked me to fill them in on my encounters (or lack thereof) with his New Delhi relatives, my exchange with the laconic Bebu, the traces of Amrita Sher-Gil I'd found in Mandi, and the Roerich chalet still decked with Amrit's furniture and dinnerware. All the while, three big stray dogs followed behind us, trotting along the waterline at a respectful distance. These three slender creatures, their tails curling upward, might have been the reason why Sunny was carrying a stick in his hands. But to me they seemed harmless and fearful, and I couldn't help turning my head now and then to cast them a sympathetic glance.

'My family wasn't like Sunny's,' Lina was saying, her white windbreaker swaying around her hips as she walked, 'although funnily enough Sunny and I belong to the same caste.' She told me her parents were from near Peshawar, in north-west India, which became

Pakistan after Independence. When disorder broke out in 1947, her father and brothers – four bankers and an engineer – had already moved elsewhere, and her grandfather, a widower, refused to leave. In the end, it was his Muslim neighbours who saved his life. They dressed him in a burka and loaded him on the last train from Peshawar to Delhi. And he never saw his home again. He lost everything.'

So loss, once again, was the ever-present backdrop – even here, in the face of what looked like the image of harmony and prosperity. Loss, and the unresolved questions of the past. Lina had been in Sunny's family long enough to remember Joginder's bad conscience. 'Sunny's grandfather had lots of regrets about Amrit Kaur. That he wasn't fair to her, that he let her go. Lots of things used to bother him . . .'

'When he came to stay with us in Poona, he used to cry,' Sunny said.

'He was sad about how he let his relationship with her die. And his second marriage, I don't think it was happy. Afterwards, his wife got too controlling. She took charge of everything he had. He became a puppet in her hands . . .'

Sunny used the word 'soft' to describe Joginder. But he stressed that he was also 'full of life, fun-loving, dancing, like my mother'. He was a ladies' man, too. 'If he liked you, the next day there would be roses sent to you, or he would drop in for coffee. When I was twenty and I was living in Bombay, he wanted to check out where I was staying as a paying guest, at the home of a French lady. A very strict lady, and very, very short. So I brought him along, and introduced him to my landlady. Then I went to change because we were going out to dinner. Suddenly when I came out, after taking a bath, I saw them dancing! And I thought: oh no, not with my landlady! What happened was that they had realised they had danced together in Paris many years before. And this is the very song that had played. She said she had the record, and so they were dancing to that . . .'

In Lina's eyes, what Joginder found attractive about a woman like his second wife Kusum was that she was unsophisticated. 'She came from nowhere and didn't even speak English. She spoke Gujarati. While Amrit Kaur was the Kapurthala princess; she had style, she was very special. I think he felt belittled beside her.'

Later, when everything changed and he was no longer able to mantain the Mandi palace, he donated it to charity. As a result, it was now left in a state of squalid, hopeless abandon.

But he, the raja without a kingdom, was able to bounce back. 'Luckily for my grandfather, after Independence many people said, why don't you stand and become our representative? A lot of maharajas did, in their former states, and were elected Members of Parliament. As did my grandfather, who won two terms for the Congress Party. Then he was appointed ambassador to Mexico, Argentina and Brazil. This was in the 1950s,' said Sunny.

'By then his second wife was fluent in English, as he had hired a governess to teach her,' Lina explained.

'But he wasn't serious about this career. It was an honorary thing. Nehru wanted people like him because they could travel abroad, socialise, and they could be useful to India in other ways. So I think he used them, until gradually the Indian Civil Service came on to the political scene and you started getting professionals who were trained.'

Dinner time was approaching and we decided to turn back, towards the house. We hadn't run into another living soul on the beach; the dogs, however, must have found something more interesting than us to follow, because they were nowhere to be seen.

For a mile or so we walked in silence, instinctually picking up the pace, each of us absorbed in our own thoughts. Then Sunny turned to me and Lina, reviving a conversation from long before, when I'd written to him from Paris about my interest in his grandmother's story. 'We were brought up hearing that my grandmother did a lot for the Jews. But I ask myself why? Why wouldn't you come to the wedding of your daughter? At least to give her your blessing! Even if she was not invited, she knew. She could have easily come . . .'

Lina: 'I think that did hurt your mother, whatever she says.'

Sunny: 'I think it affected her all throughout her life! And as much as she says about her stepmother giving her a happy childhood, later on she was not very good to her, in the sense that when it came down to the jewellery and the paintings and all the things that were from Amrit Kaur, she gave them all to her own children. She did the duty of getting Mummy married, and that was all. After that, she was quite a pain for her, all throughout. Grandfather would say: I can't do anything about it, she controls the money, she controls everything. As a matter of fact, Mummy got pushed out of all inheritance. I keep asking my mother: why weren't you sent to Cambridge or Oxford, like your brother Bebu? Or like Baby, who was educated in Switzerland?'

Then Lina said something that hadn't yet crossed my mind.

'You see, Livia, when Amrit Kaur left, maybe she was manipulated. Since there was another rani already. A lot of these women were excellent politicians, you know? Household politics, I mean. Women were really strong and really called the shots. They were so smart and clever that they never let the men feel that they were weak. That's how it was . . .'

# PART FOUR

## *Louise*

# A.K.M.

I returned to Paris with my morale at rock bottom. My trip to North India had given me an idea of the places where Amrit had lived and of the figures she'd crossed paths with. But that was it. Or at least that's what it seemed at the time.

The hypothesis that Lina Bilkha had raised, that Amrit's departure was spurred by Joginder's addition of a new wife to the nuclear family, was plausible. But I still had a hard time believing that a rival under the same roof, no matter how disagreeable her presence, could bring a mother to do something as counter-instinctual as abandoning her two children. In fact, I'd met a few 'bolters' in my life: intensely narcissistic women, ready to jettison their maternal duties and reclaim their freedom at the first opportunity. Or intellectuals, willing to put a book above their child: like one Italian author whose most celebrated novel, inspired by her turbulent relationship with her only son, shattered their bond once and for all. When I asked her, towards the end of her life, if she'd write the book again given what had happened, she answered baldly: 'Word for word.'

My trip to India felt like a failure, and I was left wondering, yet again, where to turn. The Prefecture's archives had been a disappointment, as had the Bibliothèque Nationale's. The English archives had covered only the war years. Piecing together other sources, I'd managed to form an idea of the context in which Amrit Kaur had lived up until the age of twenty-nine. But there was still a giant, murky expanse stretching from the day she left India in 1933 to the day she was arrested in Paris in 1940. The key to solving her life's mystery had to be there, in whatever had happened during those seven years. But where to look, and whom to ask?

It was then that I decided to write to Elisa Vázquez de Gey, biographer of Anita Delgado, the Spanish Cinderella who'd married Jagatjit Singh in 1908 and become the fifth Maharani of Kapurthala. So strong was her bond with Amrit that, even during the delicate time of her separation from Jagatjit Singh, Anita postponed her departure from Kapurthala to attend her stepdaughter's wedding. After that she left for Paris, where she led a luxurious life, thanks to a generous separation agreement; under this arrangement, Anita remained on good terms with her husband, whom the law forbade her to divorce.

Bubbles thought that perhaps Amrit had chosen Paris in 1933 in order to follow Anita, but it was only a hunch. Still, given that Anita seemed to be the only person who'd been truly close to Amrit, I decided to track down her diaries. I knew they existed, those notebooks written in French, because Elisa Vázquez de Gey had used them as a source in her biography of Anita, *The Princess of Kapurthala* (1997). And, more importantly, an unattributed letter mentioned in passing that Anita's diaries were the original source of the story that Amrit Kaur had sold her jewellery during the war to help Jews escape France, leading to her arrest and deportation.

Elisa replied to my probing email with a cheery 'Hola!' Of course she remembered me. It had been such a pleasure to dine together a few years back, when I first began to take an interest in this story . . . And how was my friend who'd invited us to her house on the rue Bellechasse?

Her response was not what I'd expected, given that I didn't remember Elisa, or the dinner, or drinks on the rue Bellechasse. I had no memory, in other words, of ever having met her. And when that mental slip really sank in, I was gripped by alarm, followed by a sense of nausea. Then, little by little, as I read over her words again in disbelief, from the depths arose the memory that my early days in

Paris, though exhilarating, had also been intensely difficult. And, at times, I'd reacted to the sense of loss that came with making a new start by involuntarily emptying the contents of my memory.

Naturally I kept this amnesia to myself when I rang her, telling Elisa only that I was calling to ask where I might find Anita Delgado's diaries. But she did not have good news for me.

'The diaries are no more, *ma chérie.*'

'What do you mean, no more?'

'Gone. Sold to booksellers. Disposed of.'

'Disposed of by whom?'

'By her Spanish relatives, who understood nothing. They gave me one, but it's from a year that doesn't interest you, 1913. What makes them so important?'

When I explained that they were the last place I had left to turn to, she promised to see if there were any files on her computer, but she doubted it: the book predated her current computer, and by more than twenty years.

A few hours later an email arrived.

'I'm sending you this message I received in 2009. I forwarded it to the Kapurthala family (to no response, as usual). I think it might interest you . . .' The note read:

*Dear Elisa Vázquez de Gey,*

*My name is Ginger Rosser. I live in San Diego, California. This is a serious inquiry regarding my research on the life of Amrit Kaur, daughter of the Maharaja of Kapurthala. Your book about Anita Delgado contains the only information I have found regarding the fate of Amrit and her death. The story I have to tell is compelling and there is so much to explain. I am hoping you will please pass this information along to her family.*

*I have in my possession Amrit's briefcase which contains many personal and historical items that I feel are very important. This briefcase is a museum of her life and it should be returned to her family. Amrit had friends here in San Diego. Louise Helen Hermesch and her mother Mrs Wells Goodhue. She was staying here in 1938. Somehow her luggage was left here or someone returned it from Europe after the war.*

*I do hope for a response. I want only to contact the proper people and do what is right in returning her belongings. Amrit's story is important and shouldn't be lost.*

*Sincerely,*
*Ginger Rosser*

Beneath her signature was an address in San Diego and a telephone number.

Someone had found a suitcase full of Amrit Kaur's personal papers, in California! But how could that be? And what did San Diego have to do with all this? I called Elisa back, but she threw water on the fire. 'Do you know how many people came offering me Kapurthala relics, after my book came out? Be careful, because the majority of them are frauds. You might end up spending your money on a fake.'

While she spoke I began typing Ginger Rosser's name into a search bar. And there she was, the person who'd claimed to have a 'museum' of the Rani of Mandi's life: a handsome woman, blonde, tall, shapely, Scandinavian-looking. Her social media profile said that she was a model for artists, 'retro-feminist' and was into burlesque. 'Elisa,' I said, thinking with a touch of irony about that particular form of striptease, which had just had a big moment in Italy, thanks to a certain politician and his risqué parties. 'It's not looking good here . . .'

What was I expecting to find? A neurobiologist in a lab coat standing in front of Louis Kahn's Salk Institute, the ocean fading into the horizon behind her? Meanwhile I found another link, to a video – and there was the statuesque Ginger, dressed as a waitress, white apron over a black polka-dot uniform, prowling like a lioness across

Ginger Rosser in one of her burlesque performances.

a restaurant stage, performing a striptease that ended with her lying on the ground in just a corset, a vacuum cleaner between her legs.

When I told her, Elisa burst out laughing.

'I'll call you back,' I said. And I dialled the American phone number.

The woman on the other end of the line sounded perturbed. 'How did you find me? . . . I can't speak right now,' and added, lowering her voice, 'I'm working.' I must confess that, at those words, I imagined her unbuttoning her shirt and flinging it over her head with professional flair. 'Call me back in the morning. I wake up early,' she said in a rush. Before hanging up, however, I convinced her to at least send me a few photos. And when they arrived, I understood that it truly existed, this crocodile-leather briefcase with the initials A.K.M. engraved in gold. And that it might well contain letters and documents belonging to Amrit Kaur of Mandi.

That evening, I went to bed pondering how I might come up with the money to pay her. Because, as usual, I'd understood nothing.

'Hello Livia. Here is the list of contents of the briefcase,' began the email I received the next day. 'I want to send you the entire file folder which contains the images of the items, but I am pressed for time this morning. What would be the best way to send them? I don't want the organisation to get muddled. I have 17 folders which all together contain 196 individual files, some of them copies . . . In addition there are the files from my library research which contain copies of newspaper files, cruise ship passenger lists etc. which you will probably want. I will send more info on Sunday. I have a full day today and Saturday.'

As promised, the remainder of the scanned material arrived that Sunday: photographs, letters, telegrams, a notebook, various chequebook stubs, bank slips, business cards of people Amrit had met in New York, Washington, Paris. There was even a skin analysis done by Max Factor in Hollywood, advising her to use honeysuckle cream, olive face powder and No. 18 lipstick. Though, more importantly, the note accompanying these artefacts recounted just how that crocodile briefcase had ended up in Ginger's hands.

A woman named Franziska Collier had found it while clearing out the garage after her husband Edgar Collier's death. Not knowing what to do with the briefcase, she'd passed it along to her friend Ginger, who had a soft spot for historical research. And indeed, Ginger got to work, tracking down a 1940 census that showed that Edgar Collier's mother, Frances Collier, had been a housemaid for one Louise Helen Hermesch. In their garage, Ginger also found a photo taken on the Hermesches' front lawn picturing an elegant-looking young Indian woman in a dark-coloured sari with a white floral print, bending over to pluck a blade of grass, a cigarette dangling in her other hand. The photo was dated 3 August 1938. And in yet another photo, there was the housemaid herself, Frances Collier: a slim, refined-looking African American woman wearing a pale dress with a ribbon around the collar, and a man's hat.

Frances Collier, the Goodhues' housekeeper in San Diego.

Ginger concluded her email with an equally surprising personal detail: 'I must tell you that Franziska's finding and giving me the brief-case prompted me to return to college and in 2009 I took a course in Museum Studies, got an internship at the San Diego Women's History Museum (now the Women's Museum of California) and spent three years there as an employee doing archiving and everything else too. But sadly I couldn't get the help I needed there, so that's when I took a break from all this.'

At that moment, I too felt the need for a break. After so many protracted hours spent reading, visiting archives, poring over old photographs and barely legible articles with a magnifying glass, things were suddenly moving at such a clip that I had to take a step back – almost as if my imagination needed to reclaim itself amid that onslaught of the here and now. And while I put water on for tea, as an excuse to get up from my desk, my thoughts drifted back through the years to my trip to Mumbai that day in early March – when, after a narcoleptic sleep with my forehead pressed against the aeroplane window, I opened my eyes and was momentarily witness to a scene of unsettling beauty. An ochre-coloured city surrounded by an ochre desert and ochre mountains with snow-dusted peaks appeared beneath the plane's wing, an instant before the city's street lamps flicked on in unison, the harsh pink sky turning in a flash to dark purple. What had I just seen, and where? Between the time I spent sitting with those questions and the speed of the plane barrelling east, we were immersed in the night. It took me a bit of time to regain my composure – it was like receiving a sublime gift only for it to be whisked away a moment later – but I eventually pieced together that we'd just flown over Iran, though which part of the country was anybody's guess.

To this day I dream of finding it, that city encircled by snow-capped peaks. And when, against all logic, I convince myself I'll eventually get there, desire and memory fuse; it becomes a kind of game, as I fall asleep, journeying back to that dusk and fixing it in my mind, my eyes adjusting to the shadowy neighbourhoods of the unknown city. As I sink deeper and deeper into sleep, those city streets become containers filled with names from other memories, with colours bleeding in from other worlds, scrawny-legged little boys playing barefoot, watery dawns and sooty dusks. And I fall asleep knowing that, just as with literature, the promise held by places that are so unfamiliar to us – enticing us with a new world, a fuller life – is the promise of an open sky where clouds drift unimpeded, whose mere existence is itself a consolation.

The contents of the briefcase marked A.K.M. were, in a certain sense, the opposite of that mirage: they were the elsewhere of the imagination made suddenly real, material. Not that the mystery was yet solved – all those artefacts still needed interpreting. But now that I had the information to hand, I was certain I would find what I'd been looking for.

Strewn across my desk were the remnants of a privileged life. There was a business card from Princess Fewkié ('Avec tous mes meilleurs vœux'), the daughter of King Fuad I of Egypt; one from Paul de Hevesy, a Hungarian diplomat; another from Baron Jean Pellenc, author of the book *Diamonds and Dust: India through French Eyes*. There was a Harrod's bill, dated September 1933, for various dresses, suits, jackets and children's pyjamas, all sent directly to an address in Simla, India.

There was a postcard from Jersey's Grand Hotel and a bizarre photo of a young Jagatjit Singh, probably taken at a carnival. A Christmas card with two English children sitting beneath a beautifully decorated fir tree. A portrait of a young Dutch officer in uniform bearing the caption, 'With my kindest regards, Raul van Olden, Ainhem 5 – I X – 1927', which piqued my curiosity. Could this plump officer have been Amrit's reason for fleeing?

I found a certificate of admission for 'Amrit Kaur H. H. Sahiba of Mandi' to the Theosophical Society, labelled Poona, 7 January 1927 and signed by Annie Besant, the English socialist and women's rights activist who'd exported Madame Blavatsky's theosophy to India. The certificate confirmed Amrit Kaur's connection to Nicholas and Helena Roerich. As the historian Sunil Khilnani explained to me, theosophical societies in India were a kind of sophisticated cosmopolitan club that allowed members to forge connections beyond their own limited social circles.

The briefcase also contained a list of the members of the All India Womens' Education Fund, which of course included Amrit, though I was surprised to find her husband listed there as well, along with Tibu and Bubbles. A sheet with notes written in pencil bore a few of the lines from Amrit's inaugural speech at the 1931 Asian women's congress. And among the list of speakers I spotted the name of Kamaladevi Chattopadhyay, one of the radical proto-feminists with whom Amrit felt somewhat at odds.

The real treasure in the briefcase, though, was a lined notebook with the words 'List of my things in Mandi' written in pen across the cover. In it, with nimble calligraphy, Amrit had drawn up a list, in English, of the personal belongings she'd left in India. It began with things of the widest variety: 'a fan made of ostrich feathers', '14 brocade saris from Benares', 'an incinerator for Russian Lady essential oils' and cosmetics like rice powder and essence of oregano. It continued with a complete list of her jewellery, among which I recognised the sapphire and diamond bracelets and the necklace with the extravagant sapphire pendant that I'd seen published in the Parke-Bernet auction catalogue, as well as the two rings she'd worn in the Lafayette portrait; the other pieces, however, lacked detailed descriptions – a host of pearls, diamonds, rubies and emeralds mounted on brooches, necklaces, bracelets and watches. At the bottom of the list I counted eight precious cigarette cases.

These must have been the jewels that Amrit Kaur had sold during the war, assuming she'd been able to retrieve them. This was a discovery, and I couldn't wait to share it with a few experts; though I knew that if I went knocking on doors with that note in hand, no jeweller on the rue de la Paix or the place Vendôme would ever admit to buying back a piece to bail out one of their clients.

And then, of course, there were several letters, and even the odd telegram. In order to interpret them, however, I was still lacking a few key elements.

Which, one by one, I began to track down.

# Ginger

A few days later I received another email from San Diego.

*Dear Livia,*

*I hope you don't mind if before we'll have the chance to meet, I tell you something about my life. It will make you understand why Amrit's story is important to me.*

*I've made my living as an artist's model for 30 years now, but have been a performance artist since I was in school. I loved being a topless dancer. Having to cut that career short was one of the greatest heartbreaks of my life. I did some burlesque, but the problem with burlesque was that you did it for free. Dita von Teese, who came on the scene in the early 1990s, is a millionaire now. But back then burlesque was not a moneymaker.*

*Stripping paid well. And for me, that was the key. The key was a woman's appeal. It was the only way I had to support myself, and I knew that. I knew since I was in secondary school that I would never be able to buy a house by myself, and I knew that the trick would be to find a rich guy who had an interest in me. But that didn't happen.*

*So it wasn't stripping but modeling that really changed the direction of my life. It was through modeling, in fact, that I met Franziska. And it's through her that I came in possession of Amrit's briefcase. Franzi came to me one day and said: I don't know what to do with this. I know this is the kind of thing you love, history and mystery. And she was right, I did. So every time I went modeling I took the briefcase with all its letters and notes with me and asked the artists who drew me their advice. One of these artists was also a librarian, and she offered to do some research for me, which was helpful.*

Franzi was an artists' model too. She came here from Germany as an exchange student, then she met a man, much older, a Black man. They started a relationship, and then they got married. Franziska's husband's name was Edgar Collier. He worked at the downtown post office. Then he retired, and died. When I inquired about this man's mother, Franzi told me that Frances Collier had been a housecleaner. She worked for these two women, Louise Helen Hermesch and her mother, Mrs Goodhue. I think there was a story there, but I never quite understood it.

So when Franzi's husband died Franzi moved to another place, and I helped her out. And from the moment she handed me the briefcase I dug more into the story, went back to the house a lot, and found more stuff. Franziska wanted me to help her find things that were sellable on eBay, which I did. So one day I'm standing in the garage, asking myself what's important, when I see this framed photograph of a beautiful young woman in a sari, kneeling on the lawn of a house, with a cigarette in her hand. Oh my god, I said to myself, this is the woman who owns the briefcase. She signed this photograph using the same name! That's when I started putting two and two together.

From that moment I got really involved. A woman's story like Amrit's mattered to me.

You see, I grew up during the feminist era. I was born in San Diego. It was a time when you had so many choices. In the 1970s, when I was in secondary school, I was a wild teenager, but I put up a good front. I only ditched school once. I got good grades. But there was nothing that pulled me. What am I going to do with the rest of my life? I asked myself. It doesn't sound very feminist, but I was always focused on the next boyfriend. So at first I taught swimming – I had been swimming competitively for years. I then moved to Los Angeles where I worked at the Beverly Hills YMCA, which sounds glitzy but it was just an old building with Jewish people swimming in the pool. I had some nice adventures there, taught private swimming lessons in Beverly Hills, but I realised I wasn't really moving up. I wasn't earning much money either, so I thought: maybe I'll go back to school, 'cause I'd never finished college. I wanted to major in PE and minor in Modern Dance. That's when I began to do modeling.

Amrit in San Diego, 3 August 1938.

*But in college I had trouble with the dance class – they told me I couldn't dance. I didn't have a background in ballet, so they said they didn't want to cripple me. I got very discouraged and just dropped out of college. It was then that I became a stripper.*

*And I loved it. I loved it because for the first time I had girlfriends. I felt that I was accepted. I learned to strip by watching the mature dancers as they shared the remnants of burlesque techniques. I loved being a one-woman show, picking my own music, creating theme sets and making costumes, being in control of my performance. Of course, there was all the drinking that goes with the industry of topless dancing. But I had the security of a weekly paycheck. Unfortunately, it didn't last.*

*When I began, we stripped and we served cocktails. We were employees. I was very shy, so I learned how to be with people, serve them drinks, have a conversation. Then when private dancing came in – I mean table dancing, lap dances, pole dancing – you were no longer an employee, you were an independent contractor. You had to pay a fee to the club, in order to perform. And it wasn't right.*

*We topless dancers were considered girls who lived a nice life, but there was always the stigma, 'Oh, they are all prostitutes', even though a lot of girls were working their way through college and others had homes already, because they had made enough money. If you did it right you could make a lot of money with stripping. But after the industry changed, I had to cut that career.*

*So I went back home, to San Diego. All this happened in one year. I'd gone to college, started dancing, and gone home. I was in my late twenties. Modeling helped. It enabled me to be still, not to think, and to be calm, because the rest of my life was so . . . chaotic.*

*One night I met a man and I fell in love with him. Of course I was finding guys just when their lives were falling apart, and this guy's life was falling apart. But I was determined, I had this vision. I wanted a baby. And so I got my daughter, Autumn. And then things changed. He stayed for five years, until Autumn was old enough to go to school. He is a good father, but was a lousy boyfriend.*

*So, it wasn't stripping but modeling that really changed the direction of my life. Because in Amrit's briefcase there was a story that really moved me. And there was a mystery too. Why had this woman never come back to San Diego to rescue her things? I wanted to find it out but I also wanted to save her from being forgotten.*

*To do so I needed a proper researcher. So I enrolled in Museum Studies through the Art Department of Mesa College, hoping to make connections that could be helpful. I also thought Museum Studies sounded like something I might like to do in the future. It was a three-semester program, and in the last semester we had to do an internship in a museum, and I chose the Women's Museum of San Diego. After the internship was over, they hired me. I did a bit of everything: I did office work, I organized their archives. I was happy working there for three years, but then I got fired. I was fed up with the museum's disorganization and didn't get along with the director. It was time for me to leave.*

## Ginger

*Now I work as a personal assistant to a woman and her two parrots – that's right, her two parrots. I also do some housework for two old ladies who were connected to the Women's Museum. It works well with modeling. It's all very flexible.*

*You know, last week I saw the artist who is also a librarian, the one who had helped me with some research about Amrit some years ago. I told her you were coming to San Diego to talk to me. Whenever I run into a former Museum Studies classmate I say, Hey, remember that briefcase I brought to class? Well, I found someone who cares about it just as much as I do.*
*Fill me in, when you can.*

*Ginger*

# A Mark of Shame

If we want to start from the beginning, we have to go back to December 1940, to the moment when Frances Collier rescued the crocodile briefcase marked A.K.M. It was the day that Louise Hermesch's lawyer emptied and sold her San Diego home, in order to save her life. America was still a long way from entering the war, but Louise, though American – as I was told by those who knew her – had been arrested by the Germans in Paris, together with the Rani of Mandi.

When did Louise Hermesch and Amrit Kaur meet? The answer I found in the briefcase – an impassioned telegram: 'Miss you terribly all my love – Louise' – is the summer of 1933. Back then Louise was a thirty-one-year-old widow and heiress. On her father Wells Goodhue's side she was the descendant of a weaver from Kent, William Goodhue, who'd arrived in America in 1620 aboard the *Mayflower*; among her ancestors was a signatory of the Declaration of Independence; she had a famous architect uncle, Bertram Goodhue, who counted the Rockefellers as clients; and she was related to Grace Anna Goodhue Coolidge, wife of the former American president Calvin Coolidge. On her mother Louise Graf's side, meanwhile, she had a Bavarian grandfather and a French grandmother who'd emigrated to Louisiana in the latter half of the 1800s.

In 1902, the year Louise Goodhue was born, the Texaco oil company was founded, Theodore Roosevelt became the first American president to ride in an automobile, and Wells Goodhue travelled to Atlanta to give a conference on the investment opportunities available in Georgia on behalf of the journal he published, *Bonds and*

*Mortgages*, 'the most important financial journal in the Northwest', in the words of the local paper who covered his visit.

Louise's wealth therefore came from her father – the firstborn son of a New England farmer – who'd built his own fortune, first in hardware (in 1887 he patented his 'automatic indicator', a system for signalling from within that a door is locked, like the ones we use in toilets today), then by investing brilliantly in the stock market and becoming a publisher. At his death, a year before the 1929 crisis, a *Washington Post* obituary paid homage to his career as a public speaker and as an authority in the field of international finance, which led him to spend most of his last years in Europe. Wells Goodhue was survived by a wife, a daughter – both named Louise – and a son, Eldredge Goodhue, a naval officer.

'Yes, I do remember hearing stories about Jeri, as my great-aunt Louise called her,' Vicki Sadler told me as we drove towards her farm in Maryland. Vicki was Louise Hermesch's grand-niece: a sporty, blonde seventy-three-year-old in jeans and a strawberry-pink cashmere sweater, whose days on the farm began at four-thirty and ended at sunset. We were driving through the countryside, the road lined with chiaroscuro splotches of oak and maple, crows with impressive wing-spans perched on their branches. The next morning, Vicki would be leaving with her husband for a week of horse riding through the wilderness. But today she'd carved out a little time to speak with me.

Eldredge Goodhue, Louise's brother, was Vicki's grandfather; and Louise and Eldredge's father, Wells Goodhue, her great-grandfather. 'What can I get you to drink?' she asked with a cheerful lilt, entering her cottage; all around were hills where her horses grazed at the forest edge. As she bustled about the kitchen, she began to tell me a bit about her taciturn great-aunt, trapped in a past she never spoke of, like an insect in amber.

'What I recall hearing is that my great-aunt Louise met Jeri travelling, perhaps in France, at the time when she was a young widow, having been married to a man who took his life. Her husband Harry Hermesch was a navy doctor, much older than her, and he was at sea for long periods of time,' she said, turning her periwinkle-blue eyes on me. 'There was a speculation that it was a drug overdose. But if overdose was the cause of his death, the navy would have never let that out.'

Vicki had a theory about the long periods which members of the navy spent at sea. She was convinced that these trips ate away at a sailor's nerves and led to depression, and that the excessive length of certain missions had also dealt a fatal blow to her grandfather Eldredge, who became an alcoholic and died young from cirrhosis of the liver. Eldredge and Harry, Louise's husband, were often at sea together, assigned to the same missions, and became friends.

'I don't know what happened in her marriage. Louise was very secretive . . . I think she married her husband because it was expected. Because she was from a prominent family and that's what you do. They got married in Paris with a grand ceremony,' she added with amusement. Then she set a pair of teacups on a tray and invited me to follow her into the living room.

In fact, I told her, once we'd settled into our white wicker arm-chairs, I'd read in the *New York Times* that their wedding had been held in 1926 at the Episcopal Cathedral Church of the Holy Trinity, on avenue George V. And that, upon exiting the church, the two newlyweds paraded beneath a sabre arch formed by their officer friends. They then departed for their honeymoon in Italy, where they were granted a private audience by Pope Pius XI, along with Louise's parents. 'That doesn't surprise me, because I was told that her father was somehow connected to the Vatican on behalf of the United States. The word ambassador of sorts, loosely used, was also mentioned,' she said.

'What about Amrit Kaur? What did you learn about her?' I asked.

'You mean Jeri.'

I filled her in about the letters and telegrams I'd found in a brief-case in San Diego, from which I'd learned that she and Louise had met in England, not in France, in the summer of 1933. And that Amrit had arrived from India that spring for a six-month tour of Europe, with Buckingham Palace as her first stop, to see George V and Queen Mary. Her aim, it seems, was to take a long breath of fresh air before falling back into rank.

Louise, on the other hand, had set sail from Southampton in June, accompanied by her mother. The two women – Amrit was twenty-nine, Louise two years her senior – most likely met during a holiday in Jersey, the largest of the Channel Islands. When the rani returned to London at the end of the summer, Louise sent her the telegram that spoke of how 'terribly' she missed her. Then, in early September, Louise and her mother were reunited with their new friend at London's South Kensington Hotel. And two weeks later, the three women did something unthinkable: they fled, disappearing over-night without leaving any address behind.

I knew this because the India Office Records in London still held the document reporting that one Miss Dora Swete, an American, had come to the India Office asking for help. Swete was the lady-in-waiting who was to accompany the Rani of Mandi on her Euro-pean tour, and then sail with her back to India. But on 15 September, 'Her Highness' disappeared without explanation. After two weeks of waiting, Miss Swete received a letter from the rani letting her know that her services were no longer required and that she should con-sider herself free. Miss Swete hoped the English authorities would help her return to India. And in any case, she attributed the princess's disappearance to 'two American ladies' and their 'considerable influ-ence' over her. She expressed her conviction that Amrit had left with them for the United States.

I never found out what became of that pitiable lady-in-waiting, but I do know that Amrit, not two months later, was photographed aboard the *Manhattan*, a transatlantic liner, wearing a fur-lined coat and a brightly coloured sari, an air of defiance about her as she leaned on the railing and enjoyed the ocean breeze. It was her first trip to America, according to the caption in the *Boston Globe*, which pointed out how, contrary to Indian custom, the princess was travelling without attendants. 'I don't like the fuss,' she declared, refusing to elaborate: a statement that, in the context of her culture and social standing, stung like a provocation.

No wonder I hadn't been able to find anything on her in France: for five years Amrit and Louise had been living in the United States, travelling far and wide, from New York to Los Angeles, San Francisco to Washington, Saratoga back to Hollywood, staying in luxury hotels wherever they went and stopping for the occasional respite in San Diego, at Louise's home on Point Loma.

I don't know what kind of person Louise was, I told Vicki Sadler, but Amrit had a clear-cut personality – she was stubborn, and she was passionate about women's rights. That said, even I was shocked by a photo of her from 1935, her hair slicked back with brilliantine, in a dark skirt suit and tie, looking glamorous as she arrived in Los Angeles aboard the ocean liner *Santa Elena*. This time her travel companion was 'Mrs H. R. Hermesch, socialite of Washington DC'. 'American women are the sanest on earth', the rani declared to the *Los Angeles Times*, 'so far as their dress, habits and outlook on life are concerned.' Her choice of clothing and hairstyle wasn't what one would call in line with the latest trends – that 'à la garçonne' look belonged to the 1920s, and was old news by 1935. It seemed, rather, a declaration of freedom and independence, if not something else entirely.

'So what was Louise like?' I asked Vicki.

'I only knew her towardss the end of her life, when she was heavy-set, as happens to many women. But she had the bluest eyes I had ever seen. And even then, there was a hint of something, I don't know, flamboyant. Otherwise, she was very elusive. When I was a youngster she never struck me as being particularly bright or well educated. Perhaps she was, maybe it was her personality,' she conceded. 'But I had the feeling that she was very spoiled. How these two women met so quickly and bonded right away is anybody's guess. But we know that the social norms of the day would not have accepted it as a romantic relationship. In any case, it was never discussed in the family. Just once my grandmother Annie said: maybe there was something *funny* going on there . . .'

Vicki pulled out a pair of colour snapshots from an album. In one, dated 1972, Louise stood in front of a cake – it must have been her seventieth birthday. As she blew the candles out, wearing a simple knit dress with a zigzag pattern, she stared into the lens with a look of amusement and surprise, her eyes open wide. She had short, bright-blonde hair, her pretty and proportionate face framed by modest curls.

Louise Hermesch on her seventieth birthday, San Diego, November 1972.

'The two women's friendship seems to have lasted quite a while, until after the war. The next story I remember is when they were taken prisoner. Louise was said to have slipped a postcard to one of her guards, to mail to her family in the US and to certain government officials and lawyers here, who later worked for her release. From what I understand, Jeri was released at some point because of her status, as the senior wife of the Raja of Mandi. I also recall hearing that she'd been exiled after leaving her husband, so she continued to move from country to country without citizenship or residency.'

She apologised for not having more to share. 'But . . . wait,' she said, standing up. 'There's something I'd like to show you.' She disappeared to the second floor and came back down with a cardboard box, from which she extracted a silk chiffon sari printed with apricot-coloured flowers. 'This was in the trunk I inherited from Louise, along with the few other things she left when she died. I'd like to return it to the princess's family.' Louise had died of cancer in 1978.

There were other things, as well, in that trunk Vicki had kept in her attic for nearly forty years. A large packet filled with envelopes – just the envelopes, no letters – all addressed to Amrit Kaur of Mandi, all mailed general delivery via American Express or the Thomas Cook agency. I felt a pang in my heart when I recognised a few from Bubbles, with the orange horses of the Bilkha coat of arms. Vicki thought Louise had kept them for the stamps. There were also two books: *Lord Halifax's Ghost Book*, a story collection filled with haunted houses and supernatural occurrences written by Charles Lindley, Viscount Halifax; and a Joan Kennedy novel titled *Mrs Lavender of London*, published in London in 1929, with a printed dedication: *To LOUISE HELEN, a dear American friend.* Joan Kennedy was the pseudonym of Alice Mabel Gibbs, a romance novel writer, and I wondered if Louise might have served as an inspiration, given that lilac was the colour traditionally associated with female homosexuality. But the dedication wasn't the only revelation. When I flipped through the novel, I discovered that it contained a bookplate with a nineteenth-century flair: a composition depicting a row of leather-bound volumes, three candles glowing on an antique candelabra, a helmet and an Aladdin's lamp, beneath which was a strip of parchment bearing, to my great surprise, not one but two names: 'A. K. Mandi and L. G. Hermesch'. A true couple, then: a homosexual, interracial couple who weren't afraid to say 'Us'. Perhaps this was it, I told myself – the reason why I'd encountered such hostility and suspicion back in Delhi, when I asked to meet Amrit's relatives on the Kapurthala side.

Vicki had nothing left to show me, but she suddenly had an idea. We could try to get in touch with Teresa Covey Goodhue, Louise's brother's former daughter-in-law. 'Teri' had been the principal of a school in San Diego, and Vicki hadn't seen her in forty years, but she did have her phone number, assuming it hadn't changed.

Miraculously, Teri Goodhue picked up the phone on the first ring. And without even sounding very surprised, the octogenarian ex history professor and secondary school principal answered our questions over speakerphone with the clean pronunciation of a teacher giving her students a diction lesson. 'This is a very long time ago,' she said at first. 'You have to understand that, even though I knew Louise well, everything I heard about her past comes from Annie, my mother-in-law, who had reason to dislike her.'

Annie's full name was Anne Harrison Goodhue, and she was the woman who'd married Eldredge, Louise's brother. 'She was a free spirit, a feisty woman and a woman on her own terms,' Vicki described her. 'She had her own car, a Model T, Ford's first car, and when her husband was stationed in Long Beach with the navy and she was in San Diego she would grab a bottle of gin, stick it between her legs, and drive right to see him, 120 miles away. Back in those days, driving that far was unheard of.' The image brought to mind a Mae West film.

Louise's mother was a very conservative woman, and she'd forbidden her son to marry Annie. 'Therefore when he did,' Teri cut in over speakerphone, 'Eldredge was written out of the will and Louise received everything. And spent it in what would be called today a jet-setter kind of lifestyle. So when, after the war, Louise came back to San Diego, there was . . . I don't want to say animosity, but there was a certain distance, after all those years.'

Eldredge Goohue died in 1940, of liver failure. 'I think it was the drinking that held his career back,' Teri said. 'Annie used to tell the story of the night her first son was born: when Eldredge was downstairs and was too drunk to come upstairs while she was giving birth.' The American navy punished such behaviour by denying his widow Annie a pension, which left her in a bind with two young children. Adding insult to injury, they did award a pension to Louise, even though Harry Hermesch had been caught stealing morphine for himself from the infirmary and had committed suicide to avoid dishonourable discharge.

'But how would you explain Aunt Louise going to Europe at a moment as difficult as 1938?' Vicki asked Teri.

'I can only guess, but I think it was the same reason that so many talented people and Black people went to Europe in the period between the First World War and the Second because in France they were much more broad-minded in many respects, about race and sexual orientation. When her mother died, I think Louise would have felt free to go back to Europe. She would not think that anybody like Hitler would have an impact on her life. And just as so many Jewish people somehow could not believe that the Germans could do the things that we know they did, my feeling, quite unshakeable, is that Louise didn't think it would happen to her.'

Teri dismissed the idea that Louise's mother, or her husband Harry, might have been Jewish (as the last names Graf and Hermesch might suggest). If that were the case, 'Annie would have said it. Particularly because there was animosity there.' Louise's struggles during the war, according to Teri, were the result of her own choices.

'The US was not yet at war when the princess was arrested. Louise could have come home, but she would not leave her friend. She chose not to. And the family story was that Louise received extra money from the lawyer here in the US, to try and get the princess out. Annie's feeling was that she had made all these bad choices and the only way that she could get out of them was by spending large amounts of money, supposedly as bribes. And that a substantial amount of her fortune had gone into trying to continue to live in a territory controlled by Nazi-sympathising French, the Vichy regime. Louise was not under the protection of the Vichy government, but she bribed them to try to make life easier for the princess, and then to free her from their control. This was the period when she was drinking so heavily. I remember Annie saying that when Louise came home, she was in a terrible state. And how much worse this was made by the fact that during wartime it was much harder to get an alcoholic drink, I don't know. But the ravages of long-time heavy drinking finally caught up with her.'

When Louise returned to San Diego in 1949 she was a broken woman, her house sold, her money spent. The lawyer in charge of the sale had pocketed the lion's share, according to the family. She went to live in a modest hotel in downtown San Diego, 'a very marginal kind of place', and then, when she was no longer able to care for herself, in a nursing home. She spoke little, had no friends, and seemed completely detached from the present. At Christmas or Thanksgiving Annie Goodhue would come to pick her up, so that she wouldn't have to spend the time alone, but Louise would remain silent until she'd had enough to drink, at which point she'd slip into French. She never spoke of the fortune she'd squandered, or the poverty she'd fallen into. Nor did she ever speak of any jewels.

'Whatever jewels the princess may have had, the family believed that it was Louise's money that made their lifestyle possible,' Teri said. 'The Goodhue family had been very comfortable and well-to-do throughout the entire Depression, and with her mother's death Louise would have come into every bit of that money, while the princess had been disowned by her family. Annie believed that it was the princess's family and her husband who took her jewels back.'

This was a possibility that had never even crossed my mind up until this moment. Nor did Bubbles seem to have considered it, either. But then how to explain the 1950 auction in New York, two years after Amrit's death?

Teri had her own theory. 'They could have sold them or reset them or whatever. But Annie was very clear about the family repossessing them. If you were going to sell jewels in 1950, who had the money to buy? Nobody in Europe. Everyone was selling jewels then. You had to bring them to New York.

'I really don't think that it was Louise who sold those jewels in 1950. She didn't possess the mind of a schemer. The story in the family was that her Indian friend had escaped a loveless marriage, had gone back to Europe, and in some way received a small allowance from her husband. But in terms of life spent travelling and sightseeing, she was financially at the mercy of others.

'The story I have been told,' Teri concluded, 'was that the princess's family and her husband took the jewels back: either they took them back, or kept them in India if she left them there. I frankly have no difficulty believing this, because she had disgraced them. She had run away. The fact that they didn't return them to her was meant as a mark of shame.'

# The Hungriest They've Been
## Since the Siege of Paris

On the evening of 1 July 1939, a long line of cars snaked through the gates of the Villa Trianon in Versailles. They were there to deliver the 700 guests to a ball thrown by Elsie de Wolfe, alias Lady Mendl, the ageing and indomitable American interior designer famed for throwing opulent parties and for dyeing her hair the same aquamarine as her Cartier tiara.

Elsie de Wolfe's Circus Ball, the last of pre-war Paris's grand balls, would go down in the record books as the peak of extravagance in a frantic season of social gatherings, Parisians dancing the nights away on the edge of a precipice. And this despite the rain that had turned the garden into a swamp and despite the absence of three much-awaited elephants who, with trunks flailing, had refused to leave the station in Versailles that afternoon. One of the elephants was set to make its entrance with the party's patroness on its back: Amrit Kaur's sister-in-law, Sita Devi of Kapurthala, the petite princess whose exquisite beauty had enchanted *le tout-Paris*.

Two days later, in reports of the evening, tales were told of dancing Lipizzaner horses led by a gentleman in top hat and tails; of a dog and pony show directed by the hostess; of an all-woman orchestra playing waltzes, dressed in Austrian costumes; and of the Mainbocher, Schiaparelli, Vionnet and Madame Grès dresses that revealed the bare shoulders, backs and décolletages of the most stylish guests. I searched for the Rani of Mandi's name amid so much worldly splendour, skimming others like Marie-Laure de Noailles, Clare Boothe Luce, Douglas Fairbanks, Francis Poulenc, Louis Nathaniel de Rothschild, Hedi Lamarr, Cecil Beaton and a long list of French aristocrats. I eventually realised that the presence of Amrit's brother Karam with his wife Sita would probably have dissuaded her from attending with a partner her family would never have accepted.

Piecing together a puzzle made of newspaper articles, books, photographs, ocean liner passenger lists and other various scraps – some of them supplied by Ginger – I was able to retrace the steps of these two intrepid women, who after five years of travelling across the United States seemed to have dissolved in the European clouds. Amrit and Louise set sail from Los Angeles aboard the *Europa*, disembarking in England on 11 September 1938: precisely one day before Jagatjit Singh arrived in Paris and settled in at the George V, accompanied by his entourage of sons, aides-de-camp and servants.

Amrit and her father had chosen a difficult moment to travel in Europe. Just two weeks after their arrival, the threat of war prompted Great Britain and France to sign the Munich Agreement in order to quell the ongoing Sudeten crisis. The pact, which authorised Germany to annex those parts of Czechoslovakia inhabited by German speakers, in effect paved the way for Hitler's occupation of Prague. The winds of war that led to the agreement, and the horror of *Kristallnacht* in November, when Nazis killed ninety-one Jews in Germany and destroyed thousands of shops and hundreds of synagogues in a night of anti-Semitic rage, were events that even the most clueless of travellers could not have ignored.

All of Europe was in turmoil. During the crisis that spawned the Munich Agreement, the French deployed two and a half million soldiers along the French–German border. London braced itself for aerial bombardments. The American embassy stockpiled food, gas and automobiles, sending two battle cruisers to Brest to protect the 14,000 Americans then in Paris. However, as Teri Goodhue said of Louise – and as I, by extension, assumed of Amrit – the two women must have considered themselves above the political fray of the times, and in this they seem to have been in good company. As the historian Olivier Bernier wrote in *Fireworks at Dusk*, 'Upper-class Parisians from 1937 on not only refused to see the misfortune and ugliness that increasingly surrounded them; they tried to forget that they might even exist. They had done their best to ignore the Depression for the first half of the decade; they saw no reason why they could not ignore the Nazi menace now.'

If the 1939 Circus Ball made it into the history books, it wasn't only for the graceful dancing of the Lipizzaner horses, or the graceless behaviour of the three pachyderms who threatened to ruin the evening, or the sacrificial rugs thrown over the mud so that guests wouldn't soak their silk stockings. There was another, more serious reason. That evening, Elsie de Wolfe's garden served as the stage for an informal but highly tense meeting between the French Foreign Minister, Georges Bonnet, and the German ambassador in Paris, Johannes von Welczeck. Just a few hours earlier, Bonnet had contacted von Welczeck regarding another crisis of extreme gravity: he'd asked the ambassador to inform the German government that any unilateral decisions regarding the port of Danzig, which Hitler had set his sights on, would not be tolerated by the French. In other words, that morning the French formally enjoined the Germans against annexing Danzig, which was under Polish control. Hitler, they expected, would respond in kind the next day. 'Nobody in our camp wants war,' the French general Maxime Weygand declared. 'But I affirm that if they force us to win another victory we will win it.'

Two months later Hitler invaded Poland.

Thinking back on that troubling moment, I was reminded of what one of the guests had said to me at the dinner party where I was encouraged to give up my research: 'I've never understood why

Jagatjit Singh, who was in Paris at the time, returned to India in 1939 without his daughter.' And indeed, this is precisely what I'd verified: in July 1939, Jagatjit Singh was again at the George V with his entourage, on his way back from a trip to the United States during which he met President Roosevelt, was honoured with a fifteen-gun salute at the New York World's Fair and toured the studios of 20th Century Fox in Hollywood, where he'd flirted, according to the papers, with the African American actress Nina Mae McKinney.

As usual, as soon as he set foot in Paris, the maharaja was put under surveillance by the police and the French secret service, though apart from the umpteenth accident near the hotel in his Hispano-Suiza, the authorities had little else to report this time. At that moment, the Prefecture had its binoculars trained on a Kapurthala who was neither Jagatjit nor his daughter Amrit. 'A diplomat whose francophile sentiments are known believes it useful to direct the attention of our services towards the dealings and interactions of the Princess of Kapurthala . . .' read the report sent to the prefect. It appears that one of Amrit's sisters-in-law, Sonia of Kapurthala, Prince Amarjit's Russian wife, had installed herself at the Ritz with the Hungarian actress Zita Perczel, and that the two friends were using the rooms on the place Vendôme to consort with politicians, defence contractors and French army officers, gathering, in the opinion of this francophile diplomat, information that 'could be shared with the adversary'.

When the war broke out in earnest in 1940, the Germans were in Paris within just six weeks. There ensued much confusion among the British intelligence agencies regarding the whereabouts of Amrit Kaur and her stepmother Anita Delgado. First they were reported to have been seen in Brussels, then in Paris, then Biarritz, in a series of contradictory notes. The only clear information to emerge from all the chaos was that Anita had managed to reach Lisbon and, from there, Madrid, where she spent the war years; and that Amrit Kaur had remained in Paris, where in December she was arrested at her apartment on the rue Keppler, as the mysterious Perrier reported to the Foreign Office.

The question of who this Perrier figure truly was and why he'd loaned Amrit money, as I'd told Bubbles when we first met, had led me to Lake Geneva, on the trail of a lawyer who'd served throughout the war as a go-between for Amrit, her family and the Foreign Office. And that's assuming Perrier wasn't a code name. One archive director in Paris had warned me that trying to track down his identity would be 'like looking for a needle in a haystack', words of caution that I took as a direct challenge. Could a code name really be impenetrable, with the sophisticated tools of the twenty-first century? For days on end the answer seemed to be 'yes'. My first attempt to combine the words 'Perrier' and 'Vichy' in a Google search – both of which, as my luck would have it, were extremely common brands of bottled water – turned up more than twelve million results. I tried tacking on a few other key words, and then a few others, and a few more after that, doing my best not to drown in that sea of mineral water. By chance, I landed on it, the lucky combination – the words (immediately forgotten) which achieved the impossible task of extracting that needle from the search-engine haystack: the name Paul Paillole, head of Vichy's counter-espionage network, no less, a Pétain loyalist who, when the Germans decided to invade France's unoccupied zone in 1942, fled to London, where he was soon working for the Allies and the liberation cause.

He was a peculiar fellow, this counter-espionage chief for the collaborationist government: in the memoir he published after the war, *Fighting the Nazis*, he claimed to have also been a mole for the British secret services and a supporter of the Resistance, even from the war's outset. Paillole-Perrier made himself out to be a patriot, though de Gaulle never wanted him among his ranks. And recent research done by the English historian Simon Kitson has brought some astounding details to light.

Throughout the Vichy period, Paillole arranged for the arrest of English spies, Jews and partisans all across the 'free zone'. What's surprising is just how far he went, denouncing, and in some cases executing by firing squad, 1,500–2,000 French spies employed by the Nazis. He even nabbed several 'horizontal collaborators' – women who had sexual relations with the Germans – in his counter-espionage net, forcing them to shave their heads. And this was long before partisans did the same at the end of the war, shaving the heads of women who'd collaborated or slept with the enemy – and giving rise to what the French, with a touch of black humour, later branded 'the hairdo of '44'. If all of this sounds contradictory, it's because it's a direct reflection of Pétain's very non-linear conception of Vichy's role.

Though he'd served as the principal facilitator of the German occupation, the octogenarian Maréchal took a centralised view of this collaboration, and, from his post in Vichy, was intent on maintaining a semblance of sovereignty over France – which explains why Paillole, on top of his other duties, was tasked with rooting out any acts of collaboration with Germany that did not originate from the Vichy government but were the fruit of individual efforts. And the Germans had their reasons for turning a blind eye. Strategically, the Vichy government was a way of maintaining control over an unoccupied territory, thus sparing themselves the trouble. In this way they could concentrate on northern France, from which they intended to attack Great Britain. Such was the nature of Paul Paillole's multifaceted role: he was aiding the Germans by murdering English agents and partisans and rounding up Jews, in compliance with the terms of the armistice; at the same time he was reminding Hitler, with a criminal dose of hypocrisy, that France belonged to the French and that any spies working on behalf of the Germans were not welcome.

How this officer-of-all-trades and patriot managed to get Amrit Kaur out of the Besançon internment camp remains a mystery. In any case, when the gates of the miserable Frontstalag 142 opened for her in April 1941 the rani returned to Paris with Louise Hermesch, and the Maharaja of Kapurthala wrote a thank-you letter to Marshal Pétain himself.

'Louise was not under the protection of the Vichy government,' I remembered Teri Goodhue had said, 'but she bribed them to try to make life easier for the princess, and then to free her from their control.' It had been Louise, then, who'd financed this operation, and who'd secured Amrit's favourable treatment after her release: Louise who, rather than abandon Amrit, had followed her into the internment camp instead of returning to the United States as she could have. One of the requirements for their release from Besançon and permission to re-enter Paris was that they remained traceable.

The Paris that the Rani of Mandi and Louise discovered upon their return from the internment camp must have been a different, though not unrecognisable, city. The Elsie de Wolfe and Rothschild smart set had fled, leaving behind their works of art, their silver and various other trophies, but ordinary people still crowded the streets. Everywhere there were men in uniform, public buildings were barricaded with sandbags, and strips of paper were taped across shop windows to catch the shards in the case of an air raid.

Nevertheless, the routines of daily life had mostly returned: the couturiers lifted their shutters, the *bouquinistes* continued selling their books along the Seine, and fishermen went on trying to reel in the occasional goby from the wharf. But the courtesy the Germans had shown during the first months of the occupation, when they were giving up their seats to ladies on the metro and patting children's heads – as I read in Jean-Paul Sartre's *Notebooks from a Phoney War* – had begun to wane. The Statute on Jews issued by Vichy early in the occupation, which forced Jews to register with the police and barred them from teaching, public office, writing for the newspapers or serving in the army, found favour among French anti-Semites, though it also sent a troubling signal to those who, like Amrit, counted many

Jews among their friends and family. It most certainly destroyed Albert Kahn's final days, putting an end to his dreams of tolerance.

My thoughts returned often to that Alsatian of humble origins who became a banker and then a philanthropist, because the vision of the world he pursued with such conviction – where an openness towards foreign cultures served as an antidote to war – struck me as a necessary goal. And yet, as the information I'd been collecting began to fall into place bit by bit, it seemed more and more unlikely to me that Amrit Kaur had risked her safety to aid her father's old friend.

I had to accept the truth that Kahn had died alone and bankrupt in his *hôtel particulier* surrounded by Atlas cedars, in November 1940.

One year later, in January 1942, Amrit Kaur contacted Her Majesty's British embassy in Bern from her new address at 24 rue de la Faisanderie, in Paris's sixteenth arrondissement, to appeal for medical assistance and to request a prisoner exchange that would allow her and her 'lady of honour, Madame H. R. Hermesch, American citizen' to travel to the United States. It was then, and not when she was a prisoner, as Bubbles believed, that the Germans declared themselves open to an exchange. But the writer and explorer Wilhelm Filchner was too important a spy for the English to release, especially in exchange for the daughter of a maharaja whom they privately mistrusted, not only because of Lord Curzon's negative opinion of Jagatjit Singh, or because Singh had long bragged of his preference for Paris over London. Always one to ingratiate himself with the powerful, he had travelled to Rome in 1935 to meet Mussolini; three years later, he shook hands with Hitler in the shadow of the Colosseum. This the English had not forgotten.

'My dear daughter, I much regret that owing to war conditions British government rules do not permit a remission of more than £10 per mesem to you at present. Hope you are well. Your loving father,' he wrote to her in January 1943. It was the first affectionate message he'd sent to his daughter since she'd rebelled against the family. By association, those words got me thinking about the fathers of some of her fellow prisoners in Besançon and the actions they'd taken. The young Shula Przepiorka's father, for example, even though he was Jewish, went to the police station every day to ask after his daughter, a British citizen, until he was loaded on to a train and sent to his death in Auschwitz. Or Rosemary Say's, so discreet in his efforts that only after his death, upon reading his letters, did his daughter discover what great lengths he'd gone to and how much money he'd laid down to bring her home.

With the situation rapidly worsening in France and measures of suppression only escalating, neither Amrit nor Louise could truly feel safe. Now, for every dead German, 100 French would be executed. Jews were ordered to wear the yellow star as a badge of infamy and a preliminary measure for the round-ups of the Final Solution. And the deportations began. In the Vélodrome d'Hiver round-up of July 1942, nearly 13,000 Jews were arrested in Paris alone, and again it was the French gendarmes, not the Germans, who took charge. Food was scarce, coal was scarce, the authorities even had to establish a ban on cooking cat meat in stews. The writer Jean Guéhenno noted in his diary, 'You get so cold you can't think of anything else.'

And yet, after that initial period of despondency, Paris rekindled its vital spirit. The eleven o'clock curfew left room for Maurice Chevalier, Charles Trenet, Sacha Guitry and other artists who felt no responsibility for the disaster into which France had been plunged, to sing their romantic songs and perform in the *théâtres de boulevard* for largely German audiences. The shutters rose at the Comédie-Française, opera houses and hundreds of cinemas. But once the jokes ran out, and the forced smiles faded, and the songs about wooden soles tapping along the pavements came to an end, the curfew brought Paris back to reality. From that moment until dawn, the sounds that reigned were those Ninetta Jucker described in her book *Curfew in Paris* (1960): 'Rifle shots; the sudden pepper of a machine gun – or could it be the firing squads? – the rush past of a powerful car (someone being swept away by the Gestapo perhaps) and towards the early morning, singing . . . on command.'

After the United States entered the war in December 1941, Amrit's former fellow prisoners looked on as a parade of elegant American ladies dressed in fur coats and hats arrived at the camp in Vittel. Then came the turn of another sort of prisoner: Polish Jews with South American visas or waiting on travel documents for Palestine, their faces etched with the horrors they'd suffered in Poland.

Sofka Skipwith, the Russian princess who'd stayed in Bâtiment A with Amrit Kaur, set to work immediately, giving English and French lessons to the prisoners with an eye to helping them escape. She even wrote their names on cigarette papers and passed them along to partisans, who managed to sneak into the camp as plumbers or bricklayers when repairs were needed. 'For the first time we heard the dreaded words: Auschwitz, Belsen, Dachau . . . The Final Solution,' Sofka wrote in her diary. 'We heard of deaths by torture, by starvation, the floggings, the humiliations.' The worst came in April 1944, the day the trains with wood-barred windows arrived at the station in Vittel. At the sight of them some of the Poles attempted suicide, but not all of the cyanide pills worked, and not every leap from a window proved fatal. Among those souls shoved on to the train, some already on the verge of death, Sofka Skipwith managed to save an infant, passing it to a peasant woman through a hole in the perimeter fence. Two months later, news of the Allied forces' success in Normandy began to circulate in Vittel. When Besançon was liberated, and hundreds of wounded Germans were sent to the city's hospital, the same nuns who'd suffered the shame of disrobing in front of them at Frontstalag 142 now found themselves in the ironic position of having to care for them.

I'd lived for nine years in Paris before visiting the site of the D-Day landings, but when I did go I was taken aback by just how present the spirit of that time remained, lingering everywhere. Beneath a stormy sky and beside a roiling, blue-grey sea I walked around bomb craters covered in wet grass, skirted barbed-wire fences, and entered the concrete bunkers that eerily remain standing to this day. But nothing prepared me for the American flags, planted at random in front of those little French houses with their pointed roofs, as if seventy years hadn't gone by since the landing; as if the French hadn't lost 20,000 civilians during those days of Allied bombings; as if America were still the grand, munificent democracy, poised to turn the tide of the war and save Europe from a dictator; as if the spirit of respectfulness that stopped people from playing, running or strumming a guitar along those vast and empty beaches had also prevented the construction of fast-food chains and other ghastly tourist traps, preying on the thousands of people who poured in every day to visit the tombs of their relatives and compatriots.

Leaning out over the *falaises* where the Germans made their stand, I tried to imagine the burnt-out trucks along the beach, the overturned ships, the rows of the dead draped in blankets, only their toes protruding; and all those objects abandoned on the sand, left there the next morning to tell one, ten, thousands of stories, made up of diaries, Bibles, accordions, socks lost in escape, toothbrushes, hand grenades and even tennis rackets, mixed up with the latest letters from home, their addresses clipped off, just in case.

When the Allied forces arrived in Paris, their jeeps filled with the flowers and wine and fruit that the jubilant French had regaled them with in passing, the city exploded with joy and sensuality. And one scene, among many, found a place in my imagination, right next to the images of Parisian women joyfully kissing American soldiers. On the night of Paris's liberation, 25 August 1944, hearing the sound of muffled moans around him, the French writer Gilles Perrault stopped and pricked up his ears. 'Transfixed – God forgive me – with near-religious feeling, I spent a long moment there listening to Paris making love.'

There were so many things about that extraordinary moment that Vicki Sadler might have asked her aunt Louise, on visiting her at the nursing home where Louise spent her last years, if only she hadn't been intimidated by her aunt's reserve. Had they run out into the streets with everyone else, she and Amrit? Had they celebrated, drunk, danced? Had they witnessed the surrender of 400 Germans barricaded in the Chambre des Députés, negotiated in Yiddish by a madcap, unarmed American cameraman, since the Nazis could understand that German dialect but not English? And most importantly, were they aware that three days before Paris's liberation the Raja of Mandi had contacted the British authorities, asking them to take advantage of the now imminent exchange of civilian prisoners to grant his wife permission to return 'to England and, if she so desires, to India', employing that 'if' as an acknowledgement of her freedom to choose?

One month later, the Maharaja of Kapurthala received news from the Foreign Office that his daughter was alive and was 'a guest of Countess Chasseloup-Laubat, previously Betty Earle Joplin', at number 28 rue Fabert – right there along the Esplanade des Invalides, scene of the German army's spectacular retreat. Jagatjit Singh responded to the news with gratitude and relief: Betty had been a family friend even before her second marriage, to the French explorer François de Chasseloup-Laubat. His daughter was in good hands. And as the Chasseloup-Laubats had left an archive for their heirs, I myself hoped to find out a bit more about the days when Amrit took refuge on the rue Fabert. My request to review those files, however, was turned away since, they told me, Amrit was never mentioned in them. And a follow-up letter from Bubbles went without reply.

Perhaps the archive was dedicated principally to François de

Chasseloup-Laubat's discoveries in the central Sahara, for which he was renowned. But this obstacle whetted my curiosity. And, soon enough, I stumbled upon a story that Amrit must have been aware of, since it concerned her host Chasseloup-Laubat's mother and aunt.

These two women bore the maiden name Stern, and were daughters of the Jewish banker Jean Stern and Ernesta Hierschel de Minerbi, a formidable Triestine who'd published some twenty novels under the pseudonym Maria Star and whose salon in Paris was frequented by Marcel Proust and Filippo Tommaso Marinetti. Ernesta and her daughters – whose married names were Marie-Louise de Chasseloup-Laubat and Lucie Girot de Langlade – had all converted to Catholicism before the First World War. Ernesta died in 1926. But in Nazi-occupied France her daughters remained in danger, and Marshal Pétain himself petitioned the German authorities to exempt them from the obligation of wearing a yellow star.

Following this thread, I discovered that in 1942 twenty-six such 'honourary Aryans' were named in France – that is, Jews exempted from wearing the yellow star, who, unlike the blameless Marie-Louise and Lucie, were for the large part in the service of the Reich. These included art dealers working for Hitler, Gestapo informants and the lowest of the low such as Moszek (Maurice) Lopatka, who, according to the historian Léon Poliakov, was single-handedly responsible for the arrest of hundreds of fellow Jews.

But Pétain's efforts (which remain an object of debate) to save his friend Ernesta's daughters only half succeeded: Lucie de Langlade was arrested on 20 January 1944 at her castle in Cuts, Oise, and transported to Auschwitz, where she died four days later. Pétain, who after the war was tried and condemned for treason and collaboration with the enemy, never explained why he had such a personal stake in the fates of Ernesta Stern's daughters. But his ties with the family undoubtedly had very strong roots. François de Chasseloup-Laubat was the last to visit him on the island-prison of Île d'Yeu in 1951, just days before his death.

With no way to confirm this from the Chasseloup-Laubat archive, all I knew for certain was that Amrit and Louise were stuck for what was still a considerable amount of time in a rundown Paris: just how rundown the *New Yorker* correspondent Janet Flanner tells us in her diary from 1945: 'They are hungrier than they have been any other winter of the war. They are the hungriest they have been since the Prussian siege of Paris, when their grandparents ate mice.'

People awaited trains bearing coal, but there wasn't even enough coal to operate the trains. Hot water ran only at the Hôtel de Crillon and the Ritz, and had been reserved for German officers. Electricity was turned off from dawn until dusk, except for one hour at noon, when many of the apartment buildings turned on the water which they otherwise kept off for fear it would freeze and burst the pipes. People died of pneumonia in hospitals where there were no thermometers, there was no medication and no electricity for procedures. And after Besançon, Amrit had serious health issues.

When news of President Roosevelt's death came in the spring of 1945, Parisians were gripped by a deep sense of mourning. To any American, man or woman, soldier or civilian, they offered their condolences. Reading this, I wondered what that day had been like for Louise; and if she and Amrit had attended the funeral Mass held for the president at the Cathedral of Notre-Dame. And if, after that ceremony, they'd joined the many families at the Gare de Lyon to witness the arrival of the first female civilian prisoners to be freed from the Ravensbrück concentration camp in Germany, where the Nazis had them digging trenches.

The event made waves around the city. The Germans had singled out these 300 women as the healthiest among the tens of thousands still held at Ravensbrück. Even then, eleven of them had been unable to survive the trip. When the prisoners' relatives, clutching bouquets of lilies and other spring flowers, watched them step off the train, there was no joyous outcry, only a dismayed silence. Many of them were now unrecognisable to their families. And General de Gaulle wept.

But then something changed. 'Peace is visible already,' Marguerite Duras wrote in her diary just a few days later. 'It's like a great darkness falling, it's the beginning of forgetting. You can see already: Paris is lit up at night. The place Saint-Germain-des-Prés looks as if it's floodlit. The café Les Deux Magots is packed. It's still too cold for people to sit outside on the pavement. But the little restaurants are packed too. I went out, peace seemed imminent. I hurried back home, pursued by peace. It had suddenly struck me that there might be a future, that a foreign land was going to emerge out of this chaos where no one would wait any more.'

## PART FIVE

# The Sapphires of Kashmir

# Last Jubilee

Meanwhile, in India, not one of the Raj princes seemed to realise that a revolution was imminent. Numerous monarchs among the rajas, maharajas, wadiyars, nizams, wālis, emirs, nawabs and maharawals had supported the Independence cause, without understanding that freeing themselves from the British also meant renouncing the throne. 'Even in 1945 I never thought it would end,' the Maharawal of Dungarpur would admit years later in an interview with Charles Allen. When the English writer Philip Mason arrived in Hyderabad in 1946 to tutor the nizam's grandchildren, he could hardly believe the level of denial around the palace. 'It was like the spring of 1789 at Versailles,' he wrote in his autobiography, *A Shaft of Sunlight* (1978).

Yet they were only a year away from the first Constituent Assembly, at which 2,000 princes and politicians from all over India would sit in their parliamentary seats and listen as India's future prime minister, Jawaharlal Nehru, made his historic pronouncement: 'At the stroke of the midnight hour, while the world sleeps, India will awake to life and freedom.' That joining of the clock's two hands signalled the beginning of a new India, but it also meant retirement for nearly 600 royals, some of whom could trace their lineage back to the god-sovereigns celebrated in ancient epic poems like the *Mahabharata* and the *Ramayana*. Those ex-warriors turned idlers, reviled by Lord Curzon and spoiled like grandchildren by Queen Victoria, were the last representatives of a world that had gone unchanged for centuries, if not millennia.

If the change seemed unavoidable, it was because the Second World War had left Great Britain with crippling debts, stripping the British of the resources needed to maintain their imperial network.

In the India of the 1940s, the nationalist push for independence gained enormous momentum under the direction of Gandhi, Nehru and the Muslim leader Muhammad Ali Jinnah. And the Indians who had honoured their duty, fighting alongside the Allies in Europe and Asia, were now demanding their rightful reward. Even Roosevelt understood that you couldn't ask a people to fight for the freedom and democracy of others while at the same time renouncing their own.

When leaving India became the inevitable reality, Lord Mountbatten was called upon as the last viceroy to manage a complex and hasty transition. In order to convince the princes to accede to the new arrangement calling for the creation of two states – India for the Hindu majority, Pakistan for Muslims – Mountbatten deployed every ounce of his diplomatic charm, offering seemingly unassailable guarantees, since they would be inscribed in the constitution. In exchange for ceding their titles and dominions, the princes would enjoy a gilded bourgeois life: tax-free stipends equal to 10 per cent of their former state's revenue; free health care for life; free electricity; funerals with military honours; and qualified immunity from civil prosecution – the very privileges that had allowed Bubbles and her husband Bilkha to float 'like feathers' for twenty-five years without a thought for the future.

Of course, not everyone trusted the viceroy's promises. Many scrambled to move their jewels abroad, drawing perhaps too little distinction between the jewels they owned and those that belonged to the Crown. The Maharaja of Indore tried sending his diamonds to America via Pakistan using his aide-de-camp's private jet. The Maharaja of Baroda was forced to give back emeralds and diamonds that had already set sail for Europe, and to return one particularly precious necklace to India that featured three rows of diamonds the size of olives, at the centre of which glimmered the famous 128-carat Star of the South. It is the necklace the maharani wears in Henri Cartier-Bresson's unforgettable photograph, which shows her with a strip of white organza draped over her thick head of dark hair as she selects jewels for her husband's birthday celebrations.

But convincing the princes to accede was no easy task, not even for a master in the art of persuasion like Lord Mountbatten. Many tried to negotiate their way into retaining power, not realising that without the umbrella of the British Empire an autonomous India would eat them alive. 'Do you mean I can do as I like?' the Nizam of Hyderabad blurted through his laughter when they told him that the English would be pulling out.

When the viceroy asked the princes to sign the Instrument of Accession – the legal document enabling them to choose which state, India or Pakistan, would absorb their dominions at Partition – a few dragged out the process and others resorted to dramatic gestures. At the moment of signing, the Maharaja of Jodphur pulled out a revolver and threatened Deputy Prime Minister Sardar Patel's secretary, saying he'd 'shoot him down like a dog if he betrayed the starving people of Jodhpur'. The Maharaja of Kashmir, who was Hindu but whose subjects were majority-Muslim, chose for his state to be annexed by India, sparking a controversy that to this day poses a serious threat to the subcontinent.

Others, meanwhile, treated the matter with haughty indifference. 'My father was the very last to give Mountbatten his signature,' the descendant of a great dynasty in Madhya Pradesh, Richard Holkar, told me, sitting in a cosy restaurant near the Parc Monceau in Paris. Pale-skinned, with cheeks flushed from the cold, and blue eyes inherited from his American mother, the son of Indore's last maharaja – the slender and supremely elegant Yashwant Rao Holkar, who sported the world's most coveted teardrop diamonds on his chest, was a patron of the arts who commissioned three sublime sculptures from Brâncuși (in the celebrated *Bird in Space* series) for a meditation temple to be built in India, and who had a Bauhaus-style palace erected in Indore – arrived at our meeting with a shopping trolley, since he needed to stop by the market after lunch. 'Father put that document in an envelope and sent it by post,' he told me with an amused smile, as he forked a slice of ham. 'He never could stand the English. If it were up to him, I think, he would have chosen to be American.'

Between August 1947 and the beginning of 1948, the migration of Muslims to Pakistan and Hindus and Sikhs to India produced more than fifteen million refugees. It's estimated that nearly two million died in the chaos. Now that Parisians no longer had to hide to listen to the news of *Ici Londres* (*This is London*), the BBC wartime broadcasts meant to counter German propaganda in occupied Europe, Amrit Kaur would certainly have been up to date on the bloodbath in India generated by the massive, two-way exodus that followed the euphoria of Independence.

In an interview with Charles Allen for *Lives of the Indian Princes*, Brigadier Sukhjit Singh of Kapurthala – grandson of Jagatjit and first cousin of Bubbles – who had a distinguished military career, described the situation in Kapurthala in 1947 as a catastrophe which demolished the principle of religious tolerance that his grandfather held so close to his heart, respecting the tradition of Sikhism's founder Guru Nanak.

The orderly streets with their little French-style villas that had delighted the maharaja's guests in the 1930s became the backdrop in a theatre of war: 'The whole world seemed to have gone completely crazy. The entire genesis of the problem in Kapurthala was from the refugees who came in, who having lost everything had nothing further to lose. They had no feelings for the state, therefore they had no compunction or hesitation about spreading that madness. Once the trouble spread it was really difficult to control, but luckily, because of the tremendous amity between the religions that had existed traditionally, we were spared the worst of the holocaust. We had one or two bad incidents, but these were nothing compared to what happened elsewhere in the Punjab where families were wiped out by villages.' Not far from Kapurthala, the Maharaja of Patiala set up an immense kitchen to assuage the hunger of 60,000 refugees and managed to hide 25,000 Muslims in a fort while they awaited transport from convoys. But the memory of tree branches black with vultures and ditches filled with corpses would haunt Patiala for years to come.

Because of its geographic location, straddling Pakistan and India, Punjab found itself in the most dramatic situation, flooded with millions of famished refugees whose epidemic-spreading passage provoked massacres, compulsory conversions, fires and rape. Seventy-five thousand women were victims of sexual violence. Among them, many were left disfigured and dismembered. The refugee-filled trains were targets of attack, some so frequently that they reached their destinations as long funeral wagons dripping with blood. When at last the violence came to an end, nothing was the same any more. Not a single Muslim would remain in Kapurthala, where Jagatjit Singh had built them a magnificent mosque. And no more than 1,000 Sikhs and Hindus would stay in Lahore, of the more than half a million who were living there when Bubbles and her brother had studied and played badminton at their elite boarding school.

Even Mandi was thrown into disarray, and the violence there affected some who were very close to Amrit's family. In the darkest days of Partition, her husband Joginder had to save a young Austrian named Vickie Noon from certain death. The woman's husband, the wealthy Muslim and future prime minister of Pakistan, Sir Feroz Khan Noon, was already in Lahore when the chaos broke out, and she, back in Kullu, was left to fend for herself after their servants had fled. Just as Lina Bilkha's grandfather, concealed in a burka, had been forced to bid goodbye to everything he possessed, a man came to warn Vickie Noon that they'd be setting fire to her house that night.

Vickie clung to a rifle she had no idea how to use and, when dark fell, stationed herself at a window, through which she could see the torches growing nearer as they set fire to neighbours' homes. All that saved her was an unexpected rain, which came just before midnight, clearing out the valley and extinguishing the flames. At dawn she managed to flee to Mandi, where she took refuge in her husband's friend's – the raja's – palace.

I thought of the story Bubbles had told me, about how the summer and autumn of 1947 had been a terrible period in her life – confined to bed during a difficult pregnancy in Gujarat, with no way of communicating with her family, whom she desperately missed, and news of the massacres pouring in from Punjab. At least her isolation had spared her the anguish of knowing that a band of Sikhs had threatened to abduct her brothers if Joginder Sen refused to hand over Vickie Noon. To resolve the crisis, the raja relied on an old trick: he sent the Rolls-Royce out with the shades pulled down, as if someone were hiding inside. While the Sikhs were busy pursuing the royal automobile, the young Austrian was able to escape in another car, dressed up as an Indian, her face darkened with shoe polish.

In those days, even the Donald sisters, Hilary and Barbara – who'd preserved the memory of the golden age of settlers in the Upper Beas Valley – were alerted by refugees from Lahore that the old could no longer keep the young at bay, and their house would be burned because they'd taken in Muslims. This time the aggressors were Hindu, not Sikh. 'All our servants left except the old sweeper and we thought the best way to protect ourselves was to take some of the calves indoors, then we knew the Hindus wouldn't burn the house down,' Hilary told Penelope Chetwode. After six days and six nights on watch, clutching rifles that, unlike Vickie Noon, they knew perfectly well how to use, their Muslim guests advised the Donald sisters to flee and seek protection at a police station.

Not long after, thirty armed men entered their property. The sisters approached them, fearing the end. But the men had different plans: 'Miss Sahib, we've come to protect you: there are a lot of bad men about. We will sit on your lawn from dusk till dawn and we will look after you and let no one near your house. We do not like to see our friends insulted.' This act of loyalty and chivalry saved the two women, but the Muslims they'd taken in faced an atrocious end. Split into two groups, some were tossed into a ravine and others were murdered by the police. 'The police were just as bad as anyone else during the troubles. Up here they were all Hindus. They were mad, absolutely mad – and in Muslim centres it was the other way round, the Hindus were massacred by the Muslims,' Barbara Donald lamented.

It was the end of the Raj, and it was also the end of a world that had founded its identity on the anxiety generated by two global conflicts. A few weeks later, in Naggar, Nicholas Roerich died, in the white-painted chalet where Colonel Rennick had spent his days as a hedonist philanderer and Amrit as a young and unhappy new mother. Roerich's ashes were scattered on a slope facing the purple peaks of the Himalayas, to which he'd dedicated 7,000 paintings, and his name was inscribed in Hindi on a stela that can still be found at the foot of the garden.

A month and a half later, Mohandas Karamchand Gandhi, the man who'd brought liberation to India through his message of non-violence, was shot three times and killed by a fanatical Hindu in New Delhi.

All of this fuelled my search for further texts and testimonies, each with its place in a historical framework I thought I knew, if only in broad strokes. But I was wrong: nothing could prepare me for the appalling level of barbarity displayed in the violence carried out against women in India. The Indian-born American journalist

Nisid Hajari, in his account of Partition, *Midnight's Furies* (2015), tells of how the English soldiers and reporters who'd witnessed the Nazi horrors in Europe saw the cruelty in India reach even higher levels than it had in Hitler's concentration camps: breasts chopped off pregnant women, stomachs sliced open to remove foetuses, newborns roasted on a spit. The streets of Calcutta 'resembled Buchenwald', wrote Margaret Bourke-White – no mere superficial claim, coming from a photojournalist who'd witnessed that concentration camp's liberation by the American army in 1945. 'The comparison with the death camps is not so far-fetched as it may seem,' William Dalrymple reflected, taking stock of the tragedy in a 2015 *New Yorker* piece. 'Partition is central to modern identity in the Indian subcontinent, as the Holocaust is to identity among Jews, branded painfully on to the regional consciousness by memories of almost unimaginable violence.'

This devastating wave of violence had therefore just subsided when, in 1948, the Maharaja of Kapurthala was forced to celebrate

India's Partition, 1947.

the final jubilee of his seventy-year reign in private – out of respect for the deep sense of grief that had swept over India after Gandhi's death, and for once to avoid offending a suffering population with yet another ostentatious display of his wealth. Though this didn't stop him from rallying his European friends. The ever-present André de Fouquières arrived by plane in Bombay with Denis, son of the writer Arthur Conan Doyle, and his wife, Princess Mdivani. In Bombay, the three found the city overrun by a throng in mourning. 'The famous Taj Mahal, that immense Tower of Babel whose extravagant cosmopolitanism has been the subject of reporters, is full,' the Frenchman griped. 'I'm renting, by recommendation, not a room but a bed, in a common area shared with two Englishmen and one American – the latter of whom capable of tumultuous snoring!' At the hotel restaurant he'd have to live with yet another limitation: no champagne or alcohol out of respect for the Mahatma's memory.

The account that de Fouquières left us of Jagatjit Singh's final jubilee reads as if it were written by a traveller who, on arriving in Robespierre's France, bothered only to note the fine combing of the Tuileries flower beds and the elegance of any Parisians left roaming the faubourgs with heads still attached to their necks. 'On my arrival in Kapurthala, the maharaja, whose face, beneath a pink turban, I find to be at once sweet and vigorous, speaks to me of France, of its tribulations, asks me for news of his dear Paris, his friends. One hundred questions flock to his lips in order to revive some inkling of our country, which he's not been able to see since 1939, to learn what has become of our intellectual and artistic life, whose evolution he's always followed carefully.'

Three hundred guests attended the jubilee, each accompanied by a personal attaché. Unwavering in his admiration of extravagance, de Fouquières looked past the massacres and turned his attention to birdsong. 'The aviaries remind me of those the maharaja once had in the Bois de Boulogne. Here there are parakeets dressed for the party, Himalayan bluetails, parrots from Brazil – one of which squawks: *Vive la France!* Further off, white peacocks, pink flamingos, some storks, some black ibises, some ostriches, a few silky ducks, a few golden pheasants – and tanks filled with goldfish from China.'

In the royal palace, he reserved the bulk of his admiration for certain risqué frescoes depicting 'Nothing but nudes, of the most voluptuous sort'. When an unplanned outing to attend a commemoration for Gandhi offered the maharaja the chance to introduce his aristocratic friend to Pandit Nehru, the prime minister of India, with a priceless sense of humour that completely escaped the Parisian, complimented de Fouquières on his French.

'*Voici le jour du Jubilé,*' he rejoiced in his memoir. 'Durbar Hall is aglitter with lights. Lunch is served with all the pomp of a Grand Siècle reception at Versailles. On immense tables, priceless silverware rests beside baskets of fruit in warm colours. Fifty servants carry out their duties impeccably. All wear a long, bleu-du-roi tunic with a silver belt and pink turban. His Highness presides, an emerald and diamond *sarpech* on his turban. Emeralds and diamonds on Princess Sita's sari as well, an incomparable set that had caused a sensation in Paris.'

A few days later, the maharaja would hold another reception for Lord and Lady Mountbatten. It would be the last visit to Kapurthala for the viceroy who'd made such a catastrophic blunder of the transition between the end of the British Empire and the birth of India's independence.

How different, I thought, reading the Frenchman's sugary descriptions, from the account left to us by Brinda of Kapurthala, who returned home from the war to find the state of which she would no longer be queen in ruins. 'The terrible famine after the war had brought devastation and disease to my country. My small garden was gone, dried up and run over with weeds. The house was dilapidated and the servants had fled to Pakistan. The surrounding villages were empty and desolate – it was almost as though an earthquake had destroyed the country.'

Even the maharaja's allure was now just a memory. 'My father-in-law seemed old and sick. I wanted to discuss the dreadful conditions in Kapurthala but he was too ill to be rational. The maharaja was living in the past: he could only speak of the good days. As I looked into his exhausted, lined face, I could see the pallor of death beginning to creep over his features. He babbled incessantly about returning to Europe and America and made plans for the years ahead as if he expected to live forever.'

Jagatjit Singh would die soon afterwards, on 19 June 1949, of pneumonia, in a room at Bombay's Taj Mahal Hotel while waiting to embark on one last trip to Europe. I couldn't help but think back to his grandfather, Randhir Singh, who'd returned to Bombay in a coffin while trying to get to Queen Victoria's England.

The funeral ceremony in Kapurthala would attract an enormous crowd, and the entire state would mourn.

All of this seemed to line up with what I'd come to expect of their three personalities, with which by then I'd become familiar: Bubbles' cousin Brigadier Sukhjit Singh's lucidity in the face of Kapurthala's crisis; de Fouquières' frivolity as the unapologetic socialite he was; and Brinda's despair on returning home, alone and humiliated, after Paramjit Singh had left her for a Folies Bergère dancer. And yet I was still struck by a profound sense of melancholy, knowing that neither Brinda, nor Jagatjit Singh, nor even André de Fouquières – the man who'd praised young Amrit's charm on her wedding day – had spared a single word for the maharaja's daughter, who was then living out her last days in London, far from her family.

The news on 8 November 1948, that Amrit Kaur of Mandi, at the age of forty-four, was dying of cancer at a home in Kensington under the care of Louise Hermesch, seems to have caught the attention only of the English newspapers, who carried the story in their evening edition, with photos portraying the princess at the height of her splendour. The rani who'd spoken out for women's rights long before Gandhi understood the importance of woman's emancipation, who'd rebelled against her patriarchal family and who'd paid the highest of prices for her freedom left all her jewellery to her daughter Bubbles, with an entreaty to sell as much as was needed to pay her debts, and requested that she be cremated in an orange sari embroidered with gold.

This last wish set the scene for a minor comedy, since no one at the funeral home knew how to drape a sari. As a consequence, one very embarrassed Mr Kenyon, of Messrs Kenyon and Kenyon Undertakers, left promptly for the Indian embassy to ask for clarification. There he was addressed to the embassy's cultural attaché, the journalist and writer Khushwant Singh, who found it totally appropriate to welcome him with a vulgar joke about being an expert on helping women to take their saris off, not tying them on.

# The Most Beautiful Job in the World

'. . . At a certain point, a switch flipped. And that switch flipped in 1911. No English ruler had ever set foot in India. And now here come George V and Queen Mary. And there's the famous Delhi Durbar of 1911, when all of the princes, in full regalia, present themselves to their new emperor. There were the submissive ones and the less submissive ones. The Maharaja of Alwar came and went in under a second; the Maharaja of Baroda gave half a bow, turned on his heel, and walked away with his back to the emperor; the Begum of Bhopal – India's only female head of state – had her face completely covered and never even glanced at them. And what happened? Imagine what was going through the head of a jeweller like Jacques Cartier in that moment . . .'

Addressing a remarkably crowded auditorium was Olaf Van Cleef, whom the organisers of the lecture series around the 'Joyaux: Des Grands Moghols aux Maharajahs' exhibition had introduced to the French audience as 'artist, traveller, great connoisseur of India and of jewellery'. It was May 2017, and outside the auditorium, in another corner of that immense glass and iron ship washed up by the Seine that is the Grand Palais, tourists and Parisians were lining up to see a jewellery exhibition: the display of Sheikh Abdulla bin Mohammed bin Saud Al Thani's collection, a treasure amassed by a cousin of the Emir of Qatar, where, among the diamond-studded *sarpechs* and the ruby-and-emerald-winged mythological birds, I found a few pieces owned by the Kapurthalas, such as the peacock brooch that Jagatjit Singh had acquired from Mellerio in 1905 and the half-moon-shaped emerald that, five years later, was said to have made its way from an elephant's wrinkled forehead to the pale, smooth forehead of the young Anita Delgado.

The 'Joyaux' exhibition proved a success, and a chance to admire the height of exoticism combined with the height of jewellery craft – even if for many of those Moghul-inspired *bijoux* Paris was, in truth, a homecoming. Sheikh Al Thani had been able to corral the Cartier choker, with six rows of cabochon rubies, designed for one of the maharanis of Patiala; Emperor Babur's pink diamond, which the Persian conquistador Nader Shah had claimed as war booty in the eighteenth century; the olive-shaped sapphire that the Maharaja of Indore had worn around his neck in one of the whimsical, dressing-gown-clad portraits that Man Ray had taken of him in the 1920s. Nor did his collection lack its share of striking, octagonal emeralds, flat as sheets of glass and engraved with floral patterns and verses from the Koran. Seeing them there, side by side, it was 'all a whirl of lights', as André de Fouquières put it. And yet, so powerful was their impact in their glittering glass cases that it was hard to see them for what they actually were. As if all that lustre had made them unreal.

'. . . Indian princes would come to Paris, drop their stones off with jewellers, choose their designs, and then leave for the Riviera and pick them up a year later, when they passed back through. The *maison* where I worked had made 100 pieces for the Maharaja of Patiala alone, who had four wives and hundreds of concubines. The trick was to preserve the Eastern style, but to lighten the metal and give it a certain harmony.'

Olaf Van Cleef was a reservoir of knowledge about French gold-smithery, and a seasoned lecturer. He had a face that radiated good cheer, bright-blue eyes, a wicked sense of humour and a quiver of anecdotes that made him a crowd pleaser. That afternoon he'd started things off by speaking of none other than Jagatjit Singh of Kapurthala, ridiculing certain of his delusions of grandeur, based on the fact that, in his view, the maharaja was 'a bit short' without his turban.

He then moved on to other princes, while spectacular photographs scrolled past on the screen behind him. 'The Aga Khan was the first for whom we began mixing blue and green in Paris, which is to say, adding in sapphires. You must know that sapphires were used infrequently in India, since it was believed they brought bad luck. Even the acquisition, when it came to sapphires, was done differently. What I mean is that if you were buying a sapphire, you'd then have to sleep . . . If your dream wasn't bad, you paid up. But if you did have a bad dream, you'd give it back. But you go tell Van Cleef about it!' The audience laughed.

'. . . For an order from the Maharaja of Kashmir I had to fill out a form. When I asked him his profession, he replied: "King". And the maharani's profession? "Nothing!".' And Van Cleef leaned into the *r* of that '*Rien!*', which went rolling to the back of the room, gathering more laughter along the way. '. . . The Duchess of Windsor had prominent collarbones, and it drove her crazy. So she went to see Jeanne Toussaint, who was a shrewd psychologist in addition to being Cartier's great creative director, and she had necklaces made for the express purpose of covering them up.' Meanwhile, behind him flashed images of jaw-dropping pieces such as the French heiress Daisy Fellowes' *Collier Hindou*; Wallis Simpson's flamingo brooch; the Patiala Necklace with its cascade of 2,930 diamonds, designed and made by the House of Cartier in 1928.

At the end of the conference, I approached him about setting up a time to speak. And a week later, following his directions, I found myself standing on a street in the pouring rain, in a rundown neighbourhood that seemed to have little to do with a surname like Van Cleef. Waiting outside a grey 1960s apartment building, I was certain I had the wrong address. Not so. Olaf Van Cleef came out to greet me and led me towards a tiny ground-floor apartment that looked out on to a minuscule tropical garden, which he noted with pride. And rather than join me in the living room, where he'd later show me his artwork – *haute Kitsch* portraits of Indian divinities, dotted with fragments of precious stones – he invited me to sit with him in the kitchen: not at a table, which didn't exist, but side by side, at a narrow white formica counter facing the wall.

'So tell me, then, what brings you here,' he said, handing me a cup of coffee.

I filled him in on my research, and on the obstacles I'd faced in trying to piece together the story of Amrit Kaur of Kapurthala and Mandi – explaining to him, meanwhile, that I attributed those difficulties to the fact that she'd fallen in love with a woman and was made a persona non grata. But he interrupted me right away.

'In India, maybe. But not in Paris. In Paris the Kapurthalas knew everyone, and were welcomed everywhere. In the upper class, when you're a princess or a baroness, *ca se passe très vite*, do you follow?'

I followed.

'It's the middle class that won't accept you,' and he laughed with those blue eyes the colour of Wedgwood porcelain.

'In any case, yes. I've heard about this woman's jewellery, and I can tell you exactly when. One day, many years ago, I was flying first-class back from India – and when you fly first-class, as you know, you run into important people – and I found myself sitting next to a well-known gem dealer, an elderly man who worked between Paris and Bombay. We got to talking business and, at a certain point, he bragged to me, "You know, I sold the Kapurthalas' pearls."

'He then told me how, at the war's outset, a fair number of Indian jewels and detached stones had passed through his hands, as well as a few flat, octagonal emeralds, I believe. Including a spectacular pearl necklace. He was interested, naturally, but only on the condition that he could meet the seller. And into his office walked a dark-skinned woman, which was a rare sight those days in Paris. The woman introduced herself as Madame Singh – the most common Sikh name – and only later did he discover that this was the Maharaja of Kapurthala's daughter. She explained that she wasn't selling those pearls for herself, but to help a Jewish friend. This would have been around 1939 or 1940.'

'Wasn't that a bit soon?' I asked, sceptical. The deportations didn't begin until 1942.

'Absolutely not. Many Jews began to leave as early as '37. Germain Seligmann, for example, who owned half of the place Vendôme, was already in New York in '39.'

The peerless Olaf Van Cleef, collector of gemstone histories: who would have imagined that the key to the mystery of Amrit Kaur's jewels would be sitting in an apartment near the Stalingrad metro station? Now all I needed was the name of the dealer who'd bought the necklace and perhaps the other jewels. But Van Cleef no longer remembered.

'I'm sorry, I've completely forgotten. It happened so long ago. I do remember, though, that his office was on the rue La Fayette.'

'His boutique, you mean?'

'No, no. One of those stores on the first floor, you know, with the security doors that go *clack-clack*.'

After this tale, while he was looking for a book to show me something, I asked what exactly it was he'd done before retiring to paint. And Mr Van Cleef, who bore one of the most recognisable names in international jewellery, replied with a spark of joy in his eyes, catching me off guard, 'I was a Cartier salesman for thirty-three years. The best job in the world.' Because he wasn't *exactly* a descendant of the Van Cleefs of jewellery fame, he explained, although he was careful to point out that the great Renée Puissant, who had led the Maison Van Cleef in the 1930s, was his grandfather's distant cousin.

'Do you know Renée's story? She was the daughter of an Arpels and a Van Cleef. She knew everyone in France.'

I shook my head.

'She committed suicide, or else they killed her, in 1942.'

'Are you telling me the Van Cleefs are Jewish?'

'*Bien sûr!*' he exclaimed, with an enthusiasm that bordered on mockery.

In 1970, at twenty years old, he said, he showed up looking for work at the Van Cleef boutique at the place Vendôme, and the first thing they wanted to know was whether he was of Jewish descent. He answered no, because his parents had kept it hidden from him, despite the fact that, or perhaps because, his grandfather had died at Auschwitz. In any case, he didn't get the job.

'When the Germans arrived, Renée Puissant thought she'd be protected by Josée Laval – daughter of the Vichy government's prime minister, Pierre Laval. So she took up residence in Vichy, where Van Cleef had a boutique in a hotel. Then, in November 1942, the Germans entered Vichy, and one December morning she was found dead – fallen from a window. No one knows if someone pushed her. In any case: suicide or homicide. The story I heard was that she was supporting the Resistance by buying jewellery. During the war there was a big jewellery market for supporting the Resistance . . .'

I must have raised an eyebrow, because he felt the need to double down: 'There was an *enormous* market for supporting the Resistance. And there were also many informants,' he conceded, meeting me in the middle, 'and when the Jews were deported and their houses raided, their jewellery went up for auction. Once the yellow stars were issued, in 1942, it was sell, sell, sell. And the shelters were risky places, because everyone knew that when the anti-aircraft alarms sounded people would come running with all their most valuable items. I remember one story of an Indian princess who showed up at the shelter with her hands all blue, because she'd dipped her rings in ink before she'd left. To protect them: that way no one would touch them. Who knows, maybe it was this Amrit Kaur of yours. It's true, jewellery in those days was *un marchepied pour se sauver la vie*' – a stepping stone to save your life. He then sealed things off with one of his strident '*Trrrès important!*'

As the rainstorm, so in tune with his tropical garden, seemed finally to let up, we looked at a few photo albums together and reminisced about those dark years. And it was then, speaking of his job, that he said, 'In the world of the great jewellers, you'd now and then run into an old dealer and the first thing he'd tell you was, "What *didn't* we see during the war!" Because in those years you'd come across octagonal emeralds, enormous pearls, impossible diamonds . . . You see, it was a very particular era. It was a treasure hunt in Paris, a lottery . . . you lived in fear of being robbed . . .'

Then he must have remembered the reason I'd come. 'It's strange, this story you're telling me about the Rani of Mandi, since it reminds me of those old gentlemen who'd come to me at Cartier with jewels they'd bought during the war from who knows whom, or else had received as a gift in return for offering someone protection. Yes, in my thirty-three years at Cartier I saw plenty of them . . . I told you, being a *vendeur* in a place like that is the most beautiful job in the world, you're not stuck in management, you're out meeting some-one new every day, you're travelling . . .

'The first thing someone buys when they get rich is jewellery, but jewellery is the first thing they sell when they go broke. So there's this whole group of bizarre people out there who've bought something and want to resell it, or who've been gifted a jewel and bring it to you after who knows how long . . . Believe me: it was thirty years of heaven for me. It's the school of life, really, the torment of luck, the Tantalus torment when luck abandons you. You get people who have everything and want just a little something more, but typically you get people who have nothing and think they need a big necklace to earn their badge of nobility. And it's astounding. You have to get used to it . . .'

And then, just when I was thinking it was time to leave him there with his portraits of Krishna and make my way back home, he offered me his take on the fate of Amrit 's jewels, in light of his experience.

'It won't be easy to track them down, if you ask me. Because they almost certainly weren't sold as is; most likely the stones were removed. That's the way it was done. Sure, maybe one day you'll find a little *broche* that was left untouched, but only because it wasn't important. Do you know why Mellerio's peacock brooch is still intact? Because it doesn't have big stones. In the Indian way of thinking, it was a trifle. It lacked the *arrrrrogance* of a maharani's jewellery.' I couldn't help but give a final chuckle at that rolling *r*. No one was more familiar with the dog and pony show of vanity and absurdity than this jewellery aficionado.

'And, as it were,' he said, casting me a sidelong glance, 'I personally wouldn't be surprised if it was Amrit Kaur's rival who sold her jewels. You did say the rani left after her husband took another wife, right? Perhaps this second wife of the Raja of Mandi posed as the first, used the excuse of helping the Jews as a cover, sold the jewellery, and pocketed the cash. *Vous voyez le couscous?*' (You see the dilemma?)

# From the Caucasus to the Caribbean

The man with whom Olaf Van Cleef had talked shop on a flight from Paris to Bombay in 1992 – one year before he died, as I'd discover – was named Jean Rosenthal.

I was able to track down the name thanks to Hans Nadelhoffer's book about the Maison Cartier, which described the Rosenthal firm on the rue La Fayette as the 'undisputed head of the pearl trade'. The address and the pearls lined up with Van Cleef's story, and so did the fact that Rosenthal had a presence in Bombay.

That this dashing, blue-eyed Frenchman – renowned gem dealer, partisan, Croix de Guerre recipient and Compagnon de la Libération – had been the one to purchase the Kapurthalas' pearls from Amrit Kaur struck me as both unexpected and completely logical. Unexpected because I assumed that, in the early days of the German occupation, it would be anything but business as usual for the scion of such a wealthy and conspicuous Jewish family. And logical because the Rosenthals had close connections with several Raj princes. As I'd discover after digging deeper into their history, hiding their own jewellery and the jewellery of their maharaja friends during the German round-ups and the chaos of Partition exposed them to a double Holocaust, in Europe and on the subcontinent.

The Rosenthals' story, the end of the Raj, and the Holocaust all intertwined in ways I'd never have imagined possible, had I not re-envisioned them through the eyes of Amrit Kaur. Her crocodile briefcase was still in San Diego, since I had no claim to it, and since my feeling was that it fell to the family to recover it. But even though I was eager to get back to Pune, and to Bubbles, to fill her in on all that I'd discovered in Maryland and California, learning more about the fate of the Rosenthals and the jewels that passed through their hands struck me as more than a simple curiosity. It was the closing of a circle.

From the perspective of his involvement in the struggle for France's liberation, Jean Rosenthal revealed himself to be a man worthy of his fame. He was born in Paris in 1906 and, after a brief stint in the French air force, managed to reach London in 1943, where he offered his services to de Gaulle and the French Liberation Army. It was then that he received the order to assist Richard Heslop, from the Special Operations Executive (SOE), on a pair of missions that would go down in Resistance history.

Here's how Heslop remembered him in his memoir, *Xavier*: 'Jean Rosenthal at this time was . . . just a little younger than I was, and only began to take control of the Rosenthal business of furs [*sic*] and jewellery from his famous father as the war started. His headquarters were in Paris, where he had a town house, but he was a playboy at heart and loved the beaches of southern France and the ski slopes of the Haute-Savoie, where he had yet another house. He was slim, with fair, almost gingery hair, wore glasses, and was always as perfectly dressed as you would expect of a leading French businessman-cum-playboy. He was full of energy, impetuous, and, at times, rash. But he had a great desire to rid France of Germans.'

Around the time that Amrit Kaur showed up at his office with the priceless necklace and perhaps other jewels, Jean Rosenthal had just begun working with his father, Léonard, founder of a dynasty of gem dealers who'd dominated the world's natural pearl market for forty years. With his brothers Victor and Adolphe, Léonard Rosenthal shared enormous prestige and equally enormous wealth. Then the war split them up. In 1941, Adolphe was murdered in Paris. Victor fled to India. And Léonard managed to escape to New York, where he started from scratch in an office in the Rockefeller Center. According to the *New York Times*, in 1914 his worth was valued at 415 million gold francs, the equivalent of more than a billion dollars – at least until the war came, and the Germans whisked it all away.

The Rosenthals were Tat Jews: a small community in the mountains of the northern Caucasus, a hardy people who lived their lives at 16,000 feet and spoke Russian and an Arabic dialect. In Léonard's birth city of Vladikavkaz, in North Ossetia, few children even went to elementary school. His father, Michel Rosenthal, who'd brought that brand-new surname back with him from a trip to Germany as a child, sold Baccarat crystal glasses, German porcelain and wheat. His first wife bore him eight children and died when Léonard, their firstborn, was twelve. Just three years later, the young Léonard left to seek his fortune in Paris, where, apart from a brief apprenticeship at the Baccarat headquarters on the rue du Paradis, he scraped together a living by selling a little bit of everything: umbrellas, cod-liver oil, puppies, and the occasional piece of jewellery snagged at the Drouot auctions or the pawnshop. He then enrolled in business school and brought his teenage brothers, Victor and Anatole, to Paris.

It makes perfect sense that Léonard's son Jean Rosenthal, chatting with his garrulous neighbour on that flight from Bombay to Paris, would have bragged of having purchased the Kapurthalas' pearls. No one knew better than the Rosenthals how to assess the value of those mother-of-pearl concretions whose rose, cream and yellow overtones create an iridescence known as the 'orient'. It was in 1901, in an auction room on the rue Drouot, that his father Léonard fell under the spell of his first pearl necklace. Sensing the commercial potential of those beads of light – which, according to Indian tradition, the god Krishna grew at the bottom of the sea for his daughter Pandaia to wear at her wedding – Léonard sent his brothers Victor, who was twenty at the time, and Anatole, who'd just turned seventeen, to buy them directly from the fishermen on Margarita Island, off the north-eastern coast of Venezuela, where the oyster beds and their promise of vast riches had attracted pirates and conquistadores since the days of Christopher Columbus.

The two Rosenthal brothers would spend four years on that Caribbean island. With their notable height, their bright-blue eyes, freckled skin and beards – Victor's a darker shade, Anatole's red – they must have been a sight to see amid the indigenous Guaiqueríes, who were short, dark-skinned, with straight black hair on their heads and none on their bodies. Victor, the more enterprising of the two, made friends with a Guaiquerí fisherman and fell in love with one of his sisters, a girl named Yumari. Their daughter's name, Blanca, must have been an homage to the local pearls.

Then, in two short years, everything changed. New instructions arrived from Paris. Léonard asked Victor to relocate to the Persian Gulf, where pearls of exceptional beauty and size had been harvested since the days of the Ancient Greeks. And he sent yet another brother, Adolphe, to Colombia in search of emeralds. Victor obeyed, but that didn't mean he'd forgotten about Blanca.

When the girl turned five, Victor wrote from Bahrain to his brother Anatole, still on Margarita Island: 'I must think of her future. I now have the means. She must learn her manners and receive a solid education. Her mother will never abandon her land, I no longer insist, but I want to raise this child. There's nothing to do on that Island, I don't want her to marry a fisherman, and no one gets married there anyway.' So he made a decision: he would send her to live in Samara, on the Volga – even the voyage from the Caribbean to that Russian city was hard for me to imagine – with a childless sister of his. This sister was named Amalia, and her husband was a veterinary surgeon who bought horses for the czar's army. She'd have the time to look after Blanca.

Victor's first years on the Bahrain archipelago were filled with hardship: the heat was more punishing than on Margarita; there was no fresh water, even for cooking and cleaning; and the smell of open oysters rotting in the sun was atrocious. It was also a challenge to overcome the distrust of the sheikhs, who rarely showed their most precious pearls to strangers.

Then there was the question of slaves. In Margarita, the Guaiquerí fishermen were natives who'd been enslaved by the conquistadores, but over time they'd managed to gain a certain degree of freedom. On the Bahrain archipelago, on the other hand, those descending to the depths of the oyster banks were mostly Black men – abducted as children from the coasts of East Africa and sent to work as soon as they were of age.

Slave traffic already existed on the Gulf, but in the first two decades of the twentieth century, with the increased demand for pearls, it grew out of all proportion. In 1929, an English naval officer estimated that there were 20,000 pearl-fishing slaves in Bahrain. Covered with scars from shark bites, scrapes from the coral and from stingrays, many of the men had ruptured eardrums, some had lost their vision, and the majority were sick with scurvy. But the pearls from Bahrain were the most beautiful in the world, maharajas in India had been collecting them for centuries, and no elegant woman on Fifth Avenue or in Mayfair would ever bother to wonder if the necklace adorning her bust had come at the price of another human being's blood.

When the Panic of 1907 broke out in the United States, and the New York Stock Exchange fell by over 50 per cent in just three weeks, credit institutions immediately withdrew the loans they'd given to Bombay pearl merchants, and many brokers went bankrupt. It was then that Léonard Rosenthal, with the aid of the Bloch Dreyfus bank, began investing aggressively in Bahrain, securing himself a global monopoly in natural pearls. With that venture sealed up, and a permanent agency established in Bombay to serve the Raj princes, the brothers were able to reunite in Paris as nabobs. 'Soon we'll be able to bring over everyone in our family who no longer wants to stay in Russia,' Victor wrote to his brother Anatole. 'It seems that

Rostov, Kiev, and Samara have become unlivable, with their czarists and their pogroms. For now Samara appears to have been spared, but I won't rest easy until we can all be together again . . .'

I'd gleaned this information from Léonard Rosenthal's autobiographical books, dictated to his secretary from bed after turning in early for the evening. But the true revelation was the memoir written by Blanca's daughter, Nicole Landau. *La Perle de Blanca* – or *Blanca's Pearl* – was published relatively recently in 2004, since Victor's granddaughter had to wait until Jean Rosenthal's death to print it – after the war, Rosenthal had become the head of the family and wouldn't tolerate anyone writing about them. *La Perle de Blanca* is a work of literary merit, lucid and sad. I immediately set about tracking down its author, but to my great sadness I learned from her publisher Gallimard that she'd died in 2006. Nevertheless, a month after receiving my letter, when I'd given up hoping for a response, Nicole Landau's son offered to pay me a visit.

Éric Landau, a middle-aged gentleman who would reveal himself to be both kind and wounded, arrived at rue du Bac with a dog in tow, an ivory-coloured Jack Russell to whom he'd given his grandmother Blanca's name. My own Ombra was no longer around, her heart had given out two years earlier, and the sight of that sweet little dog brought on a wave of nostalgia.

'The Rosenthals were the hardened sort, the kind of people who were left to fend for themselves at fourteen, fifteen years old. Victor had scars all over, tattoos all over. They were the brutal sort, who made their descendants suffer a great deal. All of them,' he began, taking no half-measures.

Petting his dog with a steady, rhythmic motion, he explained to me how the elder Rosenthal, Léonard, was the brains of the operation, and Victor the more adventurous one, with the closest ties to the Indian princes. Victor had enlisted in the Foreign Legion and fought for France in the First World War. He never married, but in addition to Blanca he'd had a son with his secretary. And on his death he left everything to the boy and nothing to his firstborn, 'because she was a woman', even though his Venezuelan daughter had been the apple of his eye.

As Landau spoke, I tried picturing the tattoo- and scar-covered Victor in the sumptuous *hôtel particulier* that he'd built in Neuilly-sur-Seine. In 1918, that *pierre de taille* town house, surrounded by a park where Victor kept his polo horses, opened its doors to Blanca, who had arrived from Siberia: a gorgeous, brown-skinned fifteen-year-old who spoke Russian. A few years later, when she married, Victor invited 2,000 people to a wedding celebration marked by caviar and the scent of patchouli. Even Jagatjit Singh, Amrit 's father, travelled from India to honour the half-Jewish, half-Guaiquerí bride. And so too came the Maharajas of Cooch Behar, Patiala and Baroda, and the Prince of Kashmir, the father of the bride's best friend; Victor managed his collection of precious gems, as well as his foreign investments.

Blanca's marriage to Nissim Abravanel, with his long fingers and velvety eyes, appears to have come at her own girlish insistence. But her spendthrift husband, who darted around Paris in a Hispano-Suiza with a liveried chauffeur, revealed himself to be a gambler with a taste for opium and blondes. After giving Blanca two sons and a daughter, Nicole, Nissim slipped off to Shanghai, though not empty-handed. 'When my grandmother's husband escaped to China with the jewels, my grandmother was forced to go to her father's office every week and ask for money,' Éric told me. Yet another tale of an unhappy marriage, betrayal and disappearing gems.

He continued his story by explaining that two 'catastrophes' in the 1920s had shifted the tide for the Rosenthals' business: the arrival of cultured pearls and the aftermath of the Russian Revolution. The former threw natural pearl dealers across the world into crisis, and the latter flooded the squares of London and Paris with an immense amount of jewellery all at once. It wasn't only fleeing

Russian aristocrats who wanted to sell: the Bolsheviks were in the mix too. Whenever the border patrol agents found a few diamonds or sapphires on a White Russian, they'd confiscate them and sell them at bargain prices. 'A luxuriant head of hair might serve to conceal jewels worth millions,' wrote Léonard in one of his books. 'Others who feared the rigours of persecution swallowed their diamonds, pearls, emeralds and rubies, leaving nature to return them to them. All great jewellers and dealers in gemstones knew Russian aristocrats and bourgeois who, before their eyes, threw open cases filled with magnificent jewels, saying, "Buy these, they're all that stands between me and starvation."'

Léonard Rosenthal decided it was time to diversify his investments. So he set about building the first *arcades* on the Champs-Élysées: arched passageways filled with stores, the antecedents of our modern-day shopping malls. In 1929, he financed a project out of his own pocket to transform Porte Maillot into a monumental port of entry into Paris, designed by Le Corbusier.

If Victor had built himself a *hôtel particulier* in Neuilly, with Chinese lacquer furniture and velvet tapestries, Léonard gave his own family an equally luxurious Paris residence. In a play entitled *Charm*, his daughter Rachel Rosenthal, who became a performance artist in the circle of Merce Cunningham and Robert Rauschenberg, recalled her childhood home: 'The walls were embossed dull silver lacquer, strewn about with a few Chagalls, some Monets, a couple of Pissarros, even a little Guardi . . . The salon itself, walls decorated on both sides by Jean Dunand, presented monkeys in the trees, ducks in a pond, flamingos on black ground, swans on gold ground . . .'

Dipping into philanthropy as well, Léonard financed technical schools for boys and girls, aided intellectuals such as Paul Léautaud and the Nobel Prize-winning scientist Jean Perrin, and even signed a cheque for Sergei Ėjsenštejn to make a short film entitled *Romance sentimentale*.

'Èjsenštejn?'

'That's a whole other story,' Éric Landau said, still rhythmically caressing his dog. Of course, I thought, leaning back in my chair. Outside, the wind was picking up.

'All those Russians who came running when the revolution broke out, they formed a tight-knit community in Paris, everyone leaning on each other for help. That's how Léonard met his second wife. She was a cabaret dancer who'd fled from the Bolsheviks, an absolutely sublime beauty. This community had its rich and its poor. The rich helped the poor. Not everyone was an entrepreneur or a great talent, some just wanted to drive a taxi. Every week they came to the office and we gave them money.'

But then came Black Thursday in 1929, and they fell like dominoes, one by one: banks, companies, fortunes. The Rosenthal business was liquidated.

'If the ascent had been dizzying, the fall was a nosedive,' wrote Nicole Landau. It wasn't just the jewellery that buyers abandoned – even if, in 1936, Victor Rosenthal still managed to produce a sword studded with 2,500 baguette-cut diamonds for the Maharaja of Kapurthala. The century's greatest financial disaster mangled everything, even the value of properties on the Champs-Élysées. It would take Jean Rosenthal's father, who owned twenty-six of them, ten years to recover. And when he finally did, in marched the black boots of the German army. Which was right around the time that Amrit Kaur of Mandi showed up on the rue La Fayette with her precious necklace.

I've often wondered – thinking not so much of the martyrs or the utterly ruined, but of the less fortunate human beings who lived in Europe during the first half of the twentieth century – where they found the strength to survive the horrors of two world wars, not to mention totalitarianism and genocide. The perspective on history offered by my investigation left no illusions about the increasing misery that awaited people like the Rosenthals: people who witnessed their own family's dissolution and destruction, who lost their emotional ties as well as their inheritances; who were forced to flee and start from scratch, and sometimes more than once.

The official sign that nothing would ever be the same again was the bullet that struck Adolphe Rosenthal in the temple, in the underground passageway of Porte Maillot, in September 1941. Adolphe the civil engineer, the gem dealer, had refused – much like his younger brother Anatole – to heed the coming danger. 'I was a soldier back in the First World War,' he said, 'I'm French and I studied at the Arts et Métiers. We've served France since the days of the First World War. Nothing can happen to us.'

And yet, three men dressed as policemen came to round him up that day and transport him, so they said, to a concentration camp. Then they shot him point-blank and tossed him from the speeding car. 'We never found out if it was the Germans or the French militia,' Éric Landau said. 'Shortly after, his daughter Micheline, who was sixteen years old, joined the Resistance with the Maquis de l'Ain, in and around Haute-Savoie. Which is where Jean Rosenthal later arrived.'

'What was he like?' I asked him.

'Tough, like the others,' he responded without hesitation. 'Very unfaithful. Very astute. Charming. And his physique – all the Rosenthal men were very tall, with freckles and magnificent blue eyes. Jean was the oldest of three brothers. He was a bit of a playboy: he did his fatherly duties, but he also liked to have fun. He married and then kept on with other women.'

In 1940, when Amrit Kaur stepped into his office on the rue La Fayette, Jean Rosenthal was therefore a jeweller with excellent contacts in India. Shortly thereafter, he would shed his French military uniform and leave Paris for London, where, following de Gaulle's orders, he parachuted several times into Ain, in order to evaluate and coordinate a network of partisans in unoccupied France.

Which is to say, just a few weeks before the swastika flew atop the Hôtel de Crillon, on the place de la Concorde, Amrit met not with any random jeweller, but with a young man who was poised to play a significant role in the history of the French Resistance. His partisan code name was Cantinier, while his superior, the English Colonel Richard Henslop, went by Xavier. Their most celebrated mission was the Battle of Glières, in 1944, which would become part of the myth of the Resistance, even though in reality it was a tragic failure in which hundreds of French fugitives and partisans who had taken refuge in the snowy Glières Plateau to escape deportation lost their lives. For this and other missions, General de Gaulle granted Jean Rosenthal the highest of honorary titles, Compagnon de la Libération.

His father Léonard, in the meantime, was making a new life for himself in New York, with the aid of a selective memory. I was astonished to find that in his autobiographical books – 'atrociously written', as Éric Landau put it, and not without reason – the old patriarch recounted his own successes while glossing over facts like the murder of his brother Adolphe in 1941, or the death of his sister Amalia in a concentration camp in 1944. Anatole Rosenthal, too, his dandyish brother who remained in Paris throughout the occupation, was arrested in a round-up at the hippodrome that same year and sent to his death at Auschwitz.

But the war didn't merely decimate the sprawling Rosenthal family. It also wiped out their emotional ties. After Léonard left for the United States with his 'sublime' Russian dancer, Jean and his father stopped speaking. Victor abandoned Blanca in Paris, leaving her to manage on her own with three young children, while he ran to the Maharaja of Kashmir's aid in India. And it was then, in a way no one could have foreseen, that the destinies of these Caucasian Jews and their Indian friends fused together in tragedy.

One day, according to Nicole Landau's memoir, after a covert meeting with Jean Rosenthal on the Champs-Élysées, Blanca returned home feeling deeply agitated. Her cousin had told her that time had run out: she needed to gather her children and flee. Blanca was forty years old at the time, about Amrit's age. Like Amrit she'd fought for women's rights, and like Amrit she was a beautiful woman whose skin colour would not go unnoticed in France. I wondered how she could have held out so long in Paris with a last name like Rosenthal and her married name, Abravanel.

She had certainly made some unlucky decisions. In the summer of 1942, after her German nanny disappeared overnight with no explanation, Blanca left in a hurry for the south, on the pretence that she was taking the children on holiday, and found a smuggler to help her cross the border between German-occupied France and Vichy. That day, Nicole had watched her prepare a picnic basket. Her mother had taken two enamel containers and filled them, one with butter and the other with lard. Then she'd pressed a number of emeralds, rubies and sapphires into both of them. I could hear Olaf Van Cleef's words in my ear about jewels in a time of crisis: *'Un marchepied pour se sauver la vie.'*

In the Pyrenees, at Puyoô station, German soldiers forced everyone off the train and ordered the men and boys to pull down their trousers. Blanca's two teenage sons were circumcised. Nevertheless she played the airhead, saying that she'd been adopted and even claiming that her husband was a Turk and a practising Muslim. When the Germans brought her to the Kommandantur in Salies-de-Béarn, a soldier rifled through her picnic basket, opening the enamel containers and passing a knife through the butter and lard. One by one the rubies, sapphires and emeralds rolled out. Observing the scene, Nicole's childish imagination drifted to the Count of Monte Cristo's treasure.

Blanca then turned to a female German auxiliary, claiming that her daughter was in urgent need of a lavatory, and once the door was closed began pulling multiple pouches of gems from the bun in her hair, from under her skirt, her bra, and threw them in the toilet, flushing twice. Nicole looked on as the Count of Monte Cristo's treasure disappeared down a septic tank.

The following day, the Germans brought them to the Saint-Palais internment camp in the Pyrenees, which in Nicole's words was a 'modest waiting room for the camps in Poland and Germany'. When Blanca's daughter returned there as an adult – she wanted to see what had become of those dreadful dormitories with a toilet in the centre – a young town official told her that there had never been an internment camp in Saint-Palais. That sudden slip of memory reminded me of Besançon and of the collective amnesia that seemed to have struck the witnesses I'd questioned about Frontstalag 142.

Blanca and her children were transferred to a prison in Biarritz, where she declared herself to be Victor's adopted daughter, a Venezuelan by birth, and baptised – Venezuela was a neutral country. When the embassy confirmed that she'd been born in Margarita and that she was indeed baptised, all four were allowed to re-enter Paris. But never again, they were warned, should they attempt to cross into unoccupied France.

There was a heartbreaking ending to this story. I found it almost hard to believe that the following summer, in 1943, Blanca boarded a first-class sleeper car with a few crocodile-leather suitcases, a hatbox and false papers and travelled to Cannes, where she was reunited with family members who were already in France. The best way to hide, she'd determined, was to travel as a rich woman. Her daughter Nicole took another train, under the care of friends.

Waiting for them in Cannes was Amalia Rosenthal, the adoptive mother who had raised Blanca in Russia. Throughout the summer the two women and young girl lived at the Hotel Windsor, a rooming house of sorts for those who'd fled Paris's most elegant neighbourhoods, where in the evenings a diaspora of non-practising Jews cooked Russian dishes in their own bathrooms.

But at summer's end the atmosphere changed and the residents began packing their bags. A Parisian messenger alerted them: Blanca had been reported. Under the new laws, her Venezuelan passport was no longer sufficient to protect her. She had to prepare her escape.

Blanca was the first to leave. Nicole, who was eleven at the time, followed behind her, travelling alone on a sleeper car. Blanca had insisted that it would be easier to hide in Paris, but her Aunt Amalia thought it better to meet a sister of hers in Lyons, where they could stay with her Aryan friends – pure-blooded Aryans, and therefore, according to her, 'untouchable'.

The morning after she'd brought Nicole to the train station, Amalia Rosenthal, sister of Léonard, Victor and Adolphe, and Blanca's adoptive mother, was arrested, deported to Drancy, and from there, on a sealed train, to Ravensbrück, where she met her death.

'Before leaving Paris,' Nicole wrote, 'her brother Victor had entrusted her with a small case of precious stones, half of which belonged to him, and the other half to one of his maharaja friends. The Maharaja of Jammu and Kashmir, I imagine. He was a dedicated collector of precious gems and emeralds, even though he'd been born among sapphires.' To help her arrange that heavy case in her luggage, Amalia enlisted the aid of her charming manicurist, who offered to accompany her the following day to the train for Lyons.

'Amalia accepted. The next day, the charming manicurist arrived in a car driven by her fiancé, but instead of approaching her, she got out of the car and ran off, pointing out Amalia to the driver.'

First they took the jewels; then they took Amalia Rosenthal.

In the meantime, Blanca and Nicole had managed to reach Paris. 'And Victor?' I wondered. Whatever happened to the tattoo- and scar-covered Russian Jew who'd chosen India as his second home?

Victor died in his bed, Éric Landau told me, the dog now sleeping in his lap: in Paris, and much later, having lost most, if not all, of his fortune.

But in 1947 he was in Srinagar, when Partition brought death and destruction to North India.

On the morning of 26 October, the Maharaja of Jammu and Kashmir signed Mountbatten's Instrument of Accession document, renouncing his sovereignty over Kashmir and choosing to annex his domains to India, in a move that set the ground for decades of territorial conflict with Pakistan. That night he got behind the wheel, at the head of a convoy of exiles. Beside him sat Victor Rosenthal, clutching a gun; in the back were two armed officers.

As they passed the Jammu palace, Victor heard the prince mutter, 'It's over. We've lost Kashmir.' Then he drove for a day and a night without saying another word.

# PART SIX
## Goodbyes

# A Last Visit to Pune

A few weeks after my meeting with Éric Landau, I rang up Bubbles. She greeted the sound of my voice with her usual, 'Helloooooo, when are you coming?' which by then had become the *ouverture* to all our conversations. 'Very soon,' I replied. I'd turned up a few documents and wanted to share my findings, I told her.

We agreed upon a date and then she filled me in on the latest family news. One of her beloved grandchildren, Priya, was getting married. And Tiny was soon returning from Chicago. Meanwhile, her vision had worsened, leaving her all but blind – a fact she shared with regret but not with sadness, as if she'd come to terms with it. Even so, after saying our goodbyes, I set aside the notes I was working on and went out to a store on the rue de Rennes to find her some Frank Sinatra and Dean Martin CDs. And, just to be safe, a little Nat King Cole and Elvis Presley. Even if she couldn't read any more, she could certainly still listen to the songs I knew she'd loved as a girl.

Thinking back on it now, I realise that by spending the morning figuring out just how much Bubbles would appreciate the tambourines and maracas in 'Bossa Nova Baby', I was trying to compensate for the anxiety I felt about the news I would be bringing her. At eighty-eight years old, Bubbles was a beloved mother, an adored grandmother, and a resigned widow. But she would also never cease being an orphan in pursuit of an elusive mother. Agreeing to accept, in the abstract, whatever results my research might produce was one thing. Facing the verdict was another.

★

'Well, Bubbles,' I said when I arrived at her home one January after-noon in 2017, settling into the same armchair where her husband, all those years before, had sat scanning the room in the stupor of illness. This time she greeted me in a long and mostly formless flower-print dress, though the simple white sandals peeking out from beneath the hem, on her, were the essence of chic.

'As you know, I'm here because I have news for you. I came to tell you that I found a briefcase that belonged to your mother.'

'Where did you find it?' she asked, getting straight to the point. The *how* did not interest her.

'In San Diego, California.'

'Aah.'

'Apparently she left it in Louise Hermesch's house, in 1938.'

'Must be the Louise I have met. Is she still alive?'

'No, she died in 1975, at the age of seventy-two.'

'Ooh . . .' This must have taken her by surprise. Quickly, she added, 'OK, OK,' inviting me to continue.

'Louise Hermesch sold her house in San Diego at the beginning of the war. For some reason, the housekeeper who removed her belongings kept this crocodile briefcase with your mother's mono-gram A.K.M. engraved in gold. Inside it there were photographs, letters and telegrams, some of which spoke of you.'

'Oh!'

'So I went to San Diego to meet a woman named Ginger Rosser, who has been holding on to the briefcase since it was found in a garage some years ago; and with her help, I made copies of all the documents. For you.'

'Oh, now . . . you know that I can't see . . . So just read them . . .' The briefcase itself was of no interest to her. She'd assumed, cor-rectly, that if I didn't have it with me it must still be in San Diego.

Bubbles settled into a corner of her blue-damask sofa, nearest the window that looked out on to the large Malabar chestnut; its fragrant flowers, she'd once told me, opened only after dark. Earlier, when she'd first welcomed me to her home, I noticed that she still glided through its familiar spaces with the same ease as before. The lone sign that she was now nearly blind was the bedroom door she'd forgotten to close, where her silver bed with the Bilkha coat of arms on the headboard had been left unmade.

Priya's wedding had been a couple of weeks earlier, and there'd been a constant stream of relatives coming in and out of the house, she told me, which had worn her out. And because she'd suffered a few asthma attacks at night, her two granddaughters had taken turns sleeping beside her, so she wouldn't be left alone. She'd argued that it wasn't necessary, but clearly she'd enjoyed their company. Now, however, it was just the two of us.

'All right,' I said, setting the folder I'd brought with me from Paris on my lap. The whole scene reminded me of our first encounter. 'I think I should start with the telegrams. Your mother seems to have kept all the telegrams she received when you were born. There were quite a few.'

This made her happy. 'They must be dated 12 December 1928 then . . .' she said, smiling. This too reminded me of our first meeting.

'I'm going to read to you just a couple of them, as the others are very similar. Here is the one she received from your grandfather. It is addressed "To Her Highness Rani Sahiba of Mandi, Rockwood, Simla". And it reads: "GLAD TO HEAR OF YOUR SAFE DELIVERY OF A DAUGHTER JOGIN LEAVING TONIGHT FOR SIMLA STRONGLY ADVISE YOU IN YOUR INTERESTS AND FOR MY SAKE BE AFFECTIONATE AND NICE TO HIM MUCH LOVE, FATHER."'

'Grandpa must have been worried because things were rocky . . .' she noted with a chuckle.

'So it appears. He was also giving her a strong warning not to embarrass him, don't you think? Your father's telegram in comparison was quite diplomatic. "HEARTY CONGRATULATIONS ON BIRTH OF DAUGHTER WISH SHE MAY LIVE LONG AND HAPPILY HOPE BOTH WELL ARRIVING TOMORROW, JOGINDER".' Lifting my gaze, I saw her sitting there completely still, arms folded over her chest. No comment.

'See how many?' I said, rustling the pages in my hands. 'This one is signed Betty and Tibu . . .'

'Betty was our nanny.'

'I know. Did you like her?'

'Yes. She was very strict but very nice. She was English, but maybe born in India.'

'Then there is one signed by a certain Wasir.'

'Wasir means Chief Minister.'

'And one by King George the Fifth.'

'Oh!'

At that point I moved on to Amrit Kaur's address book and read her a few names, but she didn't recognise a single one. The Harrod's bill, on the other hand – for the pyjamas her mother had bought her and her brother – elicited a giggle of satisfaction. There was a letter her grandfather had written to a woman by the name of Fairweather, about a picnic and tennis in Dalhousie, a fashionable mountain resort. And another from a man named Lionel, thanking Amrit for the enamel cigarette case and lighter that she'd given him, and sharing news of his wife, who was unwell.

Then the telephone rang and Bubbles asked if I'd like a coffee. While she ordered two from the mysterious voice on the other end of the line, a dog began barking rhythmically in the distance. The apartment was silent, as if all her neighbours had left on holiday. Outside the sun was shining, the air hot and motionless.

'The people you met in San Diego, were they cooperative?' she asked, turning back to me with a curiosity I took no note of at first.

'Very much so,' I reassured her.

'That's very nice.'

Meanwhile, I'd pulled a typewritten, hand-signed letter from my folder.

'This is from?'

'Betty.'

'My Betty.'

'Yes, your nanny Betty. It's dated almost two years after your mother left: 11 November 1935. "My dearest" – it reads – "this is my last for you from here as by the time you receive it I will be away . . . I did not want to go on leave until you returned, but as we have no idea as to when you will be back, my leave has been sanctioned as I am not fit enough to carry on with my work much longer." '

Betty wrote of her exhaustion, her shattered nerves, adding, 'I wrote and told you this and also asked you if I may go on leave but you have taken no notice of my letters and so I have been compelled to take leave before you write or arrive back . . .'

'So my mother did not reply to her . . .'

'Apparently not,' I confirmed, with reluctance. Then I went back to reading: ' "I am glad to say that Bubbles is quite well and perfectly happy and you have no need to worry about her. She has put on weight no end and is looking the picture of health. D.G. may she continue to keep fit and happy as she is now. It is going to be a terrible wrench for me to leave the children for two months, and I shall feel it very much. After eleven years in Mandi, it is more like my home I am leaving . . ." '

She then reassured her that she'd left her things in order. ' "All your boxes are properly locked and sealed with the seal you gave me. The boxes are in the godown in the Palace Annexe quite safe, protected from damp, so you need not worry about your things dear." '

For a few months, she wrote, she'd be staying with one of her brothers and would try to make herself useful in Quetta, in Balochistan, where an earthquake that year had killed tens of thousands.

' "You and the children will be much in my thoughts on the

twenty-fifth of December, the first away from the little darlings," ' I continued reading. ' "They will be in Lahore for Xmas so will have a very happy time, you may be sure. No more or else I will miss the mail . . . Tons of love and very many kisses to you dearest from Bubbles and self. Yours, Betty." '

As I read, I noticed out of the corner of my eye that Bubbles was listening with intense concentration. The mirth that had lit up her face when Betty mentioned how she was putting on more weight every day had given way to a state of thoughtful attention. For my part, I hoped she'd have time to take the letters in with calm. The next one was ridiculous, grotesque and vulgar, but could be very unsettling if interpreted literally. Which was the case, in my opinion.

'Here is another one, Bubbles. This one is in broken English. It's actually an anonymous letter, written to your mother by someone semi-literate, and it bears no date. It starts with a complaint against your father: "Oh Patriot Amrit Kamwar, we got foolish Raja," it says, and then continues: "You should not come with secretary. Public will fetch [*sic*] you are here after some months. Our raja is not a raja, he is a foolish man. He wants to take income tax!" '

This citizen of Mandi's outrage at having to pay taxes brought Bubbles' laughter back.

' "He wants to take one rupee a bigha land [2,990 square yards]!!" ' I picked back up, lightly mimicking the letter's tone. ' "He does not want to give civil posts to our graduates. Mandians are very pitiable. All castes are not happy with him, and not also with his ministry. His ministry is leading him on the wrong way. He is the puppet in the hands of donkey officers . . ." '

'Must have been some local.'

' ". . . Be careful. Take your Tikka Sahib . . ." '

'He means my older brother, Tibu.'

' ". . . otherwise he will be poisoned by new rani or stepmother. Make him as a public servant." ' Then, returning to his complaints of the raja, he concluded, ' "Public want to shoot him, and also his donkey officers such as Revenue, Engineer, Conservator, District Magistrate who has taken lands in Mandi state. All castes are unhappy. Mother sees the cases. Don't come otherwise you will be in danger." '

'I wonder who it could be . . .'

'What's interesting to me is that he writes that your mother had intended to come back to India. I'm sorry to say this, Bubbles, but I wonder if there is a grain of truth when he says that your brother Tibu was in danger, not having his mother to protect him from a stepmother who wished her own son could become raja in his place.'

'I didn't know any of this,' she said, dodging the question. 'We were too young and we were kept away from everything to do with Mummy. But this other mother he is talking about was very good to us . . . Very good to *me*,' she took care to remind me.

It was clear that those references to her stepmother were thorns in her side, so I changed the subject, instead describing the photograph of Amrit on the front lawn of Louise's home in San Diego. 'She looks young and absolutely lovely. She is in a sari with colourful flowers on a dark background, similar to the pattern of the dress you are wearing today. And she's holding a cigarette in her left hand.'

Then I started rifling through my papers again. '. . . Are you interested in Max Factor's remarks in Hollywood about how to treat your mother's oily skin?'

She shook her head, laughing.

'And here is a picture of two young children sitting under a Christmas tree. I have no idea who they could be.'

'If the boy is younger than the girl, it is Bebu and I. We always had a Christmas tree at home.'

'Oh. I had mistaken them for two little Brits, but now I see you could be right. The boy is wearing a shirt and a tie and is playing with a model sailing boat; and the girl is in a smock dress, with short curly hair parted on the side. She is holding two dolls. Both of them are too busy with their new toys to look into the camera . . .'

There was still one other letter I wanted to read. It was dated 4 February 1936, and was sent from Mouchin, in the north of France. It was written by one of Amrit's old boarding school friends: not the boarding school in Sussex that I knew of, but another, a convent in Jersey.

' *"Ma chère petite amie,"* ' I began reading, ' ". . . your kind letter, I assure you, gave me the greatest pleasure! . . . I hope with all my heart 1936 gives us a chance to meet up again; we will have so many things to say to each other, don't you think, Amrit dear?" '

As I read, a man wearing baggy trousers and slippers walked in carrying a tray with two coffee cups. Bubbles had him set the cups down on the end table beside her.

' "It's a pity that Washington is so far from here, because you really tempt me when you ask me to come to America!" ', I picked back up. ' "Take care that the gangsters do nothing to you, nor to your children if you have them there with you." '

She was tickled by the nod to Al Capone.

' ". . . You say that America is the safest country at the moment. Perhaps it's true, but Lindbergh doesn't want to stay there for the time being. In any case, I think that if war has to break out very soon, we'll have it first in France. So from that point of view you don't have to worry. I have wanted to write to you for quite some time, but for a while now I've been very tired and haven't had the strength to do anything, especially write! You know, dear friend, when one has a lot of worries, particularly in these times of crisis, it's hard to make money and I can assure you that my life is not always gay! However, things are now improving slightly and there is no point in making myself ill – on the contrary! Besides everyone's got problems and I see from your letter that you have your own, poor little thing! Why are your family bothering you, is it your brothers that are looking after you and annoying you? And how is your father getting on? I wonder if your husband isn't starting to regret what he did, and doesn't know how to get you back? You are right not wanting to hear anything, in the end they'll leave you in peace . . ." '

Bubbles interrupted me. 'I knew she didn't get along with the Kapurthala family . . . but the only time my father said something about Mummy was: "You think I didn't like your mother, but no, I was very fond of her." '

'Here the writer talks about old school friends and teachers,' I continued. 'She says she has met some of them again, and some of the nuns too. ". . . Anne de Verre asked me how you were getting on, for she could recall how 83 and 104 were often seen together, two good numbers!" '

'They called each other by number?!' Bubbles' face showed amusement and disbelief.

The rest of the letter related what had become of her old boarding school mates, and it dawned on me, reading it aloud for the first time, that there were really only two paths for those young women: either they became nuns or prisoners of an unhappy marriage. Anne de Verre took her vows and taught at a religious school in Brussels. So too did Anne de Sousberghe, though she joined a foreign mission. Another classmate, by the name of Remiette, married a rich uncle forty years her senior and burned through his fortune after he died; yet another, one Marie-Thérèse, chose the wrong man and suffered because her parents refused to see her any more. The letter ended on a nostalgic note. ' "As you know, they have very pleasant memories of you in Jersey. Remember how you used to post letters for me as you were going home, and the terrible dressing down Mother Marie-Madeleine gave me when she knew? I can assure you, I was very near to being expelled. I still get hot under the collar when I think about it, and yet it was the good old days; and as for you, how often we took delight in driving Mother Laure mad." '

The signature followed: ' "*Votre vieille 104.*" '

Up until that moment, Bubbles seemed to have been drinking in every word. But as soon as I mentioned the notebook I'd found in the briefcase, listing the things her mother had left behind in Mandi, her expression changed. I imagined these were the items Betty claimed to have safely stowed away.

'May I read you the list?'

'No, no, no, there was nothing in Mandi,' she protested. 'Not even in the trunks and suitcases she left in the godown. We opened them with my brother, much later, after my wedding, or maybe after she died. You can skip that part.'

'But what about the jewels? Didn't you want me to find out what happened to them? Here your mother wrote a list of the jewellery she had left in Mandi. It's five pages long . . .'

'*No.* Please don't read it to me. I find it upsetting.'

It was the first time I'd seen her upset. And upsetting her was, of course, the last thing I wanted to do.

So, to brighten her mood, I told her about the pearl necklace that Amrit had brought to Jean Rosenthal, declaring her wish to sell it in order to help a Jewish friend escape occupied France.

'So it's true . . .'

'I don't know, Bubbles,' I was forced to admit. I didn't want to foster any illusions, but I also didn't want to hide the fact that the answer to that question was probably more complicated.

'When I went to San Diego to look at the contents of your mother's briefcase, and matched that information with the documents I had seen in the British archives, I understood that when your mother left India in 1933, she had meant to stay away only six months.'

'Oh! . . . she was unhappy because he had married again.'

'Of course she was. She travelled to Europe with a lady-in-waiting who was to escort her everywhere. But one day in London this lady woke up to find your mother gone. Apparently, she had met two American women, and had gone to the United States with them . . .'

'I wonder who they were . . .' she said, almost in a whisper.

'This I can tell you. They were Louise Hermesch and her mother, Louise Goodhue.'

'Louise. The same one we knew. OK . . .'

'Louise Hermesch was an American heiress and a widow.'

'How did her father make his money?'

'It's not clear. Even his brother Bertram Goodhue, who was a famous architect, wondered about it in his letters. Anyway, he was in finance, but he also appears to have been on various diplomatic missions to Europe – France and the Vatican in particular. I suppose it didn't hurt that he was a cousin of the president's wife, Mrs Grace Goodhue Coolidge.'

'Was he a spy?'

I shrugged. 'Apparently in the 1920s he had lived for one year in France with his wife and Louise. So Louise too had had a French education. When they met, they must have struck a very strong alliance, I mean Louise and . . .'

'Mummy.'

'They got rid of your mother's lady-in-waiting and they ran away. I couldn't help thinking that they went to live their 1930s version of *Thelma & Louise* . . .'

'What is that?'

'*Thelma & Louise*? A film. It's a film about two best friends, brave and lovely women, who shake off the shackles of their relationships. They flee the violence of men, and the misogyny of the law, and they go on a wild road trip together. In the course of this journey across America, they get into all kinds of trouble, but they also discover the joy of freedom – and pay the price for it.'

I was trying to distract her and at the same time prepare her, so that she wouldn't be overwhelmed by what came next. So I spent a few minutes telling her about the stop I'd made on my way to San Diego, to visit Tiny and his wife Kshama at their home in the Chicago suburbs: a two-storey house, painted grey, with a front yard and one side overlooking a pond, providing the illusion that we were out in the country. A tasteful and in every way typically middle-class American home, except that here breakfast was served with Tiny's Masala tea, artfully prepared in front of the candles that Kshama kept burning for the festival of Diwali.

Tiny had come to pick me up at the airport, in one of the used Mercedes he bought when no one wanted them any more, repaired with his own hands, and, within reason, collected (he had six). One afternoon, driving through a landscape of luxurious stables like the one his father used to manage for his brother-in-law in Poona, he brought me to the glittering dealership where the SUV he was fixing was still up on the lift. The garage was empty, but his few colleagues working overtime in the office greeted him warmly.

The next morning, in the dining room, we leafed through the family photo albums, featuring several pictures of Bubbles in her youth: as a curly-haired girl, pretty and bursting with life; Bubbles and her husband at their wedding; aboard the *Queen Mary*; holding trophies from tennis tournaments; at family gatherings. One photo showed her in khaki shorts, lying on the ground with a rifle, during a clay-pigeon-shooting competition. 'She is a very good shooter. She used to shoot against the Japanese team. It's a well-known thing in the shooting world. But she could never kill a bird. Only targets . . . Look at this one,' Tiny said to me, pointing towards a different image: in this one she was standing, in a sari, looking minuscule next to her gigantic husband, a dead tiger at their feet. 'Many people came to Bilkha to shoot lions, panthers and tigers. For the shootings, we had servants and everything. You went on a jeep, you sat in a tree, tied a goat, a guy would come to tell you when it was time to shoot. The lion came in the middle of the night and you shot it . . . Not me, I was a boy . . . I went, but I never shot. Now, looking at these pictures, I feel bad! I love animals!'

Kshama had stepped away so we could chat, but not out of any submissiveness. She was an unfailingly kind woman; the mother of a son and a daughter who were both far away at college, she possessed an enviable, somewhat quizzical wisdom. Every morning she woke at dawn to work as a receptionist at a nearby Hilton, and afternoons she helped a friend who ran an Indian clothing store at a small shopping centre. Then, back at home, a little of this, a little of that. It was clear that Tiny's admiration for his mother ('she is the backbone of the family') had migrated to this woman, who had so gracefully kept him in line. 'Up to the age of twenty-five I would come home late at night and my governess would pull my socks off, pull my pants down, and put me in bed. And maybe give me a shower. If I was sick she would sit in the room and never leave till next morning,' he told me, pouring the Masala powder into the pot of milk on the stove. Then, winking at Kshama, he added, 'My wife is a very open person. She says: why don't you go back to India and marry a princess? So she'll do all the work.'

They had been three delightful days.

Bubbles sipped her coffee and listened. Then I told her how I'd gone to Maryland after Chicago to see Louise Hermesch's grand-niece. 'This woman inherited a few things from Louise, including two books with bookplates inside. I brought you a copy of these bookplates,' I told her. 'You have to imagine an old engraving of what could be interpreted as a reader's altar, adorned with a row of books, a genie lamp, the helmet of a medieval cavalier, and a candle holder. Under this image, at the bottom of the plate, the engraver drew the name of the book's owner. You would expect to find only one name inscribed there. But in this case, the names are two: A. K. Mandi and L. G. Hermesch . . .'

What I neglected to tell her was that the day before, when I arrived in Pune, I'd paid a visit to the Indian poet and novelist Raj Rao. There were no altars to reading with romantic candelabras to be found there. Glued to the desk of this gay rights activist – in India, they were still living under the same Victorian law against homosexuality that sent Oscar Wilde to prison in 1895 – was the image of a revolver whose barrel ended in a ballpoint pen.

In his role as head of the English Literature department at the University of Pune, Rao had managed to create one of the first LGBT literature courses, after his debut novel, *The Boyfriend*, became a touchstone of gay Indian fiction. 'What you've told me about the Rani of Mandi,' he said to me, stretching his impossibly long legs under his desk, 'makes me think it might be a case of "situational lesbianism": choosing lesbianism as a reaction against an oppressive marriage, or an oppressively patriarchal family.'

Bubbles had once again folded her arms over her chest and was looking at me without seeing me.

'. . . Seeing their names together in print makes one think of an intimate declaration,' I said to her. 'Don't you think? Like using the first-person plural. Like saying "our" home, "our" life, "our" library . . . I think this bookplate means that your mother and Louise were a couple, Bubbles . . . That they were in love.'

No reaction.

It took me a moment to understand.

'. . . You mean you already knew?'

How many more times would this woman pull the rug out from under me?

'No, I didn't know. I mean, no one would say it outright to me. But I also heard . . . I don't know from whom . . . long ago. You see, at that time I didn't understand . . .'

I suddenly felt tired.

'I hope the news I've brought has given you a little comfort,' I told her, though I feared I'd mostly thrown salt on old wounds.

'Yes. It has,' she tried to reassure me. 'Because sometimes one does think . . . why?'

'Well, now you have your answer, Bubbles.'

'It's true. I wish my brother Tibu was alive. I took life easier, while he never got over her leaving. He became an alcoholic. In the army, he did well . . . But whenever he was drunk he would remember her. I, I take life as it comes. Even though the "why?" was always there.'

A cloud must have drifted in front of the sun, because the room grew suddenly dark. There was still one more matter to discuss. I wished it was a more pleasant subject.

'There is one more thing I want to share with you, Bubbles, if you'll allow me. It's about the jewels. Louise's family strongly believes that your mother's jewels never left Mandi. That even though they belonged solely to her, they were kept there as a retaliation for her wanting to live a life of freedom.'

Did she grasp the implications of what I was saying? If this was truly the case, it meant not only that she and Tibu had been stripped of their inheritance, but that the story of Amrit Kaur of Mandi sacrificing her own jewels to help 'a Jewish friend' escape occupied France, as she herself told Jean Rosenthal, had been exaggerated, artfully manipulated and used as a cover for a vile and likely illegal withholding of her assets.

'That could be . . .' Bubbles said, again in a whisper, showing no sign of whether or not she'd considered such implications.

Was this how it ended, this mission I'd dedicated so much of my recent life to? No request for clarification, no reflection, no comment, nothing?

While Bubbles sat in silence, I gazed out of the window thinking of how it was going to be a shame to leave without first seeing the Malabar chestnut's flowers unfold in the dark.

'This was very nice,' she said finally. 'Good news. Thank you.' And that was all.

There, in the moment, I was left in shock. But later, on my way home, I reconsidered.

Maybe she was right. What else was there to say?

# Epilogue: Paris, 2020

For whatever we lose (like a you or a me)
it's always ourselves we find in the sea
                        e. e. cummings

Today is my birthday, and this morning when I woke up I thought I would go out and give myself a present. I walked past the centuries-old buildings along the rue de Grenelle; I stopped in front of the occasional shop window; I crossed the traffic on the rue de Rennes, ignoring the red light; and at the end of the rue Saint-Sulpice I entered a boutique across from the church. I ran my fingers through the satin shirts and Eastern-style jackets. Then I tried on a coat. And when I heard the owner, behind the counter, whisper to her saleswoman that she could offer me a discount, I left without buying it. But then I went back. It was green.

I'd been wearing only dark blue for a year and a half – that is, from the morning my mother died at a hospital in Milan, alone, even though I'd sworn to myself that I'd never let her face that moment without me. I'd spent the night on a stretcher beside her; we'd shared a few words. She was calm. Weary of living, she seemed concentrated in her anticipation of death, and was sedated with morphine. Then, the next morning, the nurse who'd come to prepare her for the doctor ordered me to leave. Five minutes later her aneurysm ruptured. By the time they reached me on the phone it was too late.

From that day on I wore only dark blue, since it was the easiest way not to think about my appearance. Which is perhaps one of grief's many symptoms; I couldn't say.

Then came the rite of passage that is clearing out and selling the home of one of your parents – my father, in love with his Kent cigarettes, had gone up in a cloud of smoke thirty years earlier. And as soon as I entered that silent apartment, with its white sofas and Empire-style furniture I knew so well, I noticed two things that my mother's absence had rendered suddenly apparent: the tragic number of X-rays, ultrasound scans, electrocardiograms, diagnoses, prescription slips, medications, bandages, elastic bands, syringes, thermometers and blood pressure monitors that had accumulated in the home of a nearly eighty-nine-year-old woman who, despite her complications, was not sick. And the fact that half of everything around the house – and I don't mean the furniture but the clothes, objects, necklaces, shoes, perfumes, books, purses, scarves, cosmetics, even the appliances – were gifts that I'd given her.

We couldn't manage to get along, my mother and I, even though we never stopped trying. The steely bond of mother–daughter solidarity had snapped long ago, the summer I was fourteen, when she lost her head over my first boyfriend, who was four years older than me. And with her quintessential taste for provocation, I watched her shed her role as my mother and become my adversary, carrying on a years-long relationship with him – behind my father's back, as far as I know. I didn't care about the boy: he was smarmy and self-seeking and I had finished with him after the first few months – never imagining that this act, of sending him away from our home, would spur my mother to lash out at me in tears, unmasking their affair. The boy didn't count, I repeat. But my mother had been everything to me. It was too great a betrayal. An irreparable break. Only many years later, with the birth of my children, did a bridge form between us, on which we approached each other warily, like two spies in our own personal Cold War. And though we still shared a bond, it was overshadowed by my resentment for the brashness with which she'd cast off her maternal role, and for her remorse that never transformed into repentance. In the web of our miscommunications, rarely did either of us let a gesture of tenderness slip through. And yet tenderness was there.

I think it would come across as strange, now, after having dragged the reader around the world, to offer the theory that I've dedicated all these years trying to do for Bubbles and Amrit Kaur what I could never do for myself and my mother. My mother: whom I've mentioned only once or twice in this story, and in passing. And yet, I undeniably grabbed hold of the lifeline thrown to me by another daughter on the other side of the world – 'Come see me' – and have been clinging to it against all reasonableness year after year, meeting after meeting, trip after trip, *story* after *story*.

And now I wonder: what if those stories were a key to this adventure? All those tales through which I'd pursued that vanished woman and attempted to recreate her world, while trying to survive my own? 'You should read "The Purloined Letter" by Edgar Allan Poe,' said a dear friend of mine as we walked one evening along the boulevard Saint-Germain, the city lit up around us. 'Maybe stories are the balm you need to cure your melancholy, and it's just so obvious you don't realise it. It's like when you go looking for a lost letter, and you can't find it because it's right before your eyes, just sitting there, on the mantelpiece.'

I began this narrative by saying that my first trip to Mumbai coincided with a moment in my life when a pervading sense of loss had obscured my past and future. And that a powerful need for change had led me to abandon Italy. The fact that I had no job in Paris, nothing tying me there at all, meant that my choice of self-exile was not without its unknown pleasures.

Many of these unknowns helped sustain the promise of a life more in line with my desires. But I think the time has come to admit that, in my adjustment to this foreign reality – rendered all the more intense by the excitement of sharing it with my lovely daughter, on the verge of adolescence – I was also contending with an invisible enemy. Not the one that my friend, with his compassionate euphemism, had referred to as my melancholy; but with an insurmountable sadness that, for years on end, had been waking me every morning, as punctual and unstoppable as the motion of a tide.

The first black wave came with the separation from the love of my life. When it crashed over me, it felt like being fractured along a line that ran down my skeleton from head to toe, precisely along the old, calcified fracture from my teenage years. Then, after thirteen long years of recurring tides, when I'd given up even fighting them any more, those old waters receded and the illness dissolved. Mechanically. As if an invisible key had turned and disabled some mechanism. Power on. Power off.

Naturally, I spent a long time wondering about the reasons behind this metamorphosis, which had realigned the rhythms of my interior life with the moving spectacle of the world. But the answers I landed on were all too rational to really hit the mark. Nor did it help to think back on the words of Ramesh Balsekar – to that morning in Mumbai, in his bourgeois living room in Malabar Hill, when he warned me that prolonging the pain of loss is an act of ignorance. All these years later, his words still struck me as they'd struck me then: as an authoritative form of abstract meditation, which unfortunately left me cold.

Then one evening it snowed – unexpectedly, since it was already spring. It was the beginning of April and I was heading out to meet a friend when I opened the front door and was startled by the sight of a transformed rue du Bac: as if that rather austere street had suddenly morphed into the enchanted set of a Tim Burton film. Filled with wonder, I stood there admiring the heavy snowflakes falling in slow motion through the conical beams of the street lamps while the golden glow of the brasseries illuminated the Saturday evening crowds, drinking, laughing and smoking at outdoor tables, sheltered by canopies stretched over the pavements. And in that moment, in the euphoria provoked by that scene, I felt a revelation drift down over me along with the snow.

Reconciling Bubbles with her mother had been the key that set me free.

These days, I learned, we have a scientific explanation for what I felt in that moment. I also know that there is a reason why such apprehensions, which Emily Dickinson called 'God's introductions', arrive in the most unexpected circumstances, when your thoughts are elsewhere. They occur when the brain's neocortex, which controls reason, pauses for a moment, and certain neural networks, able to relate pieces of knowledge that we've accumulated in the past and to establish connections, can operate freely, without running into the obstacle of logic.

Naturally, I didn't share any of this with Bubbles. She had plenty to think about with her own story, no need to take on the extra burden of mine. She'd got the answers she was looking for. I'd found one I didn't even know I was after. Only the issue of whether or not the Rani of Mandi had truly used her jewels to save lives was still open to question – even if I'd been left with a bitter taste in my mouth, knowing that an ugly truth might be hiding beneath that supposedly heroic gesture.

My search had come to an end, and I'd left Pune with the buoyant heart of someone who'd accomplished her mission. Yet I still harboured the regret of never having had the chance to watch Bubbles enjoy the music she'd loved as a girl. When I handed over, with great apprehension, the package of CDs I'd chosen for her, she dashed my expectations by telling me that her CD player was broken and she might even have thrown it out.

A few months later, I dialled her number.

'Helloooo, when are you coming?'

'Not so soon, this time,' I replied, reminding her that the moment had arrived to put it all on paper, this story that had grown almost spontaneously in my hands, and that I could now feel buzzing around me like a forest awakening in spring.

'OK, OK,' she said in her usual way. 'But don't take too long!' she jeered, hinting at the possibility that it might be too late by the time I got there.

Then she told me about the children who'd just come to see her and those who were on their way; about her approaching ninetieth birthday; about Priya, who'd adapted to her new married life, and Pooja, who had graduated and found a good job.

The conversation was winding to a close and we'd said our good-byes when, all of a sudden, she remembered something.

'Almost forgot to tell you that we fixed the CD player! Oh what a joy to listen to Elvis Presley and Dean Martin again. And Sinatra! Sinatra is my favourite . . . Did I ever tell you I once met him at a party in Rome? . . .'

# Acknowledgements

I would like to thank Jonathan Galassi at Farrar, Straus and Giroux for the fundamental role he played in bringing this book into being; Clara Farmer at Chatto & Windus for her invaluable contribution; and my Feltrinelli family, Carlo Feltrinelli, Gianluca Foglia, Laura Cerutti, Giovanna Salvia and Theo Collier for accompanying every step of the Italian edition. Thank you to Katherine Liptak, Vera Linder and Amanda Waters for coordinating our shared work. Special thanks to Alberto Rollo for his generous attention from the very beginning. And to everyone, from New York to London to Milan, who worked behind the scenes.

Thanks to Tash Aw and Adam Thirlwell for helping me set this project in motion; and to Peter Straus at RCW Literary Agency and Melanie Jackson of the Melanie Jackson Agency for taking it under their wings.

Thanks to Mariarosa Bricchi, Jenny McPhee and Alexander Stille for their early reads and guidance.

Thanks to the entire Bilkha family, to Madame Gillet, Teri Goodhue, Richard Holkar, Eric Landau, Zakiya Powell and Vicki Sadler for sharing their family memories.

Thanks to Naheed Mazaruddin Khan of Surat for her generous help as my cultural interpreter, for her passionate critique, and for hosting me in Pune with her husband Hamid.

Thanks to Amin Jaffer, former director of the Asian Art department at Christie's and now curator of the Al Thani Collection, and to Susan Stronge at the Victoria and Albert Museum for sharing their knowledge of Kapurthala's jewels.

*Acknowledgements*

Thanks to Elisa Vázquez de Gey and Ginger Rosser for going out of their way to give me access to essential research materials; and to Franziska Collier and Jimmy Fox for the same.

Thanks to Sumita Mukherjee at the University of Bristol; to Sunil Khilnani, former director of the India Institute at King's College London and now at Ashoka University, India; to R. Raj Rao at the University of Pune; and to the Sanskritists Fabrizia Baldissera at the University of Florence and Silvia D'Intino at the CNRS in Paris – all of whom helped me with the cultural context necessary for interpreting this history.

Thank you to everyone who in any way provided me with information, ideas, contacts, suggestions or leads: Subhash Agrawal, Antonio Armellini, Peter Bance, Viren Bhagat, Célestine Bohlen, Cristina Carenza, Come Carpentier, Tanuja Chandra, Vikram Chandra, Audrey Chapuis, Brenda Cullterton, Eric and Gabrielle Deroo, Fausta and Johnny Eskenazi, Gaia Franchetti, Wendy Goldman Rohm, Russell Harris, Siddarth Kasliwal, Momin Latif, Antonio Martinelli, Michael Ockenden, Eline de Potter, Marie-Hélène de Taillac, and the faithful Tofurno.

Thanks to Verdella Caracciolo for her hospitality in Normandy; to Priscilla de Moustier and Beatrice von Rezzori for allowing me to work in their homes.

Thanks to my family: to Aimone Sambuy for his unfailing support throughout these years, and to our children Costantino and Maria Edmée for their kind critiques.

Lastly, a special thank you to Judith Thurman, for *everything*.

# Bibliography

## Books

Charles Allen and Sharada Dwivedi, *Lives of the Indian Princes*, Century (London, 1984)

Anita Anand, *Sophia*, Bloomsbury (London, 2015)

Anita Anand and William Darlymple, *Koh-I-Noor*, Bloomsbury (London, 2017)

Gisèle Armelin, *Un Voyage aux Indes*, Albert Messein (Paris, 1935)

Jean Pierre Azéma, *1940 l'Année Terrible*, Seuil (Paris, 1990)

Peter Bance, *The Sikhs in Britain*, Coronet House (London 2012)

Nick Barnard, *Indian Jewellery*, V&A (London, 2008)

Olivier Bernier, *Fireworks at Dusk: Paris in the Thirties*, Little, Brown (Boston, 1993)

Margaret Bourke-White, *Halfway to Freedom*, Simon and Schuster (New York, 1949)

Frederick Brown, *The Embrace of Unreason: France, 1914–1940*, Knopf (New York, 2014)

Penelope Chetwode, *Kulu: The End of the Habitable World*, Times Books International (New Delhi, 1972)

Ian Copland, *The Princes of India in the Endgame of Empire 1917–1947*, Cambridge University Press (Cambridge, 1997)

Yves Courrière, *Joseph Kessel ou Sur la Piste du Lion*, Plon (Paris, 1985)

Alain Daniélou, *La Via del Labirinto*, Casa dei Libri (Padua, 2004)

Diwan Jarmani Dass, *Maharajah* (1969), Hind Pocket Books (New Delhi, 2008)

Diwan Jarmani Dass, *Maharani*, Hind Pocket Books (New Delhi, 2018)

# Bibliography

Wendy Doniger, *The Ring of Truth: And Other Myths of Sex and Jewellery*, Oxford University Press (Oxford, 2017)

David Drake, *Paris at War: 1939–1944*, Harvard University Press (Cambridge, MA, 2015)

Marguerite Duras, *La Douleur*, P.O.L. (Paris, 1985)

Marguerite Duras, *The War: A Memoir*, Pantheon (New York, 1986)

Marguerite Duras, *Cahiers de la Guerre*, P.O.L. (Paris, 2006)

Janet Flanner, *Paris Was Yesterday 1925–1939*, Viking (New York, 1972)

Janet Flanner, *Uncollected Writings 1932–1975*, Hartcourt Brace Jovanovich (New York, 1981)

Janet Flanner, *Paris Journal 1944 –1955*, Hartcourt Brace Jovanovich (New York, 2011)

Rosita Forbes, *India of the Princes*, The Book Club (London, 1939)

André de Fouquières, *Au Paradis des Rajahs*, Fontemoing (Paris, 1912)

André de Fouquières, *Cinquante Ans de Panache*, Pierre Horay (Paris, 1951)

J. C. French, *Himalayan Art*, Oxford University Press (London, 1931)

Patrick French, *India: A Portrait*, Allen Lane (New Delhi, 2011)

Giovanni Galli, *La Signora in Nero: Albert Rausch, il Lambro e la Ricerca del Graal*, Carlo Pozzoni (Como, 2009)

David Gilmour, *Curzon*, John Murray (London, 1994)

David Gilmour, *The Ruling Caste: Imperial Lives in the Victorian Raj*, John Murray (London, 2005)

David Gilmour, *The British in India: Three Centuries of Ambition and Experience*, Allen Lane (London, 2018)

Charles Glass, *Americans in Paris: Life and Death under Nazi Occupation 1940–1944*, HarperPress (London, 2009)

Côme Carpentier de Gourdon, *Memories of a Hundred and One Moons*, Har-Anand (New Delhi, 2016)

Lepel H. Griffin, *The Rajas of the Punjab* (1873), Munshiram Manoharlal (New Delhi, 1998)

Jean Guéhenno, *Journal des Années Noires*, Gallimard (Paris, 1947)

# Bibliography

Navina Najat Haidar and Courtney Ann Stewart, *Treasures from India: Jewels from the Al Thani Collection*, The Metropolitan Museum of Art (New York, 2014)

Richard Heslop, *Xavier: A British Secret Agent with the French Resistance*, Biteback Publishing (London, 2014)

Antonia Hunt, *Little Resistance: A Teenage English Girl's Adventures in Occupied France*, Secker & Warburg (London, 1982)

Anna Jackson and Amin Jaffer, *Maharaja: The Splendour of India's Royal Courts*, V&A (London, 2010)

Amin Jaffer, *Made for the Maharajas: A Design Diary of Princely India*, New Holland (London, 2006)

Amin Jaffer, *Beyond Extravagance: The Al Thani Collection*, Assouline (New York, 2013)

Kumari Jayawardena, *Feminism and Nationalism in the Third World in the 19th and early 20th centuries*, Zed Books (London, 1994)

Angma Dey Jhala, *Courtly Indian Women in Late Imperial India*, Pickering & Chatto (London, 2008)

Paul Jourde, *L'Inde des Maharajas*, Libreria Hachette (Buenos Aires, 1943)

Manju Kak, *Nicholas Roerich: A Quest and a Legacy*, Niyogi Books (New Delhi, 2013)

Sudhir Kakar and Katharina Kakar, *The Indians: Portrait of a People*, Penguin Books India (2007)

B. L. Kapoor, *History and Heritage of the Western Himalayas*, Agam Kala Prakashan (Delhi, 2001)

Maharani Brinda of Kapurthala, *Maharani: The Story of an Indian Princess*, Henry Holt (New York, 1954)

HH The Raja-Rajgan Jagatjit Singh of Kapurthala, *My Travels in Europe and America 1893*, George Routledge and Sons (London, 1895)

HH The Raja-Rajgan Jagatjit Singh of Kapurthala, *My Travels in China, Japan and Java 1903* (1905), Facsimile press (2016)

Princesse Prem Kaur de Kapurthala, *Impressions de Mes Voyages aux Indes* (1915), Forgotten Books (London 2015)

John Keay, *India: A History* (2000), Grove Press (New York, 2010)

Joseph Kessel, *La Vallée des Rubis*, Gallimard (Paris, 1955)

Omar Khalidi, *Romance of the Golconda Diamonds*, Mapin Publishing (Middletown, NJ, 1999)

Sunil Khilnani, *The Idea of India*, Hamish Hamilton (London, 1997)

Sunil Khilnani, *Incarnations: A History of India in 50 Lives*, Allen Lane (London, 2016)

H. B. Khoury, *Glimpses Behind the Veil*, Sampson Low, Marston & Co. (London, 1935)

Simon Kitson, *The Hunt for Nazi Spies: Fighting Espionage in Vichy France*, The University of Chicago Press (Chicago, 2008)

Pramod Kumar, *Posing for Posterity: Royal Indian Portraits*, Roli Books (New Delhi, 2012)

Katherine Lack, *Frontstalag 142: The Internment Diary of an English Lady*, Amberley (Stroud, 2010)

Nicole Landau, *La Perle de Blanca*, Gallimard (Paris, 2004)

Momin Latif, *Bijoux Moghols*, Societé Génerale de Banque (Bruxelles, 1982)

A. J. Liebling, *The Road Back to Paris*, Doubleday (New York, 1944)

A. J. Liebling, *Just Enough Liebling*, North Point Press (New York, 2004)

A. J. Liebling, *World War II Writings*, The Library of America (New York, 2008)

John Lord, *The Maharajas*, Random House (New York, 1971)

Janet Malcolm, *Two Lives*, Yale University Press (New Haven, 2007)

Michael R. Marrus and Robert O. Paxton, *Vichy France and the Jews: Second Edition*, Stanford University Press (Stanford, 2019)

Katherine Mayo, *Mother India: Selections from the Controversial 1927 Text*, edited and with an Introduction by Mrinalini Sinha, University of Michigan Press (Ann Arbor, 2000)

K. P. S. Menon, *Many Worlds: An Authobiography*, Oxford University Press (London, 1965)

Vincent Meylan, *Mellerio dits Meller: Joaillier des Reines*, Éditions Télémaque (Paris, 2013)

Man Mohan, *A History of the Mandi State*, Mandi Durbar (Lahore, 1930)

Marco Moneta, *Un veneziano alla Corte Moghul: Vita e Avventure di Nicolò Manucci nell'India del Seicento*, Utet (Milano, 2018)

Lucy Moore, *Maharanis: The Lives and Times of Three Generations of Indian Princesses*, Penguin Books (London, 2005)

Hans Nadelhoffer, *Cartier: Jewellers Extraordinary*, Harry N. Abrams (New York, 1984)

David Okuefuna, *The Dawn of the Colour Photograph: Albert Kahn's Archives of the Planet*, Princeton University Press (New Jersey, 2008)

David Okuefuna, *The Wonderful World of Albert Kahn*, BBC Books (London, 2008)

Ian Ousby, *Occupation: The Ordeal of France 1940–1944*, Pimlico (London, 1999)

Paul Paillole, *Services Speciaux 1935–1945*, Robert Laffont (Paris, 1975)

Paul Paillole, *L'Homme des Services Secrets*, Julliard (Paris, 1995)

Paul Paillole, *Fighting the Nazis*, Enigma Books (New York, 2004)

Paul Paillole, *Notre Espion chez Hitler*, Nouveau Monde (Paris, 2011)

Anthony Penrose, *The Lives of Lee Miller*, Holt, Rinehart and Winston (New York, 1985)

Gilles Perrault, *Paris under the Occupation*, André Deutsch (London, 1989)

Abhishek Poddar and Nathaniel Gaskell, *Maharanis: Women of Royal India*, Mapin Publishing (Ahmedabad, 2015)

Katherine Prior and John Adamson, *Bijoux de Maharadjas*, Assouline (Paris, 2000)

Michael Pym, *The Power of India*, G. P. Putnam's Sons (New York, 1930)

Alan Riding, *And the Show Went On: Cultural Life in Nazi Occupied Paris*, Knopf (New York, 2010)

Raj Rao, *The Boyfriend*, Penguin India (New Delhi, 2003)

Nicholas Roerich, *Indian Journals 1933–1946*, International Roerich Memorial Trust (Naggar, 2000)

Léonard Rosenthal, *Au Royaume de la Perle*, Payot (Paris, 1919)

Léonard Rosenthal, *Au Jardin des Gemmes*, Payot (Paris, 1922)

Léonard Rosenthal, *L'Esprit des Affaires*, Payot (Paris, 1925)

Léonard Rosenthal, *Faisons Fortune* (1924), Hachette-BNF (Paris, 2018)

Judy Rudoe, *Cartier 1900–1939*, The British Museum Press (London, 1997)

Laurent Salomé and Laure Dalon, *Cartier: Le Style et l'Histoire*, Ministère de la Culture (Paris, 2013)

Jean-Paul Sartre, *Les Carnets de la Drôle de Guerre: Septembre 1939–Mars 1940*, Gallimard (Paris, 1983)

Rosemary Say and Noel Holland, *Rosie's War: An Englishwoman's Escape from Occupied France*, Michael O'Mara (London 2011)

Charlie Scheips, *Elsie de Wolfe's Paris: Frivolity Before the Storm*, Abrams (New York, 2014)

Elsa Schiaparelli, *Shocking Life* (1954), V&A (London, 2007)

Anne Sebba, *Les Parisiennes: How the Women of Paris Lived, Loved and Died in the 1940s*, Weidenfeld & Nicolson (London, 2016)

Nicholas Shakespeare, *Priscilla: The Hidden Life of an Englishwoman in Wartime France*, Harvill Secker (London, 2013)

Umrao Singh Sher-Gil, *His Misery and His Manuscript*, Photoink (New Delhi, 2008)

Khushwant Singh, *A History of The Sikhs*, vols I and II (1963), Oxford University Press (New Delhi, 1999)

Khushwant Singh, *Ranjit Singh: Maharaja of the Punjab* (1962), Penguin Books India (New Delhi, 2001)

Patwant Singh, *The Sikhs*, John Murray (London, 1999)

Brigadier H. H. Sukhjit Singh and Cynthia Meera Frederick, *Prince Patron and Patriarch: Maharaja Jagatjit Singh of Kapurthala*, Roli Books (New Delhi, 2019)

Susan Stronge, *Bejewelled Treasures: The Al Thani Collection*, V&A (London, 2015)

Vivan Sundaram, *Amrita Sher-Gil: A Self-Portrait in Letters and Writings*, vols I and II, Tulika Books (New Delhi, 2018)

Alex von Tunzelmann, *Indian Summer: The Secret History of the End of an Empire*, Simon and Schuster UK (London, 2007)

Unknown author(s), *Kapurthala State: Its Past and Present* (1921), Facsimile Publisher (New Delhi, reprint 2016)

Ruth Vanita and Saleem Kidwai, *Same-Sex Love in India: A Literary History*, Penguin India (New Delhi, 2008)

Elisa Vázquez de Gey, *La Princesa de Kapurthala* (1997), Planeta (Barcelona, 2008)

Alexander Werth, *Les Derniers Jours de Paris* (1940), Slatkine & Cie (Paris, 2017)

Romy Wyllie, *Bertram Goodhue: His Life and Residential Architecture*, W. W. Norton (New York, 2007)

Coralie Younger, *Wicked Women of the Raj: European Women Who Broke Society Rules and Married Life*, HarperCollins (New Delhi, 2003)

Sofka Zinovieff, *Red Princess: A Revolutionary Life*, Granta Books (London, 2007)

# Anthologies

*Albert Kahn. Singulier et Pluriel*, Lienart (Paris, 2015)

*Reporting World War II, Part One: American Journalism 1938–1944*, The Library of America (New York, 1995)

*Reporting World War II, Part Two: American Journalism 1944–1946*, The Library of America (New York, 1995)

# Academic journals

Madhu Kishwar, 1985, 'Gandhi on Women', *Economic and Political Weekly*, 20 (41), 1753–8

Sumita Mukherjee, 2017, 'The All-Asian Women's Conference 1931: Indian Women and Their Leadership of a Pan-Asian Feminist Organization', *Women's History Review*, 27 (3), 363–81

Mrinalini Sinha, 1994, 'Reading Mother India: Empire, Nation, and the Female Voice', *Journal of Women's History*, 6 (2), 6–44

Mrinalini Sinha, 1994, 'Suffragism and Internationalism: The Enfranchisement of British and Indian Women Under an Imperial State', *Indian Economic & Social History Review*, 36 (4), 461–84

## Films in DVD

*The Wonderful World of Albert Kahn*, produced by David Okuefuna, BBC DVD, 2008

*L'Insaississable Albert Kahn*, by Robin Hunzinger, Bix Films – France Télévisions, 2011

# Illustration Credits

**p. 7** Rani Shri Amrit Kaur Sahib. The Lafayette Studio, London, 1924 ©
Lafayette Collection / Victoria and Albert Museum, London; **p. 19**
Amrit's father and mother: Maharaja Jagatjit Singh of Kapurthala and
Rani Kanari, *c.*1890 © Roli Collection. Unknown photographer; **p. 20**
Amrit's sister-in-law, Sita Devi of Kapurthala, also known as Princess
Karam, photographed by Cecil Beaton for *Vogue*, 1934. Cecil Beaton
Archive © Condé Nast; **p. 22** Albert Kahn on the balcony of his bank,
Paris, 1914. Negatif noir et blanc, 12 x 9 cm, Inv. No. I 135 X © Départe-
ment des Hauts-de-Seine / Musée Départemental Albert-Kahn,
collection des Archives de la Planète. Photograph by Georges Chevalier;
**p. 40** Maharaja Jagatjit Singh on the Kapurthala throne © Peter Bance
Collection. Unknown photographer; **p. 54** Exterior view of the Jagatjit
Palace, Kapurthala from the Rani of Mandi's wedding album. Matt gelatin silver print, 1918–24, 190 x 282 mm. ACP: 95.0010(39) © Alkazi
Collection. Unknown photographer; **p. 55** Interior of the Royal Palace
from the Rani of Mandi's wedding album. Matt gelatin silver print,
1918–24, 227 x 263 mm. ACP: 95.0010(35) © Alkazi Collection. Unknown
photographer; **p. 56** Square in front of the Jalao Khana, the ancient
palace complex in Kapurthala, Punjab, India, November 1927.
Autochrome, 9 x 12 cm, Inv. No. A 59 322 S © Département des Hauts-
de-Seine / Musée Départemental Albert-Kahn, collection des Archives
de la Planète. Photograph by Roger Dumas; **p. 61** The three princes and
princess of Kapurthala from the wedding album of Sri Tikka Paramjit
Singh of Kapurthala with Princess Brinda of Jubbal. Platinum print,
1911, 222 x 163 mm. ACP: 98.57.0001(4) © Alkazi Collection. Photograph
by Bourne and Shepherd; **p. 62** View of the guest camp from the Rani of
Mandi's wedding album. Matt gelatin silver print, 1918–24, 207 x 278 mm.

ACP: 95.0010(32) © Alkazi Collection. Unknown photographer; **p. 63** The drawing-room tent (guest camp) from the wedding album of Sri Tikka Paramjit Singh of Kapurthala with Princess Brinda of Jubbal. Platinum print, 1911, 181 x 307 mm. ACP: 98.57.0001(22) © Alkazi Collection. Photograph by Bourne and Shepherd; **p. 64** HH the Maharaja of Kapurthala in front of the Jagatjit Palace from the Rani of Mandi's wedding album. Matt gelatin silver print, 1918–24, 281 x 226 mm. ACP: 95.0010(36) © Alkazi Collection. Unknown photographer; **p. 69** Lunch at Elsie de Wolfe's in honour of Gertrude Stein, spring 1938 © Roger Schall Archive. Photograph by Roger Schall; **p. 71** Princesses of Kapurthala © Maidun Collection / Alamy; **p. 113** Bubbles with her brother Tibu, *c.*1933 © Peter Bance Collection. Unknown photographer; **p. 126** Jacques Cartier with Indian gemstone dealers. Photo from Jacques Cartier's album recording his voyage to India in 1911. Cartier Archives © Cartier; **p. 135** Refugees leaving Paris after the fall of France, *c.*1940 © Anthony Potter Collection / Hulton Archive / Getty Images; **p. 142** A sketch of daily life in Frontstalag 142 by Mabel Fanny Twemlow, courtesy of Paul Lack; **p. 152** Wedding portrait of Nirvana Devi and Jashwant Singh of Bilkha, 1946 © private collection of Nirvana Devi of Bilkha. Unknown photographer; **p. 160** Portrait of the Raja and Rani of Mandi after their wedding from the Rani of Mandi's wedding album. Matt gelatin silver print, 1923, 202 x 142 mm. ACP: 95.0010(16) © Alkazi Collection. Photograph by Frederick Bremner; **p. 162** Her Highness the Rani of Mandi from the Rani of Mandi's wedding album. Matt gelatin silver print, 1918–24, 275 x 210 mm. ACP: 95.0010(3) © Alkazi Collection. Unknown photographer; **p. 163** HH the Maharaja of Kapurthala along with his family and entourage with the Prince of Wales from the Rani of Mandi's wedding album. Matt gelatin silver print, 1922, 216 x 280 mm. ACP: 95.0010(10) © Alkazi Collection. Unknown photographer; **p. 164** Victoria Bridge in Mandi, India. British Empire and Commonwealth Collections, Bristol Archives, UK © Bristol Archives / Winthrop Collection / Bridgeman Images; **p. 184** Nicholas Roerich standing beside a live leopard in

Naggar, 1937 © Roerich Museum Collection, New York. Unknown photographer; **p. 205** Ginger Rosser in one of her burlesque performances © Ginger Rosser. Photograph by Bags Orbit of Top This Photography; **p. 207** Frances Collier, the Goodhues' housekeeper in San Diego © private collection of Franziska Collier. Unknown photographer; **p. 213** Amrit in San Diego, 3 August 1938 © private collection of Franziska Collier. Unknown photographer; **p. 221** Louise Hermesch on her seventieth birthday, San Diego, 1972 © private collection of Vicki Sadler; **p. 252** Sikhs migrating to a Hindu section of Punjab after the partitioning of India © Margaret Bourke-White / The *LIFE* Picture Collection / Shutterstock.

*Plate Section*

Rani Amrit Kaur of Mandi. The Lafayette Studio, London, 1924 © Lafayette Collection / Victoria and Albert Museum, London.

Group portrait during the jubilee celebrating fifty years of the reign of Maharaja Jagatjit Singh at Kapurthala, Punjab, India, November 1927. Autochrome, 9 x 12 cm, Inv. No. A 59 298 S © Département des Hauts-de-Seine / Musée Départemental Albert-Kahn, collection des Archives de la Planète. Photograph by Roger Dumas.

Princess Brinda of Kapurthala © Peter Bance Collection. Unknown photographer.

Princess Sita Devi of Kapurthala, 1934 © Peter Bance Collection. Photograph by André Durst.

Princess Indira of Kapurthala, Brinda and Paramjit's eldest daughter, Delhi, mid-1930s © Peter Bance Collection. Photograph by Kinseys Studios.

Indira Devi. Unknown date, 203. History and Art Collection / Alamy.

Amrita Sher-Gil, *Self-Portrait as a Tahitian*, 1934. Public domain.

Amrita Sher-Gil, 2. History and Art Collection / Alamy.

Photograph of Maharaja Jagatjit Singh of Kapurthala with his turban ornament. India, 1928. Gelatin silver print. Inv. PF04_CL_P017_01. Archives Cartier Paris © Cartier.

Advertisement from The Spur. Cartier Paris. Turban ornament belonging to the Maharaja Jagatjit Singh of Kapurthala, created in 1926. Inv. PF18_MOD_P25. Cartier Archives © Cartier.

Anita Delgado's half-moon emerald. By kind permission of Christie's.

Anita Delgado, Maharani Prem Kaur of Kapurthala, London, 1912 © Collection of Elisa Vázquez de Gey. Photograph by Rita Martin.

Egyptian goddess vanity case. Cartier Paris, 1928–30. VC 28 A28–30. Nils Herrmann, Cartier Collection © Cartier.

Boucheron's platinum and diamond turban *sarpech* for the Maharaja of Kapurthala, 1913 © Boucheron Archive.

Mellerio's famous peacock brooch, bought by the maharaja in 1905 and offered to Anita Delgado. By kind permission of Christie's.

The wedding dowry from the Rani of Mandi's wedding album. Matt gelatin silver print, 1918–24, 211 x 280 mm. ACP: 95.0010(51). Unknown photographer.

The rani's library bookplate © private collection of Vicki Sadler.

Rani Amrit Kaur of Mandi © private collection of Nirvana Devi of Bilkha. Unknown photographer.

# Index

Page references in *italics* indicate images.

## Index